1916 in Global Contex

The year 1916 has recently been identified as "a tipping point for the intensification of protests, riots, uprisings and even revolutions." Many of these constituted a challenge to the international pre-war order of empires, and thus collectively represent a global anti-imperial moment, which was the revolutionary counterpart to the later diplomatic attempt to construct a new world order in the so-called Wilsonian moment. Chief among such events was the Easter Rising in Ireland, an occurrence that took on worldwide significance as a challenge to the established order. This is the first collection of specialist studies that aims at interpreting the global significance of the year 1916 in the decline of empires.

Enrico Dal Lago is Professor of American History at NUI Galway. He is the author of several books, the latest of which are *The Age of Lincoln and Cavour: Comparative Perspectives on Nineteenth-Century American and Italian Nation-Building* (2015), and *Civil War and Agrarian Unrest: The Confederate South and Southern Italy* (2018).

Róisín Healy is Lecturer in Modern European History at NUI Galway. Her publications include *The Shadow of Colonialism on Europe's Modern Past* (2014) and *Poland in the Irish Nationalist Imagination, 1772–1922: Anti-Colonialism within Europe* (2017).

Gearóid Barry is Lecturer in Modern European History at NUI Galway. His books include *The Disarmament of Hatred: Marc Sangnier, French Catholicism and the Legacy of the First World War, 1914–45* (2012) and *Small Nations and Colonial Peripheries in World War I* (2016).

Routledge Studies in Modern European History
https://www.routledge.com/history/series/SE0246

1916 in Global Context
An Anti-Imperial Moment

Edited by Enrico Dal Lago,
Róisín Healy, and Gearóid Barry

Routledge
Taylor & Francis Group

LONDON AND NEW YORK

First published 2018 by Routledge

2 Park Square, Milton Park, Abingdon, Oxfordshire OX14 4RN
52 Vanderbilt Avenue, New York, NY 10017

Routledge is an imprint of the Taylor & Francis Group, an informa business

First issued in paperback 2019

British Library Cataloguing in Publication Data
A catalogue record for this book is available from the British Library

Library of Congress Cataloging in Publication Data
A catalog record for this book has been requested

ISBN: 978-1-138-74999-3 (hbk)
ISBN: 978-0-367-34891-5 (pbk)

Typeset in Sabon
by codeMantra

Contents

List of Figures

Notes on Contributors

Gearóid Barry is Lecturer in Modern European History at NUI Galway. His books include *The Disarmament of Hatred: Marc Sangnier, French Catholicism and the Legacy of the First World War, 1914–45* (2012) **and** *Small Nations and Colonial Peripheries in World War I* (2016).

Geoffrey Bell is an independent historian and writer. He studied at Magee College Londonderry/Derry, Trinity College Dublin and the University of Leeds. His books include *The Protestants of Ulster* (1976), *Troublesome Business* (1982), *The British in Ireland* (1984) and *Hesitant Comrades: The Irish Revolution and the British Labour Movement* (2016).

David Brundage is Professor of History at the University of California, Santa Cruz. His recent publications include *Irish Nationalists in America: The Politics of Exile, 1798–1998* (2016), "Remembering 1916 in America: The Easter Rising's Many Faces, 1919–1962," in *Remembering 1916: The Easter Rising, the Somme and the Politics of Memory*, ed. Richard Grayson and Fearghal McGarry (2016).

Charles-Philippe Courtois is Associate Professor of History at the Royal Military College Saint-Jean, Québec, Canada. Specialising in Quebec intellectual history, his latest book is a collection of essays co-edited with Laurent Veyssière, *Le Québec dans la Grande Guerre. Engagement, Refus, Héritages* (2015).

Enrico Dal Lago is Professor of American History at NUI Galway. He is the author of several books, the latest of which are *The Age of Lincoln and Cavour: Comparative Perspectives on Nineteenth-Century American and Italian Nation-Building* (2015), and *Civil War and Agrarian Unrest: The Confederate South and Southern Italy* (2018).

Cecelia Hartsell is completing a postgraduate degree in History at University College Dublin. Her research focuses on the issues of politics, history and memory in the 1966 and 2016 commemorations of the 1916 Easter Rising, as well as the parallels between them and the fiftieth and hundredth anniversary commemorations of the American Revolution.

Róisín Healy is Lecturer in Modern European History at NUI Galway. Her publications include *The Shadow of Colonialism on Europe's Modern Past* (2014) and *Poland in the Irish Nationalist Imagination, 1772–1922: Anti-Colonialism within Europe* (2017).

Timothy D. Hoyt is Professor of Strategy and Policy and the John Nicholas Brown Chair of Counterterrorism Studies at the U.S. Naval War College in Newport, Rhode Island. Hoyt is the author of *Military Industry and Regional Defense Policy: India, Iraq and Israel* (2006), and over 50 articles and chapters on international security and military affairs.

Jonathan Hyslop is Professor of Sociology and African Studies at Colgate University, Hamilton, New York, and Extraordinary Professor at the University of Pretoria. He is the author of *The Classroom Struggle: Policy and Resistance in South Africa 1940–1990* (1999) and *The Notorious Syndicalist: J.T. Bain – A Scottish Radical in Colonial South Africa* (2004).

Stephen McQuillan was awarded a PhD in History from Trinity College Dublin in 2017 for a dissertation entitled "The Pre-independence Nexus: Irish Radical Subversive Connections, 1900–1923." In 2015, he was a Spectress fellow at Jawaharlal Nehru University, New Delhi.

Andrew G. Newby is Marie Skłodowska-Curie COFUND Senior Research Fellow at the Aarhus Institute of Advanced Studies, Aarhus University. His publications include *Ireland, Radicalism and the Scottish Highlands* (2007); *Famines in European Economic History* (2014); and *"Éire na Rúise": An Fhionlainn agus Éire ar thóir na saoirse* ["The Ireland of Russia": Finland and Ireland in search of freedom] (2016).

Erin O'Halloran is a DPhil Candidate in Global & Imperial History at St Antony's College, Oxford, working on a thesis entitled "Cairo between Worlds: Britain, India and the Middle East, 1936–1942". She has received the T.E. Lawrence-All Souls Scholarship in History and the Mary Le Messurier Award for the Study of History.

Michael Provence teaches Middle East history at University of California at San Diego, where he is director of Middle East Programs. He is the author of *The Great Syrian Revolt and the Rise of Arab Nationalism* (2005) and *The Last Ottoman Generation and the Making of the Modern Middle East* (2017).

Danielle Ross is an Assistant Professor of Asian History at Utah State University. She has published on Islamic education and Russian Muslim participation in the First World War in journals such as *Kritika* and *Ab Imperio*. Her current project focuses on Russian imperial and economic expansion and Islamic religious revival in the Volga River Basin.

Daniel Marc Segesser is an Adjunct Professor in History at the University of Bern in Switzerland. His publications include *Der Erste Weltkrieg in globaler Perspektive* (2014). Together with Roman Rossfeld, he is Section Editor for Switzerland of *1914–1918 online. International Encyclopedia of the First World War.*

Vanda Wilcox teaches modern European history at John Cabot University, Rome. Her current research focuses on the Italian Empire in the era of World War I. Her publications include *Morale and the Italian Army during the First World War* (2016).

Acknowledgements

The present volume arises from an international conference on "1916 in Global Context: Connections and Comparisons", held at the Moore Institute in NUI Galway in June 2016 as part of the national commemorative programme for the centenary of Ireland's 1916 Rising and of NUI Galway's "A Nation Rising" initiative, coordinated by Dr. Mary Harris. We would like to express thanks to the Irish Research Council, which generously funded the conference through the "Marking the National Decade of Centenaries" strand of its New Foundations Scheme. We are particularly to its chair, Prof. Jane Ohlmeyer, and John Concannon, director of the Ireland 2016 Centenary Programme, for opening the conference. We also wish to thank the Moore Institute and its director, Prof. Daniel Carey, for hosting the conference and the administrative staff of the Discipline of History, School of Humanities, Helena Condon and Maura Ó Cróinín, and Dr. Cathal Smith and Joseph Dobransky for their assistance.

Section I

Transnational and Comparative Approaches to 1916

1 Globalising the Easter Rising

1916 and the Challenge to Empires

Enrico Dal Lago, Róisín Healy
and Gearóid Barry

The year 1916 has recently been identified as "a tipping point for the intensification of protests, riots, uprisings and even revolutions."[1] Many of these constituted a challenge to the international pre-war order of empires and thus collectively represent a global anti-imperial moment, which was the revolutionary counterpart to the later diplomatic attempt to construct a new world order in the so-called Wilsonian moment.[2] As Keith Jeffery has pointed out, "The Easter Rising in Ireland … was far from being the only rebellion against imperial rule during 1916."[3] The Rising was an attack, in late April 1916, on British rule by a group of approximately 1,000 committed revolutionaries, who seized key strategic positions in Dublin and other parts of Ireland, but were defeated by circa 20,000 British forces. The Rising was marked by the destruction of the city centre and the deaths of over 400 civilians. It was followed by the arrest of the combatants and thousands of alleged sympathisers across the country, the execution of fifteen of its leaders for treason after secret courts martial and the public trial and hanging of the famous humanitarian turned revolutionary Roger Casement in London in August 1916.[4]

Some historians have interpreted the Rising as an attempt to mobilise popular opinion against British rule rather than defeat it militarily and as anti-democratic in that the majority of the population supported Home Rule rather than separation, and rejected physical force nationalism. Moreover, 200,000 Irishmen were fighting in British uniforms in World War I to secure the former.[5] In this volume, we argue that the Rising was a serious attempt to overthrow British imperial rule in Ireland. The planners took over several major public buildings, including Dublin's General Post Office, one of the principal communications nodes of the capital, and used modern technology, such as radio, to broadcast the collapse of British rule in a major city in the Empire's metropolitan core city to the world. Moreover, the Proclamation of the Irish Republic was profoundly anti-imperial in its assertion of "the right of the people of Ireland to the ownership of Ireland … asserting it in arms in the face of the world."[6] It provided a clear democratic and pluralist framework for the new state that the rebels hoped to establish. Many of the principles contained therein enjoyed broad support among nationalists. At the same time, in terms of tactics, the constitutional tradition tolerated violence in certain political circumstances.[7]

From a global and anti-imperial perspective, the fact that the Rising took place in Europe granted it, as Lenin, the foremost contemporary critic of Europe imperialism, observed at the time, "a hundred times more political significance than a blow of equal weight would have in Asia or Africa."[8] Indeed Richard Bessel has argued in a recent synthesis on revolution in the era of World War I, that "What happened in Dublin in 1916 and its aftermath needs to be understood not just in an Irish or European context, but in a broader global framework."[9]

Part of its significance was the inspiration it offered anti-imperial forces in both Europe and beyond.[10] Lenin welcomed the Easter Rising as a blow against imperialism, although he wrote, "It is the misfortune of the Irish that they rose prematurely, before the European revolt of the proletariat had *had time* to mature." At the same time, he viewed the Rising as an important training ground for future revolutions, including the one that the Bolsheviks were planning in Russia. He wrote, "it is only in premature, individual, sporadic and therefore unsuccessful, revolutionary movements that the masses gain experience, acquire knowledge, gather strength, and get to know their real leaders, the socialist proletarians."[11] Significantly, the Easter Rising of 1916 was followed by a series of anti-imperial revolts, which culminated in the Russian Revolution of October 1917, just as the Revolution of February 1848 in France had set in train a series of revolts against the Restoration order which lasted into 1849, not just across Europe but as far beyond as New Granada and Brazil in Latin America.[12]

With this edited collection, we intend to provide a global perspective on the Easter Rising by means of over a dozen case studies, which highlight the contemporaneity of multiple anti-imperial occurrences and their links with the Irish rebellion. In so doing, we seek to explain the temporal clustering of anti-imperial revolts in 1916 and the particular place of the Easter Rising on an international canvas. Following Niall Whelehan's insight, we argue that "discussions of the 1916 Rising raise ... questions about what transnational perspectives can bring to the historiography of the Irish Revolution of 1912–1923."[13] In this connection, this volume is novel in several respects. It is the first collection of specialist studies that aims at interpreting the global significance of the year 1916 in the decline of empires. It brings together analyses of anti-imperial movements in chapters which span the globe from Ireland to Central Asia and from Finland to Australia. It looks beyond the conventional context of national histories to emphasise the transnational and global connections of anti-imperial risings in different parts of the world. The combination of studies of the Easter Rising and other analogous events helps to highlight the peculiarities and commonalities, alongside the mutual connections, of the various revolutionary episodes that characterised the global anti-imperial moment of 1916. These national anti-imperial movements often supported one another, although, in their drive for the liberation of their own homelands, they were sometimes forced to make strategic alliances with the imperial powers against which their own empires were in conflict.

According to Fearghal McGarry, a transnational perspective on the Irish Revolution promises to provide insights into "the significance of broader factors, such as the destabilising impact of the First World War, the postwar shift of power from imperial state to nation-state, and the acceptance of self-determination as the principal source of political legitimacy."[14] Recent historiography has recognised the potential of transnational perspectives in the study of modern Ireland, most notably Niall Whelehan's work on the Fenians and the well-established scholarship on Irish-Indian and Irish-South African connections.[15] Studies of Irish nationalists have exposed the extent of their sympathy for anti-imperial causes elsewhere in the British Empire.[16]

There have been some attempts in recent years to explore links between the rebels of 1916 and contacts with the Irish diaspora in various parts of the English-speaking world. For example, Tom Garvin has discovered that half of the 304 nationalist leaders active in the period from 1858 to 1928 had lived outside Ireland.[17] The constant movement of people and ideas between Ireland and established Irish communities in Britain, North America and Australasia had a major impact on the shaping of Irish nationalism. In 2016 alone, two books highlighting the significance of American links for the Irish revolutionaries have appeared.[18] The importance of these links was apparent in the realm of cultural nationalism which was so critical to the formation of the 1916 revolutionary generation. The founders of the Gaelic League drew inspiration from the efforts to protect the Irish language among the immigrant community in America.[19] One of the most committed activists of the Gaelic League and later executed for his part in the Rising, Thomas Kent had himself been active in the Philo-Celtic Society based in Boston in the 1880s.[20] The Irish Republican Brotherhood, founded in New York in 1858 and colloquially known as the Fenians, exemplified the close intellectual and political contact between revolutionaries across the English-speaking world.[21] As Niall Whelehan points out, there has not yet been a comprehensive analysis of the impact of foreign residence on the "revolutionary generation", and how its exposure to global intellectual trends influenced their ideas, particularly in relation to nationalism, revolution and labour. Indeed, recent scholarship on paramilitary violence has emphasised the global connections between "revolution, imperial collapse and ethnic conflict".[22]

Some valuable research has been undertaken, however, on prominent individuals involved in the Rising. Robert Schmuhl has emphasised the importance of John Devoy in conceiving, financing and executing the Rising from his base in New York.[23] Joost Augusteijn has shown the importance of Patrick Pearse's sojourn in America in his political development.[24] Fearghal McGarry has pointed out that five of the seven signatories of the Easter Proclamation spent time in America.[25] Indeed many of them led transnational lives. Tom Clarke was imprisoned in Britain for fifteen years before he went to the United States. Joseph Plunkett was educated at the elite English Catholic boarding school, Stonyhurst. Most notoriously, Roger Casement was a British consul and spent periods of his life in Africa, Latin America and the United States. Michael Mallin, an Irish Volunteer commandant who was executed for his part in the Rising, had served in the British army in the Tirah campaign on the Indian-Afghan border in 1897–1898. James Connolly spent his early life in Britain and had extensive contact with syndicalists and socialists throughout the world, especially during his time in the United States, where he became active in the Industrial Workers of the World, also known as the Wobblies.[26] Indeed prosopographical analyses of the rank and file participants in the Rising indicate that these included foreign-born children of Irish immigrants. The most notable of these were the so-called "Liverpool Lambs", a company of the Irish Volunteers drawn from the Irish community of Liverpool and other British cities, including the three King brothers, John, Patrick and George.[27]

In addition to the transnational connections we have outlined above between the rebels and the Irish diaspora, Fearghal McGarry has called for a comparison of the different Irish settlements across the world in order to determine their part in the global reverberations of the Rising.[28] This type of comparative study would resonate with the current historiography of the British Empire, which focuses on the intra-imperial connections between the metropole and its peripheries and between the different colonies.[29] These connections consist of "cultural and social networks built by migrants, as well as market forces, new technologies, and imperial armies."[30] In attempting to develop a full understanding of the reception of the Rising across the British Empire, historians need to look to Melbourne, Bombay, Cape Town and Toronto, as well as London. Indeed, it would be worthwhile to examine the role of the Irish diaspora in comparison with other diasporic nationalist movements, such as those of the Poles and Zionists, in anti-imperialism at home.[31]

Anti-imperialist forces were gaining strength in the early years of the twentieth century, as exemplified by the formation of the Subject Races International Committee in 1907, which brought together not only activists pleading the causes of Europeans, such as Irish and Poles, but also those of non-Europeans, such as those represented by the Aborigines' Protection Society and the Egyptian Committee.[32] World War I itself weakened the existing imperialist world order. As Richard Bessel has pointed out, "Not only did the war bring destruction to the three main continental European empires; it also shook the belief in the solidity of European global domination" constituting "a revolutionary challenge to imperial power, in Cairo no less than in Dublin."[33] This present volume treats the Easter Rising as the first major anti-imperial revolt on European soil in 1916 in a series of anti-imperial episodes which together constitute a global anti-imperial moment which would culminate in the

October Revolution in Russia the following year. From the outbreak of World War I, Irish radical nationalists were plotting a revolt, following the long-time Irish republican dictum that "England's difficulty was Ireland's opportunity." They decided to strike in April 1916 rather than later because of both the national and international contexts. By early 1916, the planners felt that public opinion was more sceptical about the War, especially in light of the delay in granting Home Rule, and feared that the War might end before they had an opportunity to strike. Keeping in mind the international context of World War I, this collection therefore considers the global framework of 1916, both transnationally, by means of little-known links between the rebels and different parts of the world, and comparatively, by means of a series of case studies of contemporaneous anti-imperial revolts across the globe.[34]

At the time of the Rising, Dublin was far more cosmopolitan than historians have acknowledged. According to the 1911 census, there were 18,905 people resident in Ireland who had been born outside the United Kingdom. These included approximately 6,000 Europeans. Of these, 1,985 were born in Russia, most of whom were Jews fleeing persecution there. The remainder came principally from France, Germany, Austria-Hungary, Italy, the Low Countries and Scandinavia.[35] Just as in London, Paris or Vienna, residents of Dublin could avail of Turkish baths in the city centre. The Hammam Family Hotel and Turkish Baths, established in 1869, occupied a prominent position on the city's main thoroughfare and epicentre of the Rising, O'Connell Street. Moreover, many of the Rising's leaders and some of the rank and file had spent time on the continent, exploiting artistic, intellectual and Catholic networks. One combatant, Liam Ó Briain, had studied in Berlin, Bonn and Freiburg and later became professor of modern languages at University College Galway.[36] The most famous female combatant, Constance Markievicz, owed her unusual surname to the Polish artist she met while studying in Paris. Indeed, there are numerous more underexplored examples of continental connections which lend themselves to a full-length study. Word of the Rising spread quickly throughout Europe and encouraged anti-imperial sentiment in several places, such as Poland.[37] Hungary provided a model for Arthur Griffith, whose Sinn Féin Party benefitted from the radicalisation of Irish nationalist opinion in the aftermath of the Rising.[38] Roy Foster has drawn parallels between the Irish "revolutionary generation" and the contemporary Russian intelligentsia.[39]

Irish observers of the Rising were particularly familiar with the anti-imperial tradition of Latin America, as a result of the participation of Irish expatriates, most notably Bernardo O'Higgins, in the nineteenth-century revolts against Spain and Portugal. In Easter Week, one witness described an old captain as having "just arrived from the home of revolutions, South America".[40] In fact, in the same years of the Irish Revolution, one major Latin American country, Mexico, was in the throes of its own revolution, which involved in part resistance to American imperial interference.[41] In addition, Argentina was home to a large Irish expatriate community, one of whom, Eamon Bulfin, fought in the G.P.O.[42]

Events in Africa also provided a frame of reference for the Easter Rising. A journalist, who was staying in a hotel opposite the G.P.O., compared the Rising to Hail Columbia, an encounter in the Anglo-Boer War.[43] He might also have noticed the slouch hat, worn by the Irish Volunteers. According to Keith Jeffery "Some Irish Volunteers of Easter 1916 styled themselves 'De Wets', and ostentatiously adopted Boer commando cocked hats."[44] In October 1914, De Wet helped launch a rebellion against South Africa's participation in the British war effort with a view to establishing a provisional republican government in South Africa, but was defeated in January 1915.[45] Bill Nasson has called the Boer Rebellion of 1914–1915 "a warm weather version of the 1916 Easter Rising".[46] The War sparked further rebellions in Africa, especially in 1916, most notably the Senussi Rebellion against British and Italian forces in Libya.[47] In French Africa alone in this year, there were rebellions in the Maghreb and Madagascar.[48]

News of the Easter Rising also reached other continents. It was reported extensively, if somewhat generically, for instance, in the Persian press.[49] Meanwhile, just five weeks after the surrender in Dublin, Grand Sharif Hussein of Mecca, supported by British intelligence and troops, most notably Colonel T. E. Lawrence of Arabia, led a major attack on the Ottomans in an attempt to unite the Arab people and establish an independent Arab state, but was eventually overcome by Ottoman forces.[50] A little more than a month after the outbreak of the Arab Revolt, hundreds of thousands of Muslims in Central Asia, provoked by the expansion of labour conscription, rose up against their Russian imperial rulers.[51] In India, Annie Besant, a nationalist and women's rights activist of mixed Irish and British heritage, founded the All Indian Home Rule League in September 1916 to challenge British imperial rule. She became president of the Indian National Congress in 1917.[52] The Rising intensified anti-imperial sentiment among the Irish living abroad. One of the most spectacular examples of this was the conversion of the Irish-born Archbishop Daniel Mannix of Melbourne from constitutional nationalist to republican sympathiser, a change which informed his vigorous interventions against the imposition of conscription in Australia in 1916.[53]

All the above examples demonstrate the type of methodology we suggest as the best way of studying 1916 in a global context. A methodology that looks both at transnational connections and parallels between the Irish Easter Rising and contemporaneous events throughout the globe as part of a synchronous anti-imperial moment is required. As a history of 1916 as a global anti-imperial moment, this volume considers connections and parallels between multiple manifestations of anti-imperial discontent in different parts of the world, of which the Easter Rising is one specific local manifestation and the earliest major one in chronological terms. Within the global framework of World War I and the challenge it posed to empires, by 1916, this anti-imperial discontent had reached a critical point and acquired a momentum that reached a climax in the Russian Revolution of October 1917. The combination of the severe pressures placed on all their subjects by imperial authorities for the purposes of the war effort and the strategic opportunities provided by the conflict of empires produced a perfect storm for the creation of an anti-imperial moment. The evidence for this lies in the multiple revolts and protests against imperial rule that flared up across the world in 1916.

This book is divided into four sections. Section 1 provides a discussion of the methodology behind the issues addressed in the volume and highlights the long-term significance of the Easter Rising in the context of anti-imperialism in a European and global setting. The introductory chapter acknowledges the wealth of scholarship situating the Easter Rising within the Irish, British-Irish and Irish-American contexts, but argues for an expansion of horizons to include connections and comparisons with other parts of the world. The following chapter by Timothy Hoyt contextualises the Easter Rising within the history of anti-imperial violence across the world over the course of a century. Hoyt places Ireland's 1916 Easter Rising in a broad geographical and temporal context, arguing that the lessons learned from the Rising "not only enhanced the effectiveness of the Irish rebellion to come (the Anglo-Irish War of 1919–1921 [more commonly known as the Irish War of Independence]) but also of other revolts throughout the [British] Empire and, after the Second World War, in the postcolonial world." By contrasting the reasons for the failure of the Rising in organizational and military terms – i.e., the excessive secrecy and the decision to focus on Dublin – and in political terms – specifically, the lack of a broad political support – with its long-term implications, "both unanticipated and revolutionary", Hoyt argues in favour of the Rising's importance both for subsequent Irish historical developments and for anti-imperial and postcolonial movements worldwide.[54]

Section 2 examines the Atlantic World from North America to South Africa, a region that current scholarship has identified as characterised by increasing interconnectedness well into the twentieth century. Two chapters consider comparable social and political upheavals among French Canadians and African Americans in response to the pressures of a prolonged war and racism at home, respectively. Two other chapters in this section reflect on the links between challenges to empire from non-white communities based in New York City and by miners in South Africa. In the first chapter of this section, Charles-Philippe Courtois takes an innovative approach to the Atlantic dimension of the Easter Rising by looking at parallels with the 1918 Conscription Crisis in the province of Quebec as comparable events in an anti-imperial moment against British rule, which encompassed both Ireland and French Canada in World War I. In Courtois's analysis, the echoes of the Easter Rising emerge as an important factor that galvanised

French Canadian nationalists in the years preceding the Conscription Crisis, as Quebecois separatist and nationalist papers such as *La Croix* and *Le Devoir* praised the 1916 Irish revolutionaries, making either implicit or explicit references to the situation in French Canada.[55] In the following chapter, Cecelia Hartsell focuses on a contemporaneous event to the Irish Easter Rising in another part of the Atlantic World, the start, in 1916, of the First Great Migration of African Americans to the northern cities of the United States. Hartsell argues that the Great Migration created room for African Americans to develop strategies of political resistance to the racist politics of Woodrow Wilson's administration, and that those political strategies became increasingly radical, also as a result of contact with Irish and other foreign anti-imperialists. Ultimately, she concludes that "the activist ethos of the Great Migration, which began in earnest during the same year of the Easter Rising", led to a new urban form of African American protest whose origins fall within "the revolutionary tradition of 1916".[56]

In his chapter, David Brundage approaches the important Atlantic dimension of 1916 by focusing specifically on New York as a central node of the political activities of Indian nationalist Lala Lajput Rai in his struggle against British imperial rule in the years of the Irish Revolution. By inserting Rai's activism within the "vibrant multinational anticolonial movement" in New York during and after World War I, which found a major source of inspiration in the Easter Rising, Brundage is able to trace the changing influence that Irish nationalism had on Rai as he transitioned from an initial support of Home Rule in Ireland to an increasing identification with Irish revolutionary republicanism.[57] In the final chapter in this section, Jonathan Hyslop looks at the Rand Rebellion carried out by British and Afrikaner miners in South Africa in 1922 and at the 1916 Easter Rising in Ireland, emphasising both the parallels between the two "armed insurrections against British imperial authority" and the connections between the two events' insurgents, dating back to the Second Anglo-Boer War (1899–1902). He emphasises specifically the concept of "contemporaneity" as a way to understand separate events as parts of particular "global conjunctures". Thus, in his view, Ireland's 1916 Rising and South Africa's 1922 Rebellion, though separate events, occurred "in the context of a particular global concatenation of forms of warfare, labour movement and nationalism that prevailed from roughly 1911 to 1923."[58]

Section 3 addresses anti-imperial activity in North Africa, Asia and the Pacific. The first three chapters in this section examine anti-imperial activities in the British Empire and the Ottoman Empire and links between them. The next two chapters look at the reception of the Easter Rising abroad, both in terms of media coverage in Central Asia and direct political impact on the Australian contribution to the imperial war effort. In Chapter 7, Michael Provence considers events in the Middle East in 1916 in their global context, reviewing the strategic position of the Ottoman Empire since

1911, so as to help explain the Entente powers' political manipulations and military interventions in the region from 1914 to 1916. The late spring of 1916 brought bad news for the British Empire, first from Ireland and then, within a week, that of the catastrophic British surrender to Ottoman forces at Kut in Mesopotamia. Provence argues that 1916 was a moment of acute anxiety for the prestige and security of the British Empire which presaged future troubles.[59] In Chapter 8, Erin O'Halloran considers the British Empire's response to the Silk Letters Conspiracy, a secret anti-imperial plot discovered by British intelligence in 1916, which implicated a range of Indian, Arab and Afghan Muslim leaders. Hidebound by religious stereotypes, British officials – in Cairo and especially in Delhi – underestimated the potential threat just as they misread the emerging phenomenon of joint Muslim-Hindu opposition within India itself. O'Halloran concludes that, in fact, "nationalist and anti-imperial sentiments were at least as important as communal or sectarian identities in driving political opinion – and anti-British action" in south Asia in 1916.[60] In Chapter 9, Stephen McQuillan examines in transnational perspective the wartime collaboration of Irish and Indian radical nationalists against "the combined subjection of Ireland, India and Egypt to English rule", as the US-hosted Irish Race Convention described it in March 1916. A daring (but foiled) arms shipment to India in 1915 involving Irish, Indian and German intrigue – and whose nerve centre was San Francisco – was but one (sensational) act of solidarity. Energised by the Rising, the international Friends of Irish Freedom and the Indian National Committee fraternised again in Stockholm in 1917, worrying British intelligence, but also, in McQuillan's words, "conferring legitimacy upon [their] respective claims to independence".[61]

In Chapter 10, Danielle Ross considers the range of attitudes to empire and to anti-imperial violence amongst Russian Muslims – and amongst the ethnic Kirghiz intelligentsia in Turgai province in particular – during the Easter Rising and the extensive Central Asian revolt of the summer of 1916. Local press coverage of the Rising reveals Muslim opinion to be divided on rebellion as a strategy. The July 1916 urban insurrection led by Alibi Jangil'din in Turgai paralleled aspects of the Irish rebellion: whilst not imitative, it demonstrates for Ross the "existence of models, ideals, and rituals in anti-imperial revolt and state-founding" that transcended imperial boundaries during World War I.[62] In Chapter 11, Daniel Marc Segesser places Irish-Australian reactions to the Easter Rising in a broader imperial context by looking at how, in 1916, the relationship between the imperial centre in London and the Dominion of Australia was influenced by a conglomeration of global factors, mostly beyond Prime Minister William Hughes' direct control. All these factors – a crisis in grain production related to climatic conditions, wheat farmers' disgruntlement with British import policy and the dramatic events in Ireland – contributed to the defeat of conscription in a referendum in October

1916, making this plebiscite a "national event with global ramifications and a strong Irish imprint".[63]

Section 4 considers the reverberations of the Easter Rising in Europe, focusing on the specific examples of Britain, Italy, Finland and Poland. The first two chapters examine responses to the precedence of national over socialist goals in the anti-imperialist activities of James Connolly and Cesare Battisti, both executed by imperial authorities in 1916, within the context of World War I and a history of mixed national and imperial loyalties. The next two chapters examine responses to the Easter Rising in Finland and Poland and the validity of alleged parallels between these parts of Europe and Ireland, as territories subject to imperial authority and denied independent statehood. In Chapter 12, Geoffrey Bell argues that most members of the British labour movement were highly critical of the Easter Rising and vilified Connolly in particular for putting nationalism before socialism. He ascribes their hostility to the Rising to a lingering resentment at the establishment of separate Irish trade unions before the War and either support for the British war effort or a commitment to pacifist principles. He also suggests that the British labour movement was not actually anti-imperial, quoting Ramsay MacDonald as typifying its view that the British Empire "must exist, not merely for safety or order, or peace but for richness of life".[64] In Chapter 13, Vanda Wilcox examines the conviction and execution of Cesare Battisti for treason in July 1916 within the context of anti-imperialism in the Austro-Hungarian Empire. She shows that while the Austrian authorities regarded the Austrian subject from the Tyrol as a traitor for having joined the Italian army, Italians saw him as a hero for having put his nation before his empire. The harsh treatment of Battisti, especially the distribution of photographs of his corpse, and other Italian "traitors" during the War exposed the incompatibility of loyalty to both the Empire and the nation and sealed the fate of the Austro-Hungarian Empire.[65]

Andrew Newby begins the following chapter with the well-known story of the presence of a Finnish volunteer in the GPO during the Easter Rising to explore anti-imperialism in Ireland and Finland. As subject peripheries of the Entente Powers, Finland and Ireland followed similar trajectories during World War I, including small-scale collaboration with the German enemy. "In this respect," he concludes, "both countries conform to a more general sense that 1916 was an 'anti-imperial moment', forming part of a tapestry of causally (if sometimes loosely) connected reactions against imperialism, drawing on long-term resentment, the particular socio-political flux caused by war, and the interference and encouragement of the imperial powers' enemy."[66] In the final chapter, Róisín Healy argues that there are strong parallels between the Easter Rising and the Poznanian Uprising of 1918/1919 as highly organised anti-imperial rebellions fought with minimal outside assistance. She explains the considerable time lapse between them in terms of the very different geopolitical positions of Ireland and

Poland in World War I. Unlike Ireland, Poland's strategic position at the heart of Europe led each side to woo it with promises of greater autonomy. While impressed with the Easter Rising, the Poznanian Poles feared confronting the Germans until they were assured of their defeat in 1918.[67]

In Ireland, the radicalisation of Irish nationalist opinion which followed the Easter Rising and the threat of conscription in 1918 resulted in a landslide electoral victory for Sinn Féin, the political party most committed to seeking independent statehood for Ireland, in December 1918. The Irish Republican Army, heirs of the IRB and the Volunteers, supported the establishment of an Irish government with a renewed military struggle in the Irish War of Independence from 1919 to 1921. Meanwhile, in 1920, the British government granted self-government to the northern six counties of Ireland, where Unionists who had resisted rule from Dublin held a majority. The truce that ended the War of Independence was followed by the Anglo-Irish Treaty of December 1921, which established the Irish Free State in the remaining twenty-six counties, but unleashed a Civil War (1922–1923) between those for and against the Treaty.[68]

In global perspective, the transnational significance of the Easter Rising long outlived the anti-imperial moment of 1916–1917. International interest in Irish affairs remained strong into the Irish War of Independence and Civil War. Maurice Walsh has pointed out that the outrage caused by foreign journalists' reports of British atrocities in Ireland in the War of Independence put pressure on the British government to reach a settlement in Ireland.[69] Anti-imperial forces abroad continued to look to the example of the Easter Rising in their efforts to free themselves from their own empires. Indeed, armed Indian anti-imperialists took direct inspiration from the events of 1916 in Ireland when launching their own rebellion against British rule in Chittagong in the Bengal region of India in 1930.[70] The later president of India from 1969 to 1974, V.V. Giri, claimed himself to have been inspired by the Easter Rising to work towards Indian independence. He had witnessed the Rising as a student in Dublin and had even been tutored by one of the executed leaders, Thomas MacDonagh.[71] As a founding moment for the Irish state, the Easter Rising left a legacy of anti-imperialism, which has defined the image of Irish foreign policy and the reputation of Ireland abroad, particularly in relation to the process of decolonisation in Africa and Asia.[72]

Notes

1 Klaus Weinhauer, Anthony McElligott, and Kirsten Heinsohn, "Introduction," in Weinhauer, McElligott and Heinsohn, ed., *Germany 1916–23: A Revolution in Context* (Bielefeld, 2015), 21.
2 Erez Manela, *The Wilsonian Moment: Self-Determination and the International Origins of Anticolonial Nationalism* (Oxford, 2009).
3 Keith Jeffery, *1916: A Global History* (London, 2016), 4.
4 Fearghal McGarry, *The Rising: Ireland: Easter 1916*, new ed. (Oxford, 2016).

5 Fearghal McGarry, Easter Rising (Great Britain and Ireland), in: 1914–1918-online. International Encyclopedia of the First World War, ed. by Ute Daniel, Peter Gatrell, Oliver Janz, Heather Jones, Jennifer Keene, Alan Kramer, and Bill Nasson, issued by Freie Universität Berlin, Berlin 2014-10-08. doi: 10.15463/ie1418.10076. For a critical introduction to the vast historiographical debate on the Easter Rising, see Diarmaid Ferriter, *A Nation, Not a Rabble: The Irish Revolution, 1913–1923* (London, 2015), 56–96.

6 The Proclamation of the Irish Republic, www.taoiseach.gov.ie/eng/Historical_Information/State_Commemorations/Proclamation_of_Independence.html.

7 Brian Hanley, "The Ireland of Our Ideals," Paper Delivered at "Proclaiming the Revolution" Conference, National University of Ireland Galway, 22 January 2016 (posted 26 January 2016, https://cedarlounge.wordpress.com/2016/01/26/the-ireland-of-our-ideals-paper-delivered-at-proclaiming-the-revolution-conference-brian-hanley/).

8 V. I. Lenin, *British Labour and British Imperialism: A Compilation of Writings by Lenin on Britain* (London, 1969), 164–68.

9 Richard Bessel, "Revolution," in Jay Winter, ed., *The Cambridge History of the First World War*, vol. 2, *The State* (Cambridge, 2014), 139.

10 Liam Ó Ruairc, "Easter Rising (1916)," in Immanuel Ness and Zak Cope, eds., *The Palgrave Encyclopedia of Imperialism & Anti-Imperialism: Volume 1* (Basingstoke, 2016), 622.

11 Lenin, "The Discussion of Self-Determination Summed Up," *Lenin's Collected Works* 22 (Moscow, 1964), 320–60. www.marxists.org/archive/lenin/works/1916/jul/x01.htm.

12 Jürgen Osterhammel, *The Transformation of the World: A Global History of the Nineteenth Century* (Princeton, 2014), 543–58.

13 Niall Whelehan, "Introduction," in Niall Whelehan, ed., *Transnational Perspectives on Modern Irish History* (London, 2015), 6. For an example of broader perspectives on the Rising, see Ruán O'Donnell, ed., *The Impact of the 1916 Rising: Among the Nations* (Dublin, 2008).

14 Fearghal McGarry, "'A Land Beyond the Wave': Transnational Perspectives on Easter 1916," in Whelehan, ed., *Transnational Perspectives*, 182–83.

15 Niall Whelehan, *The Dynamiters: Irish Nationalism and Political Violence in the Wider World, 1867–1900* (Cambridge, 2012); Kate O'Malley, *Ireland, India and Empire: Indo-Irish Radical Connections* (Manchester, 2008); *Forgotten Protest: Ireland and the Anglo-Boer War* (Belfast, 2003). For an example of a transnational life of an Irish nationalist between Ireland and South Africa, see Daithí Ó Corráin, "'A most public spirited and unselfish man': the career and contribution of Colonel Maurice Moore, 1854–1939" *Studia Hibernica* 40 (2014), 71–133.

16 Paul A. Townend, "Between Two Worlds: Irish Nationalists and Imperial Crisis, 1878–1880," *Past and Present* 194 (2007), 139–74; Sean Ryder, "Ireland, India and Popular Nationalism in the Early Nineteenth Century," in Tadhg Foley and Maura O'Connor, eds., *Ireland and India: Colonies, Culture and Empire* (Dublin, 2006), 12–25; Jennifer Regan, "'We Could Be of Service to Other Suffering People': Representations of India in the Irish Nationalist Press, c. 1857–1887," *Victorian Periodicals Review* 41 (2008), 61–77.

17 Tom Garvin, *Nationalist Revolutionaries in Ireland, 1858–1928* (Dublin, 2005), 53–55.

18 Miriam Nyhan Grey, ed., *Ireland's Allies: America and the 1916 Easter Rising* (Dublin, 2016); David Brundage, *Irish Nationalists in America: The Politics of Exile, 1798–1998* (Oxford, 2016).

19 Úna Ní Bhroiméil, *Building Irish Identity in America, 1870–1915: The Gaelic Revival* (Dublin, 2003).

20 Gearóid Barry, "Thomas Kent: Total Abstainer," in David Bracken, ed., *The End of All Things Earthly: Faith Profiles of the 1916 Leaders* (Dublin, 2016), 57–60.

21 Whelehan, *The Dynamiters*, Jonathan Gantt, *Irish Terrorism in the Atlantic Community, 1865–1922* (New York, 2010); Fearghal McGarry and James McConnel, eds., *The Black Hand of Republicanism: Fenianism in Modern Ireland* (Dublin, 2009); Shane Kenna, *War in the Shadows: The Irish-American Fenians Who Bombed Victorian Britain* (Dublin, 2013).

22 Robert Gerwarth and John Horne, eds., *War in Peace: Paramilitary Violence in Europe after the Great War* (Oxford, 2012), 7. For a sceptical view of the impact of the Easter Rising on events abroad, see Roy Foster, *Vivid Faces: The Revolutionary Generation in Ireland, 1890–1923* (London, 2015), xvii.

23 "John Devoy: The Intrigue of Exile," in Robert Schmuhl, ed., *Ireland's Exiled Children: America in the Easter Rising* (Oxford, 2016), 15–44. For another example of a transatlantic Irish republican activist, see Eileen McGough, *Diarmuid Lynch: A Forgotten Irish Patriot* (Cork, 2013).

24 Joost Augusteijn, *Patrick Pearse: The Making of a Revolutionary* (Basingstoke, 2010), especially 41–43.

25 McGarry,"A Land Beyond the Wave, 169; Gerard MacAtasney, *Tom Clarke: Life, Liberty, Revolution* (Dublin, 2013).

26 Donal Niven, *James Connolly: A Full Life: A Biography of Ireland's Renowned Trade Unionist and Leader of the 1916 Rising* (Dublin, 2006). For a female socialist participant in the Rising also born in Scotland, see Lawrence William White, "Skinnider, Margret," in James McGuire and James Quinn, eds., *Dictionary of Irish Biography* (Cambridge, 2009). (http://dib.cambridge.org/viewReadPage.do?articleId=a8112). Arthur Wicks, a former British wobbly who moved to Ireland, joined the rebels in the Easter Rising. See "Arthur Wicks," in Jimmy Wren, ed., *The GPO Garrison Easter Week 1916: A Biographical Dictionary* (Dublin, 2015), 374–75. Tom Glynn, who spent periods in Ireland, South Africa and Australia, is another example of a transnational labour activist.

27 "George King," "John King," and "Patrick King," Wren, *G.P.O. Garrison*, 154–55.

28 McGarry, A Land Beyond the Wave, 182. See Kevin Kenny, "Diaspora and Comparison: The Global Irish as a Case Study," *American Historical Review* 90 (2003), 133–62.

29 Gary B. Magee and Andrew S. Thompson, *Empire and Globalisation: Networks of People, Goods and Capital in the British World, c. 1850–1914* (Cambridge, 2010).

30 Niall Whelehan, "Playing with Scales: Transnational History and Modern Ireland," in Whelehan, ed., *Transnational Perspectives*, 11.

31 On diasporas generally, see Kevin Kenny, *Diaspora: A Very Short Introduction* (Oxford, 2013). Specifically, on the Irish diaspora in comparative context, see, for an earlier period, Matthew Frye Jacobson, *Special Sorrows: The Diasporic Imagination of Irish, Polish and Jewish Immigrants in the United States* (Berkeley, CA, 1995) and Donald Akenson, *Ireland, Sweden and the Great European Migration: 1815–1914* (Liverpool, 2012) and, on World War I a whole, Michael Neiberg, *The Path to War: How the First World War Created Modern America* (Oxford, 2016).

32 Róisín Healy, *Poland in the Irish Nationalist Imagination, 1772–1922: Anti-Colonialism within Europe* (London, 2017), 224–25.

33 Bessel, "Revolution," 143.

34 Gearóid Barry, Enrico Dal Lago, and Róisín Healy, "Towards an Interconnected History of World War I: Europe and Beyond in Gearóid Barry, Enrico Dal Lago and Róisín Healy, ed., *Small Nations and Colonial Peripheries in World War I* (Leiden, 2016), 1–18.
35 William Buck, "POWs and Civilian Internees in Ireland during World War I," in Barry, Dal Lago, and Healy, eds., *Small Nations*, 73.
36 For more detail on Liam Ó Briain's transnational connections, see online exhibition at NUI Galway, "A University in War and Revolution, 1913–1919: The Galway Experience," http://exhibitions.library.nuigalway.ie/s/nuigalway-1916/page/evolving-university-changing-ireland
37 See *Macallaí san Eoraip: Scéal éirí amach na Cásca i nuachtáin na hEorpa* [*Echoes in Europe: The Story of the Easter Rising in Europe's Newspapers*] (Dublin, 2016).
38 Thomas Kabdebo, *Ireland and Hungary: A Study in Parallels* (Dublin, 2001).
39 Foster, *Vivid Faces*, xviii–xxiii.
40 John Higgins, "The Chivalry, the Madness, the Inevitable End," in Mick O'Farrell, ed., *1916: What the People Saw* (Cork, 2013), 95.
41 Douglas W. Richmond and Sam W. Haynes, eds., *The Mexican Revolution: Conflict and Consolidation, 1910–1940* (College Station, TX, 2013).
42 "Eamon Bulfin," in Wren, *G.P.O. Garrison*, 15.
43 O'Farrell, *1916*, 179.
44 Jeffery, *1916*, 218.
45 Bill Nasson, *Springboks on the Somme: South Africa in the Great War, 1914–1918* (Johannesburg, 2007), 210.
46 Nasson, *Springboks on the Somme*, 41–55.
47 Richard Bosworth and Giuseppe Finaldi, "The Italian Empire," in Robert Gerwarth and Erez Manela, eds., *Empires at War, 1911–1923* (Oxford, 2014), 42–43.
48 Richard Fogarty, "The French Empire," in Gerwarth and Manela, eds., *Empires at War*, 120–23. On the Maghreb Amal Ghazal, "Counter-Currents: Mzabi Independence, Pan-Ottomanism and WWI in the Maghrib," *First World War Studies* 7 (2016), 81–96.
49 Correspondence from Prof. Stephanie Cronin to the editors, 10 November 2015.
50 Mustafa Aksakal, "The Ottoman Empire," in Gerwarth, Manela, eds., *Empires at War*, 31–32.
51 Jonathan Smele, *The "Russian" Civil Wars, 1916–1926: Ten Years that Shook the World* (Oxford, 2016).
52 Anne Taylor, *Annie Besant: A Biography* (Oxford, 1992).
53 Brenda Niall, *Mannix* (Melbourne, 2015).
54 See Timothy Hoyt, Chapter 2 in this volume.
55 See Charles-Philippe Courtois, Chapter 3 in this volume.
56 See Cecelia Hartsell, Chapter 4 in this volume.
57 See David Brundage, Chapter 5 in this volume.
58 See Jonathan Hyslop, Chapter 6 in this volume.
59 See Michael Provence, Chapter 7 in this volume.
60 See Erin O'Halloran, Chapter 8 in this volume.
61 See Stephen McQuillan, Chapter 9 in this volume.
62 See Danielle Ross, Chapter 10 in this volume.
63 See Daniel Marc Segesser, Chapter 11 in this volume.
64 See Geoffrey Bell, Chapter 12 in this volume.
65 See Vanda Wilcox, Chapter 13 in this volume.

66 See Andrew Newby, Chapter 14 in this volume.
67 See Róisín Healy, Chapter 15 in this volume.
68 Ferriter, *A Nation*, 170–278; Michael Laffan, *The Resurrection of Ireland: The Sinn Féin Party, 1916–1923* (Cambridge, 1999).
69 Maurice Walsh, *Bitter Freedom: Ireland in a Revolutionary World 1918–1923* (London, 2014). For examples of international interest in the War of Independence, see the study of a French Christian Democrat activist by Gearóid Barry, *The Disarmament of Hatred: Marc Sangnier, French Catholicism and the Legacy of the First World War, 1914–45* (Basingstoke, 2012), 66–67 and, on Italian irredentists, see Mark Phelan, "'Prophet of the Oppressed Nations: Gabriele D'Annunzio and the Irish Republic, 1919–21," *History Ireland* 21 (2013), 44–48.
70 O'Malley, *Ireland, India and Empire*.
71 Conor Mulvagh, *Irish Days, Indian Memories* (Dublin, 2016).
72 Gerard Keown, *First of the Small Nations: The Beginnings of Irish Foreign Policy in the Interwar Years, 1919–1932* (Oxford, 2016); Kevin O'Sullivan, *Ireland, Africa and the End of Empire* (Manchester, 2012).

2 The Easter Rising and the Changing Character of Irregular Warfare

Timothy D. Hoyt

On 24 April 1916, approximately 1,000 armed members of the Irish Volunteers and the Irish Citizens Army seized control of key locations in Central Dublin. Each group emerged from domestic political turmoil (Home Rule and labour agitation) in Ireland in the 1912–1914 period. Each had connections with the Irish Republican Brotherhood (IRB), and the first action of the rebels was to declare an Irish Republic and assume provisional leadership of that notional new state. The British military reacted rapidly to the new threat, concentrating superior forces in Dublin and gradually isolating or eliminating key Republican outposts. On 30 April, the leaders of the rebellion surrendered – the notional Republic only lasted a week. The idea, however, persisted and became a unifying concept for a more successful revolt – the Anglo-Irish War of 1919–1921. That war ended in the partition of Ireland and the establishment of an Irish Free State with Dominion status, which has since evolved to become the Republic of Ireland. The Republican idea still motivates political violence today, as splinter factions of the Provisional Irish Republican Army (IRA) continue to carry out attacks and threats in pursuit of a united Ireland. The lessons learned from the Rising created the conditions for success in 1919–1921, and continue to provide a useful model for mobilizing political support for insurgency and secession a century later.

The Easter Rising of 1916 was a very traditional *Irish* revolt. It was, after all, directed by a secret society of self-selected elites, organizing clandestinely in the name of a virtual Republic – a concept dating back to the French Revolution.[1] Secret societies opposed to English rule had attempted rebellion in the 1790s, 1803, 1848, and 1867. The ever-present *threat* of political violence enabled enormous strides in the nineteenth-century constitutional nationalist movement, including Catholic Emancipation, disestablishment of the Church of Ireland, land reform, and three Home Rule Bills.[2] In other circumstances, the passion and enthusiasm behind the Rising, and perhaps even its leaders, might have provided additional leverage for the Irish Parliamentary party to secure a more accommodating Home Rule Bill, as the Land League had provided leverage for Parnell in the 1880s.

The leaders of the Rising, however, chose to work in secret, cloaked in the mantle of the IRB. The need for generational rebellion, articulated in the 1916 Proclamation, represented a rejection of constitutional politics. The leaders of the Rising hoped to mobilise the public through a symbolic occupation of the capital, and to utilise outside military, political, and economic support from both America and Germany. The planning, insofar as we can tell, reflected important lessons from the failed rebellions of 1798, 1803, 1848, and 1867. It was a *very* Irish rebellion.

The Rising also exhibited important connections with recent European revolts. Like other nineteenth-century revolutionary movements, the Rising's leaders attempted to mobilise the nation through a kind of "propaganda by the deed." This term is normally associated with terrorism, but is also a fitting description of a military seizure of a capital city, intended to dramatically demonstrate national opposition to a ruling regime and create popular fervour and support.[3] Seizing the capital city not only demonstrated the power of the rebels and the incompetence of the ruling authorities, but also paralyzed governance and significantly affected the local economy. Ending as it did with the crushing of the rebels by the vastly superior forces of the state, the Rising again demonstrated common features with revolts throughout Europe in the early and mid-nineteenth century, and most recently the Paris Commune in 1871.

In retrospect, however, the Rising also heralded the beginnings of a new era of organised irregular warfare – a distinctive change in what Carl von Clausewitz would call the "character" of twentieth-century warfare.[4] The Irish Republican movement, which for all its apparent traditionalism was already showing signs of creative and revolutionary thought, was a learning organisation. From the errors, inadequacies, and tragedy of the Rising, a new leadership emerged that was both innovative and pragmatic. This new leadership evaluated the Rising critically, and derived valuable lessons from it. Those lessons not only enhanced the effectiveness of the *Irish* rebellion to come (the Anglo-Irish War of 1919–1921) but also of other revolts throughout the Empire and, after the Second World War, in the postcolonial world.

The first, and most important, lesson learned by the new leaders of Sinn Fein and the Irish Volunteers concerned both the strengths and the weaknesses of secret organisations. The IRB played a key role in organizing and launching the Rising. Its Military Committee (later Military Council) successfully concealed preparations from the leadership of the separate Irish Volunteer organisation – in which they were covertly embedded as senior officers – until the week before the Rising.[5] Discovery of the secret plot led to a countermanding order cancelling planned exercises on Easter Sunday by the commander of the Volunteers, who was not a member of the IRB. The Rising, therefore, was delayed a day, and carried out with a much smaller force than planned.

By keeping knowledge of the revolt to such a small number of people, the leaders achieved tactical surprise to the dismay of both the British authorities and of Irishmen who might have either supported them or counselled patience and caution. The Supreme Council of the IRB, having approved preparations for a revolt in 1915 and early 1916, was never informed of the actual date. They therefore were unable to use other embedded personnel in political organisations (Sinn Fein) or in various administrative positions across the country to assist the Rising. The overall Volunteer organisation was similarly surprised. It is not clear, for example, if coherent plans had ever been disseminated to Volunteer units outside of Dublin.

Secrecy and the need to preserve secure communications, however, severely hampered and ultimately undermined the effort to secure German arms. Orders were sent to the *Aud* – a disguised German ship carrying arms and ammunition for the rebellion – changing the planned date for landing the arms after the German vessel had already left port. The Military Council was apparently unaware that the ship had no wireless communication or contact with either Germany or Ireland! Efforts to mobilise parties of Volunteers and transport for the arms were left until literally the last minute, and collapsed from an inability to coordinate men who had never met, and in some cases, were utterly unfamiliar with the coastline.[6]

A second, related lesson concerned the efficacy of revolts in capital cities. Seizure of the capital was a critical step in the French Revolution, and a key objective in nineteenth-century popular revolutions. In economies that were largely agrarian, the capital became a "center of gravity" – the political, economic, and administrative centre of a country.[7] Government forces had difficulty fighting in congested urban areas, where narrow curving streets and centuries of urban build-up constrained manoeuvre space, tactics, and the utilisation of artillery. The redesign of major cities with wide boulevards and circles in the mid-nineteenth century was deliberate, both for aesthetic and security reasons.

Revolutionary activists viewed the seizure of capitals as a viable tactic in the late nineteenth century. The Paris Commune of 1871 demonstrated the possibilities associated with improvements in firepower – breech-loading rifles with a higher rate of fire and longer range that were easily operated by non-professional troops. City fighting was viewed as a significant force multiplier for revolutionary forces. This fact was demonstrated in the battle of Mount Street Bridge, where a handful of determined Volunteers held up the advance of a British brigade for hours, inflicting very heavy casualties.

Dublin was, in many respects, still a nineteenth-century capital. It remained the administrative and economic centre of the island, as well as the transport hub. British authorities, remembering Emmet's failed rebellion in 1803, had ringed the city with garrisons, and Dublin's ports and rail lines allowed rapid reinforcement from the Curragh, Belfast, and the rest of the United Kingdom. The rebels were aware of this, and positioned forces to cover many of the garrisons and rail lines, although full coverage was prevented by the lack of troops due to the partial mobilsation. British reinforcements arrived rapidly, however. In addition to those sent, hundreds of thousands of partially trained troops were available if necessary from training installations in England and Wales – the products of the new conscription policy for the Great War in Europe. In this respect, the old assumption that "England's difficulty was Ireland's opportunity" proved demonstrably flawed – in the absence of significant outside assistance, Ireland could not possibly field a force that the vastly expanded British Army could not defeat in short order.

A key assumption on the part of the rebels, especially socialist leader James Connolly, was that the British would be reluctant to destroy the city itself.[8] This assumption proved gravely flawed. Although reports that the British used "heavy artillery" are simply wrong, the four eighteen-pounder field artillery pieces and the twelve-pounder naval cannon on a gunboat proved both useful and quite destructive. As a 1966 study of the military aspects of the Rising pointed out, the most effective use of these modest artillery pieces was to start fires.[9] These forced the Volunteers out of the G.P.O. and devastated significant sections of central Dublin.

The destruction caused in the Rising, and the surrender and arrest of thousands of Volunteers at its end, demonstrated the limits of urban insurrection to future Republican leadership. Leaders of the Cork Volunteers proposed a "rolling Rising" in late 1919 – a Rising in Cork, and then six months later a Rising in Galway, and then later in another city. The idea was rejected by Chief of Staff Richard Mulcahy.[10]

Mulcahy had, in fact, been a key player in one of the few major engagements outside of Dublin – the successful ambush of a Royal Irish Constabulary (RIC) patrol at Ashbourne. Volunteers under the command of Thomas Ashe and Mulcahy moved into the countryside, patrolled aggressively, and killed or captured a number of police when given the opportunity. In 1919–1921, the Volunteers were careful to keep a balanced approach, supporting guerrilla activities in the countryside (referred to in one key strategic document as "the war zone") while maintaining a constant presence in, but not occupation of, Dublin.[11] The only mass military action carried out in Dublin after the Rising was the storming of the Customs House, at the express demand of De Valera, in May 1921.

The use of guerrilla tactics, demonstrated at Ashbourne and later adopted as the preferred tactic of the IRA, created significant problems for the British administration. As Charles Callwell pointed out in the first major doctrinal text on irregular warfare, guerrilla tactics were a very difficult problem for a conventional force to combat.[12] From 1919 to 1921, guerrilla tactics allowed the IRA to fight effectively despite its inherent limitations in training, tactics, and weapons, and to create a series of increasingly complicated problems for the RIC, the British Army, and Dublin Castle. Guerrilla tactics allowed rebel forces to continue demonstrative resistance over a protracted period, rather than risking all the rebellion's assets in the opening stages of a revolt.[13]

As mentioned above, the Easter Rising was a classic Irish revolt, led by a secret society determined to prevent infiltration of its ranks, even as it infiltrated various other nationalist organisations. The tactical value of secrecy was outweighed, in many respects, by the failure to capitalise on potential widespread public support. The IRB constitution, and many of the organisation's leaders, stated that there should be no military uprising until the country was adequately prepared, reflecting the failure of the Fenian rebellion in 1867.[14] The Rising, with its unique combination of both secrecy and shoddy organisation, failed to capitalise on broader political dissatisfaction. As Charles Townshend has pointed out, the Irish population did not have time to express support, but events in May suggest that considerable sympathy existed for the rebels.[15] As the IRB and Volunteer leadership rebuilt after the Rising, the new leadership recognised the need for political preparation and mobilisation, and political organisation became an integral feature of the 1917–1919 radicalisation of Irish politics, ending with the creation of Dáil Éireann.

The concept of broad national political resistance to British rule was not new. James Fintan Lalor had written about the possibility of national resistance in the mid-nineteenth century. The IRB, as mentioned above, had altered their Constitution to prohibit military action until the country was properly prepared. Bulmer Hobson, one of the leaders of the IRB until 1914, and a key figure in the Volunteers, had written a treatise on defence that examined different methods of protracted resistance – primarily nonviolent or political, but implicitly including "physical force tradition" as well.[16] Hobson's opposition to the Rising was rooted in the IRB Constitution, even though he had been dismissed from the IRB in 1914.

After the Rising, Sinn Fein and Volunteer members were imprisoned together for months. This created greater bonds between the organisations. The IRB had infiltrated both groups – Sinn Fein in the early 1900s, the Volunteers in 1913–1914 – but the overlap in membership and perspective remained quite limited. Sinn Fein members imprisoned for a so-called "Sinn Fein Rebellion" in which they played no role found they had more in common than expected with the political views of Volunteers. Parliamentary by-elections offered an opportunity for Sinn Fein to run candidates that were associated with the Rising in 1917. The October 1917 conventions of both Sinn Fein and the Volunteers were held on consecutive days. The conventions elected Executive Councils for both organisations. These Councils had a 30 per cent overlap in membership, with Eamon De Valera named as the president of each.[17]

This overlap, and the informal civil-military relationship that emerged from both the Executives and later Dáil Éireann, proved an important strategic asset for the rebels and a model for future insurgencies.[18] Sinn Fein carried on a nationwide campaign that organised and mobilised nonviolent resistance, including an ostracization campaign against the police. This incremental campaign of radicalisation provided the base of broader support for the physical force effort that evolved gradually in 1919 and early 1920.

The combination of political mobilisation and gradual military escalation allowed increasing pressure to be brought to bear on British authorities, ensured greater popular support when British reprisals became official policy, enabled greater success for the IRA and its guerrilla tactics by providing shelter and intelligence, and protracted the war and raised costs for the British government, which contributed to their willingness to find a negotiated solution.[19]

Necessity forced the IRA and the Republican movement to adapt and find a new strategy for rebellion. In the past, Irish rebels had fielded virtually all their forces initially and staked the results of their efforts on a single battle or action. The new political-military strategy, however, allowed the Irish to continue resisting with only a fraction of their total supporters in the field. While this created a war of pin-pricks rather than great battles, each incident caused increasing pressure on the British, and many prompted disproportionate British retaliation, further eroding British reputation and legitimacy. The corollary aspect was the ability of Irish forces to absorb losses and continue functioning, learning from each setback and continuing to adapt in new and effective ways.[20]

The Republican movement became a coalition of nationalists, cooperating towards a vague but common goal, which enabled them to integrate and use people and groups who were *not* committed to armed struggle. Although secrecy and covert organizing continued, primarily in the form of the reinvigorated IRB, new approaches emerged from the experience of 1916 and the need to create and sustain a broader movement. Information became a critical element of Republican strategy. The Ministry of Information became an important part of political outreach (see below), mobilising the domestic population as well as providing powerful alternative arguments to the official British policy statements.

In addition, the first Director of Information for the Volunteers was Michael Collins, who later became the Director for Intelligence. Collins was obsessed with secrecy, but also recognised the failings of the Rising leadership.[21] While the IRB remained clandestine and almost completely under his personal control, he also created an intelligence organisation to compete for information and deny the British any opportunity to penetrate a larger and more public leadership. The opening blows of the war of independence in 1919 were directed against the "G" Division of the Dublin Metropolitan Police, which investigated political crimes. Selective assassinations and intimidation rendered it ineffective within a matter of months. British efforts to infiltrate agents into the IRA were dealt with ruthlessly. By winning the battle for intelligence early, and winning a second round on "Bloody Sunday" in November 1920, Collins and his small unit bought time for the Republican cause to mature and grow, and denied intelligence to the British. The intelligence battle – denial, deception, and murder – has also become an important aspect of contemporary revolts and revolutions, counterinsurgency operations, and counterterrorism efforts.

The Rising was, effectively, a coup d'etat by a secret military organisation. As mentioned above, the Council's obsession with secrecy – understandable, in historical context – inhibited both military planning and political organizing. The result, however, was that neither the Volunteer organisation nor the public at large were prepared for the Rising. Units in the countryside were disorganised and confused. The Rising's short duration precluded effective mobilisation of either popular or international support. The signers of the Proclamation, who constituted the provisional government of the new Republic, were the seven members of the secret Military Council of the IRB – hardly a representative body of the Irish people.[22]

The creation of a shadow government in January 1919 opened new opportunities for competition with the British authorities for political legitimacy in Ireland. Dáil Éireann, established on the basis of the November 1918 national elections across the United Kingdom, could argue plausibly that it represented the majority view of the Irish people. Of 105 Parliamentary seats in Ireland, 73 were won by Sinn Fein, whose newly elected representatives refused to go to Westminster, met in Dublin instead, and swore allegiance to the Irish Republic proclaimed by the leaders of the Rising. The new Dail sent "ambassadors" to other countries, many officials to the United States, and a team to represent the interests of the Irish nation at the Versailles Peace Conference. It acted, on the international stage, as an independent government, taking full propaganda advantage of the commitment of both the British Empire and the Allies to the independence of small nations. Although its foreign policy efforts were ultimately unsuccessful (no country recognised the Irish state until after the Treaty in 1921), they did create an aura of legitimacy and symbolic authority in competition with British claims, and created the public perception – particularly in the United States – of being the underdog.[23]

Establishment of an alternative government is only one step in the competition for legitimacy, however. What made the Dail particularly effective was its ability to contest Dublin Castle in the provision of services to the public. The Dail established numerous ministries which competed – with varying degrees of effectiveness – with the British for local governance and services. Sinn Fein's increasingly impressive victories in local, town, and county elections left Republicans in formal political control of many localities. Alternate courts and police systems, funded by a National Loan (run by Michael Collins as the Minister of Finance), shifted the responsibility for the rule of law in many areas from Dublin Castle to the rebels.

None of this would have been possible without the ongoing military efforts of the Volunteers, later renamed the IRA. Civil-military relations between the IRA and Sinn Fein were informal. Richard Mulcahy met with his Dail superior and Minister of Defence, Cathal Brugha, on a regular basis.[24] Mulcahy himself was a Sinn Fein TD, as was Michael Collins. De Valera was, in theory, President of the Executive of both Sinn Fein and the Volunteer organisation. After his departure in April 1919 for America, however, the Volunteer organisation began to decline. Once "real war" broke out in 1920, its functions were effectively subsumed into the General Headquarters of the IRA. The IRA passively resisted efforts by the Dail to assert control over its actions, and the Dail and De Valera both showed only modest inclination to accept responsibility for IRA military actions until relatively late in the war of independence. Despite the lack of formal control, the IRA and Sinn Fein both declared allegiance to the Irish Republic, and the IRA's continued resistance and periodic military success contributed to Sinn Fein's legitimacy as the representative body of the Irish people.

The combination of continuing political resistance and escalating military violence created a unique set of problems for the British Empire. The first was a question of the value of the political object – how vital *was* control of Ireland in the aftermath of World War I. The second was a matter of morality and principle – Ireland was, after all, a part of the United Kingdom, and Britain's reluctance to resort to martial law and to declare the conflict a "small war" lay in part in an unwillingness to admit that a portion of the homeland might be engaged in a separatist revolt. A third was the issue of priorities – in the aftermath of Versailles, Britain had to assert control over one million square miles of new empire in the Middle East, negotiate the Versailles agreement, manage the collapse of the Ottoman Empire, cope with a significant economic recession, and find ways to manage the expansionist naval programs of Japan and the United States. Given the willingness of Britain to consider Home Rule in 1914, a negotiated settlement was certainly a viable alternative to significant military escalation and a possible longer, bloodier war. All these factors contributed to the British government's decision to negotiate with the rebels in 1921, and to the Truce and Treaty that followed (as well as the tragic civil war).

The Irish struggle proved a complex problem for Britain. The Rising was crushed militarily within a matter of days, but the political aftershocks – especially the public response to the executions of the leaders – were both unanticipated and revolutionary. The Rising changed political conditions in Ireland, creating a symbol (the notional Republic) that rallied and united disaffected Irish of all political classes and beliefs. From the ashes of defeat, a new generation of Irish leaders emerged.

The British Army proved curiously resistant to attempting to learn lessons from the Irish conflict – a resistance that also was seen regarding the changing character of *conventional* warfare.[25] The official histories written on the conflict gathered dust on shelves for decades, and the new small wars manuals written in the 1930s barely reflected the unique aspects of the Irish war.[26] It was not until 1940, when the Special Operations Executive began to investigate methods for organizing revolts in occupied Europe, that the Irish war began to receive attention as an example of a new form of revolutionary warfare. This was, in some ways, a timely lesson – for in the aftermath of the Second World War, colonial rebellions begin to demonstrate many of the same characteristics of the successful Republican revolt.

Many rebellions in the inter-war period and the postcolonial world replicated aspects of the Irish rebellions. The struggle for legitimacy through an organised political movement, the protraction of resistance to raise long-term costs to overstretched imperial powers, the increasing use of guerrilla tactics rather than direct conventional confrontation, and the limits of city combat were all lessons that were reflected in some successful insurgencies, and learned painfully by others. An important aspect of these tactics included creating opportunities for the enemy to over-react and make delegitimizing mistakes.

The manner in which the lessons of the Irish war were learned by other future rebels was both direct and indirect. Some movements attempted to learn directly from Irish example. Bengali rebels studied the biographies of Irish rebels, particularly Dan Breen. Jewish nationalists in the Palestinian Mandate also looked to Irish examples and tactics.[27] The Irish provided an example of successful revolt by a small nation against imperial rule – and that demonstration effect was noted by generations of future rebels. Finding ways to gain and increase legitimacy compared to imperial governors, to raise military and security costs for those governors, and to protract that resistance became staples of postcolonial wars of independence and of secessionist and other revolutionary struggles since that time.

The Easter Rising, viewed in isolation, is a peculiar act of military incompetence, which had fortuitous political effects due to British political ineptitude. This cynical view only presents part of the picture. The Rising represents, in fact, both the end of one era and the beginning of another – a turning point in the changing character of twentieth-century irregular warfare.

Carl von Clausewitz, in his epic *On War*, states bluntly in the first pages that "...in war, the result is rarely ever final."[28] The Proclamation of the Irish Republic in 1916 certainly reflected this idea, noting the six armed rebellions against British rule and the generational tradition of armed resistance – the famous "physical force tradition" of Irish nationalism. Clausewitz insists that the nature of war is unchanging – organised political violence used for the achievement of implicit or explicit political aims. But he also notes that the character of war can change, depending on the "spirit of the age" or the nature of the political systems of the various combatants.

Studies of the Easter Rising rarely discuss the broader military implications of the revolt for the international community. The emphasis, understandably, is on the political impact of the Rising as a pivotal moment in the Irish national struggle. Studies of the military aspects of the Rising focus instead on discreet tactical engagements (Mount Street Bridge, St. Stephens Green), or the overall futility of both military resistance and efforts at broader national mobilisation.

Viewed in historical context, however, the Easter Rising might be viewed as the third or fourth in a series of episodes that led, in the period from 1912 to 1923, to the creation of the modern Irish state.[29] The militarization of Irish nationalism occurred in phases, and the Rising is a pivotal moment not only in the political history of Ireland, but also in the changing character of twentieth-century warfare. The methods of the IRA, and the demonstrated effectiveness of the Irish national revolt from 1919 to 1921, were the result of lessons learned from 1916. The IRA's successes not only encouraged anti-colonial movements but also provided a template for successful resistance in Bengal, Palestine, and other parts of the Empire. While the Rising may not have significantly affected many of the other political revolts around the globe in 1916–1918, its consequences were felt across the imperial system for decades, and as a model of national resistance remain viable even today.

Notes

1 Florrie O'Donoghue, *No Other Law* (Dublin, 1954), 68–74.
2 Charles Townshend, *Political Violence in Ireland: Government and Resistance since 1848* (Oxford, 1983).
3 The concept of "propaganda of the deed" originated with the Russian terrorist group Narodnaya Volnya ("People's Will"), which believed symbolic acts of violence would mobilise the masses more quickly and effectively than peaceful political organization. See http://terrorism.about.com/od/groupsleader1/p/NarodnayaVolya.htm. The idea that the Irish revolutionary tradition includes a kind of propaganda of the deed has been applied as far back as the United Irishmen. See Nancy Curtin, *The United Irishmen: Popular Politics in Ulster and Dublin, 1791–1798* (Oxford, 1998).
4 Carl von Clausewitz, *On War*, edited and translated by Michael Howard and Peter Paret (Princeton, NJ, 1976), 220, 593–94.
5 The committee expanded from three members to seven, and eventually included all the signatories of the Proclamation. Leon O'Broin, *Revolutionary Underground* (Lanham, MD, 1976), 155–58, 167; Diarmuid Lynch and Florrie O'Donoghue, *The I.R.B. and the 1916 Insurrection* (Dublin, 1957), 25, 47–48.
6 Desmond Ryan, *The Rising: The Complete Story of Easter Week* (Dublin, 1949), 101–14.
7 Clausewitz, *On War*, 595–96.
8 Tim Pat Coogan, *1916: The Easter Rising* (London, 2005), 97.
9 P.J. Holly, "The Easter 1916 Rising in Dublin: The Military Aspects," *The Irish Sword* 7.29 (1966), 313–26; P.J. Holly, "The Easter 1916 Rising in Dublin: The Military Aspects (Part II)," *The Irish Sword* 8.30 (1967), 48–57.
10 Maryann Gialanella Valiulis, *Portrait of a Revolutionary: General Richard Mulcahy and the Founding of the Irish Free State* (Lexington, KY, 1992), 49; Mulcahy Papers, University College Dublin Archives, P7/D/66.
11 Mulcahy Papers, University College Dublin Archives, P7/A/17 "The War as a Whole" Staff Memo 24 March 1921.
12 Charles Callwell, *Small Wars: Their Principles & Practice*, 3rd ed. (London, 1906), 31, 37, 99 126.
13 Florrie O'Donoghue, "Guerrilla Warfare in Ireland 1919–1921", *An Cosantóir* 23 (1963).
14 "Constitution of the I.R.B. (Irish Republican Brotherhood)," Bureau of Military History, Dublin, C.D. 8/3. This is a typescript copy provided by Bulmer Hobson with a signed affidavit of authenticity. This version was adopted after

the I.R.B. was reorganised in 1873, and remained in force until sometime after 1916.

15 Charles Townshend, *Easter 1916: The Irish Rebellion* (Oxford, 2005), 269–320 discusses the rapid shifts in political sympathy for the rebels and their platform, which *might* have been mobilised more effectively.

16 Marnie Hay, *Bulmer Hobson and the Nationalist Movement in Twentieth-Century Ireland* (Manchester, 2009), 75–76. Hobson's pamphlet *Defensive Warfare: A Handbook for Irish Nationalists* (Belfast, 1909) influenced plans for resistance, even if Hobson himself was repudiated by the Military Committee and imprisoned just before the Rising. See also Townshend, *Easter 1916*. On pp. 90–100, Townshend discusses the planning process for the Rising, which considered but ultimately rejected the type of broader national resistance favoured by Hobson.

17 Richard Mulcahy, "The Irish Volunteer Convention 27 October 1917," *Capuchin Annual* 34 (1967), 408–9.

18 Tim Hoyt, "Military Innovation in Ireland, 1916–1923," *Defence Forces Review 2016*, 9–20.

19 Charles Townshend, *The British Campaign in Ireland 1919–1921: The Development of Political and Military Policies* (Oxford, 1975) remains the seminal study on Britain's side of the conflict.

20 For an excellent recent history of the conflict *after* the Easter Rising, see Michael Hopkinson, *The Irish War of Independence* (Montreal and Kingston, 2002).

21 Tim Pat Coogan, *The Man Who Made Ireland: The Life and Death of Michael Collins* (Niwot, CO, 1992), 53–54.

22 A comparison with the signatories of the American Declaration of Independence is instructive. The Continental Congress was composed of representatives of a broad portion of the political and economic elites in the thirteen colonies.

23 An exhaustive study of the emergence of the new Irish republic – which extends to the tragic Civil War that followed – is Dorothy MacArdle, *The Irish Republic* (New York, 1965). The most recent study, using recently opened archival sources, is Charles Townshend, *The Republic: The Fight for Irish Independence* (London, 2013).

24 Risteard Mulcahy, *My Father, The General: Richard Mulcahy and the Military History of the Revolution* (Dublin, 2009), 43.

25 Williamson Murray and Allan R. Millett, eds., *Military Revolution in the Interwar Period* (Cambridge, 1998).

26 Charles W. Gwynn, *Imperial Policing* (London, 1934).

27 Bruce Hoffman, *Anonymous Soldiers: The Struggle for Israel, 1917–1947* (New York, 2015).

28 Clausewitz, *On War*, 80.

29 Those episodes might include the formation of the Ulster and Irish Volunteers (1912–1913), the Home Rule Crisis of 1914, the Rising, the conscription crisis of 1918, the establishment of the Dáil, the beginnings of formal military operations in 1920, the Treaty, and the Civil War that followed.

Section II
The Atlantic World

3 Echoes of the Rising in Quebec's Conscription Crisis

The French Canadian Press and the Irish Revolution between 1916 and 1918

Charles-Philippe Courtois

Studies of Ireland in the period from 1916 to 1922 take into account debates on World War I in the United States and Australia.[1] In contrast to this, Canada receives much less attention in the historiography of Ireland's revolutionary period. Irish Canadian support for Sinn Féin, the movement that was the political beneficiary of the Easter Rising, was simply not comparable to the prominent role played by other parts of the Irish diaspora. At the same time, those claiming Irish origins represented the third largest national group within Canada at this time, behind those identifying as English and French but ahead of those identifying as Scots. Arguably, French Canadian nationalists were more sympathetic to Irish freedom than large sections of Irish Canadian opinion, even amongst Irish Canadian Catholics.[2] In many ways, Irish immigration to Quebec had been distinct. Unlike English-speaking "new Worlds," Quebec was mostly Catholic; through intermarriage and adoption, many French Canadians had ended up with Irish surnames.[3] Quebec was also receptive to anti-imperialism.

The Quebec Legislative Assembly adopted motions in favour of Home Rule in 1887 and 1903. During the Irish War of Independence (1919–1921), Quebec's archbishops, Cardinal Bégin of Québec and Mgr Bruchési of Montréal, petitioned the king in favour of peace; massive demonstrations of solidarity, including commemorative masses, followed the death of Terence McSwiney, attracting at least as many French Canadians as Irish Quebeckers.[4] The reaction to the "Irish Revolution" had therefore a distinct character in Quebec.[5] The nationalist press not only denounced the repression of the Rising, but also the lack of response of Irish Canadians in 1916. Robert McLaughlin reckons that the relationship between Irish nationalism and French Canadian nationalism in Canada in the early twentieth century "is an area of research crying for further investigation."[6] French Canadian nationalism's relations with the Irish has mostly been studied with regard to the 1837–1838 Rebellions, when local Irish Catholics were important allies of the Parti patriote; comparisons between Ireland and Quebec, some centred on the forced unions of 1801 and 1840, are few.[7] For the early twentieth century, the rivalries within the Catholic Church in North America have been the focus of attention.

In my view, the Irish Revolution's appeal for French Canadian nationalists was bound up with an evolution towards a nationalism more centred on the Quebec polity rather than on the entire Canadian federation. During World War I Canada experienced a severe clash between English and French Canada over the rights of the French language and the question of participation in imperial wars. The imperial dimension of this issue is too often neglected, at least in the Canadian literature, yet conscription was bitterly debated in most Dominions and opposed by non-English nationalities, in Ireland and Quebec. However, comparison between anti-imperialism in Quebec and Ireland during World War I is uncommon in the limited historiography on the Conscription Crisis.[8] Recent studies have analysed specific aspects of the crisis but rarely consider its international dimensions.[9] Moreover, very few studies analyse Quebec's reaction to the Irish Revolution. An exception to this is Simon Jolivet, although his analyses of French Canadian reactions to the Irish Revolution do not cover the Rising specifically.[10] In contrast to the Irish Canadian Catholic press, whose main papers, the *Catholic Register* and the *Catholic Record*, condemned the "Insane Folly of the Sinn Féiners" and their "unjustifiable" revolt in 1916, even if Irish Catholic newspapers' stances would begin to shift from 1917.[11] The French Canadian nationalist press was more immediately sympathetic.

The chapter on the coverage of the Rising in the French Canadian press two pairs of newspapers on both ends of the spectrum, from the most nationalist, *Le Devoir*, edited by Henri Bourassa, and separatist weekly *La Croix*, to the most Loyalist, *L'Événement* and *L'Action catholique*. It will compare their initial representation and later coverage of the Irish Revolution in the years 1916–1918 in connection with Quebec's Conscription Crisis. The chapter attempts to explain why French Canadians were so interested in the Irish Revolution; why ethnic rivalries with Irish Catholics did not dampen their solidarity with Ireland and the lasting effects of the nationalists' support, by situating their attitudes within the broader context of Canada's unity crisis and relations between Irish and French Canadians. Such an analysis should shed new light on the evolution of French Canadian nationalism during World War I as well as exploring a little-known facet of the Easter Rising's influence.[12]

The clash that culminated in the Conscription Crisis of 1917–1918 had been brewing since the beginning of the decade over the issues of the imperial wars and bilingual rights. Sir Robert Borden's Conservative government at federal level had rapidly estranged itself from French Canadians since its election in 1911, beginning with its military policies. The Ontario Tories adopted "Regulation XVII" in 1912 which made English the only language of instruction in the province, ending French Canadians' bilingual school system within Ontario's separate Catholic schools. Franco-Ontarians were the biggest French-speaking minority in Canada and the closest to Quebec. Their growth in Ontario to 8 per cent of the population by 1911 alarmed Orangemen, who had obtained the anglicisation of public schools in most other provinces.[13] Regulation XVII led to formidable mobilisation against the measure in Quebec throughout the war. It became a major argument against greater recruitment or conscription. French Canadian nationalists decried the "Boches" of Ontario and pointed to the inconsistency of dying in the defence of liberty and small nations in Europe while French Canadians' rights were being crushed at home. French Canadians argued that the confederation's official bilingualism had been recognised in the 1867 constitution; given the privileges granted to Anglophones and Protestants in Quebec, the separate francophone Catholic schools in Ontario were considered a measure of reciprocity.

This crisis was escalating in 1916, with further resignations from government by French Canadian Conservatives and major demonstrations in Ottawa. Borden's incomprehension remained complete, dismissing the protests, in the words of his recent biographer, as "all this whining when a war for civilization raged."[14] Borden wrote in 1916: "The vision of the French Canadian is very limited. He is not well informed and he is in a condition of extreme exasperation by reason of fancied wrongs supposed to be inflicted upon his compatriots in other provinces."[15] Originally, Borden's government had a goal of deploying 50,000 troops (mainly on the Western Front) and promised to avoid conscription. The government rapidly increased the size of the Canadian Expeditionary Force. By New Year's Eve in 1915, Borden suddenly declared it would reach 500,000 men, disregarding the warnings of generals and industrialists on the limitations of training and industrial needs.

Borden continued to declare his intention to avoid conscription when a National Registry was imposed in 1916, a measure supported by the Catholic hierarchy in Quebec which nonetheless provoked new riots. Archbishop Bruchési of Montréal, in particular, accepted Borden's denials that the National Registry was not, as *nationalistes* claimed, a step towards conscription, which was in fact what it became.[16] The hierarchy alienated its flock and some argue Mgr Bruchési never fully recovered from the political humiliation. Nationalists criticised his first pronouncements in favour of recruitment in 1914, asserting Mgr Bruchési's declaration would "delight Irish imperialists" in Canada (implicitly referring to churchmen such as Mgr Fallon) and already contested Bruchési's authority on such matters.[17] The contestation of bishops' authority by laymen had been unknown in Quebec since the demise of radical republicanism in the late nineteenth century.[18]

Voluntary recruitment declined in Quebec in 1916. Two-thirds of recruits were British-born (much more than their proportion in the population). Much of the English-speaking press pointed the finger at French Canadians, presented as "white race" with the lowest recruitment. The Canadian Forces had since 1867 consistently failed to accommodate French Canadian identity, a reality only reinforced by the policies of Federal Defence Minister Sir Sam Hughes.[19] In this context, French Canadians were already rejecting the possibility of conscription advocated by others to force them to "do their duty." The first anti-conscription riots occurred in Quebec in

1915. French Canadians rejected the notion that it was their patriotic duty to participate in a British war. Arguments about helping Belgium, France and Britain in the war were acceptable; imposing conscription for a foreign war and service in a British army was not. Solidarity with France swayed French Canadian opinion little. France had abandoned Quebec since 1763; as demonstrated in the 1837–1838 Rebellions, no power would help French Canadians in a struggle for independence. The Third Republic's anti-clericalism further tipped the scales against sympathy for France as French Canada had reinforced its Catholicism after the 1837–1838 Rebellions.

Borden decided in favour of conscription on foot of his participation in the Imperial War Cabinet in the spring of 1917 and the persuasive efforts of British Prime Minister David Lloyd George.[20] When Sir Wilfrid Laurier, leader of Canada's opposition, refused to back the measure, demanding a referendum as in Australia, Borden convinced most English-speaking Liberal MPs to join his new "Union" government that supported conscription. Violence erupted in protests across Quebec in the summer of 1917, culminating in the Easter riots of 1918 in Quebec City and the imposition of martial law in Quebec.[21] Borden sought a new mandate from the people in the autumn of 1917 in an election described as "one of the few in Canadian history deliberately conducted on racist grounds."[22] Election campaigners intentionally pitted English against French with slogans such as "The slacker must not rule Canada."[23] Unionist candidates in the election risked their lives, as did recruitment officers. Equally, the Quebec population refused to cooperate. Laurier's divided Liberals were reduced mostly to seats in Quebec, yet in terms of the popular vote Borden's victory was much narrower, despite unprecedented gerrymandering. If this served Borden's unpopular government well initially, this advantage would not prove enduring; the Conservatives never recovered in Quebec and the Liberals became Canada's "natural governing party" in the medium term.

The "unity crisis" also led to important reorientations of French Canadian nationalism, which was dominated in 1914 by Henri Bourassa, founder of *Le Devoir* and its *maître à penser* since he broke with Prime Minister Laurier in 1899 over participation in the Boer War.[24] Very critical of imperialism and colonialism, he advocated the greatest possible autonomy for Quebec and bilingual rights. His prestige marginalised other *nationaliste* currents in favour of his pan-Canadian ideal. Acknowledged as very influential over French Canadians, Catholic affairs and Canadian politics, more generally, Bourassa was often received by foreign leaders, including Irish leaders on different occasions. Indeed, he considered himself a friend of the Irish Parliamentary Party (IPP), the constitutionalist nationalist party in Westminster.[25] Bourassa approved of Canadian participation in the War in 1914, as long as it served Canada's interests. *Le Devoir* regularly situated the debate on Canadian military involvement within its imperial context.[26] Bourassa began defending Benedict XV's pacifism in 1915, putting him at odds with Quebec's hierarchy.[27] In 1916, *Le Devoir* denounced Borden's new recruitment targets. Even though Bourassa embodied Quebec's resistance and was the *bête noire* of imperialists, the force of the unity crisis, involving Regulation XVII and conscription, also spelled the decline of his dominance. A rift would occur between Bourassa and his former followers in 1923 over separatism, such that thereafter French Canadian nationalism split into autonomist and separatist camps.[28]

Broadly speaking, French Canadians' interest in the situation in Ireland was based upon the aspiration for emancipation from empire, resistance to assimilation and a shared Catholicism. French Canadians felt their existence to be close to unknown (even in France) and misunderstood, if not scorned, in North America. Comparisons with the much more famous resistance to religious and political assimilation in Ireland could be used to help "normalise" French Canada's own resistance to the British Empire. This was still very much the case in the 1910s: their position on the war was generally misunderstood. French Canadian interest in Ireland flourished, beginning with the "Patriotes" (who were fond of comparing their leaders to Daniel O'Connell) and under the leadership of Eamon De Valera in the 1930s, although began to wane after World War II.[29]

Any international comparison of this type must be approached with caution and nuance. The hardships faced by French Canadians since the British conquest of 1763 were not of the same severity as those of Ireland's people. The Oath of the Test was eliminated by means of the Quebec Act of 1774. This reversal of policy concerning assimilation marked the beginning of the French Canadian Catholic Church's Loyalism, reinforced by church opposition to the French Revolution and by the excommunication of French Canadian rebels in 1837–1838. This did not prevent the Church from resisting renewed assimilation policies or pressures, but its cultural resistance remained coupled with its Loyalism, well expressed by a pastoral letter of the bishops in 1914 and their position in 1916 regarding the National Register.[30] As well, some form of Home Rule, however limited, had been granted to Quebec with Confederation in 1867. There was no equivalent of the IPP after 1867: French Canadians had integrated pan-Canadian parties (Henri Bourassa rejected the party system). Finally, in Ireland, religion tended to converge with national identity during the Irish Revolution; in Canada, the language question superseded religion, even though most French Canadian nationalists were also fervent Catholics.

Ireland had many similarities in World War I, including difficulties with integration into a British army, especially given the refusal to form an Irish Division and a French Canadian brigade. To what extent were these nations' interests at stake in a British war? The discrepancy between the purported British mission of defending small nations and the denial of rights at home, whether by postponing Home Rule or implementing Regulation XVII, stood out in both countries.[31] Yet for French Canadian nationalists, differences were also of interest. The most striking contrast was probably the difference in attitude of the Catholic Church to anti-imperialism. For separatist or anti-imperial Catholics in Quebec any discussion of the Easter Rising was also a discussion of Catholic theology on insurrection as presented in Quebec by church leadership. No bishop in French Canada criticised the British Empire in a manner that could be remotely compared to the outspoken Irish duo of Bishop Edward Thomas O'Dwyer of Limerick and Archbishop Daniel Mannix of Melbourne who forcefully denounced British repression in the wake of the executions of the Irish rebel leaders in May 1916. Although Cardinal Bégin criticised the introduction of conscription in Canada in 1917, he could find no extenuating circumstances for the violence of the Easter 1918 riots in Quebec against the new law and he unreservedly condemned the idea of insurrection. The declaration by Irish priest Fr Thomas Duggan that he and "[his] generation [of trainee priests] in Maynooth [seminary] embraced the ideals of Easter Week with a hundred percent fervour" would not have been uttered by a French Canadian priest and few voices in official Quebec Catholicism praised the Easter Rising rebels like the popular publication, the *Catholic Bulletin*, did in Ireland.[32]

Relations between Irish and French Canadians also influenced the coverage of the Irish Revolution. French Canadians were interested in contrasting Irish Canadian support for assimilation with the assertiveness of nationalism in Ireland. An estimated two-thirds of the Irish community in Canada were Protestants, with the notable exception of Quebec, and their influence over the evolution of the Dominion was extensive.[33] The Orange Order was very influential in Canadian politics, especially the Tory Party outside Quebec.[34] By some estimates, one Protestant adult in three became a member by the turn of the century.[35] Many Federal Prime Ministers, Ontario Premiers, most Toronto Mayors (where 12 July became "a public holiday in all but name"), were members of the Order.[36] The Order's *bête noire* in the Dominion was the French Catholic element and their demands for linguistic and religious rights, which they opposed using the slogan "One flag, one language, and one school, equal rights for all, special privileges for none."[37] Orangemen also often expressed this view in more violent language.[38] Orangeism played a leading role in the polarisation between French and British Canada after 1867, in each major crisis from the Red River Rebellion (1869) to the Ontario Schools Controversy of 1917.[39] During World War I, Orangemen pointed the finger at French Canadian "slackers." In Borden's cabinet, Sam Hughes was a well-known Orangeman, and indeed, his right-hand man, Arthur Meighen, determined to spare nothing in the defence of Britain, was of Ulster Presbyterian heritage.[40]

Irish nationalism was discreet in Canada where, in contrast to Irish-Americans' "diasporic" nationalism, Irish Canadian Catholics focused on assuming a new Canadian identity, first promoted by the Irish

Catholic "father of Confederation" Thomas D'Arcy McGee.[41] This implied agreeing with the English character of the Dominion and the British connection, a phenomenon Mark McGowan has described as "The Waning of the Green."[42] There certainly was no "waning of the Orange" in Canada. Robert McLaughlin has noted the Canadian financial support of Ulster Unionist paramilitarism during the Irish Home Rule Crisis (1912–1914).[43] He is also one of the few to challenge the "waning of the Green" thesis, dominant in Irish Canadian studies, pointing to the real mobilisation around the Self-Determination for Ireland League of Canada, notably from 1919 to 1922.[44] Adding further nuance, Simon Jolivet argues that a disproportionate amount of Irish Canadian Catholic support for the Irish Revolution was found in Quebec, where assimilation into English Canadian identity was slower and solidarity with French Canadian nationalism greater.[45] Indeed, many of the demonstrations of solidarity analysed by McLaughlin took place in Quebec and involved Irish Canadian leaders and politicians from Quebec.[46] Nevertheless, "Green" and "Blue" relations were not always harmonious.

Their rivalry within the Catholic Church in North America, in areas where French Canadians had important diasporas, such as Ontario or New England, is well documented.[47] The French Canadian hierarchy resented a perceived push by Irish clergy to take over dioceses in Canada where French Canadians still retained either a majority or plurality of Catholics, favouring anglicisation of Church institutions, a process backed to some extent by the Apostolic Delegates.[48] The Holy See entertained hopes at this time of converting North America and Britain and thus seems to have favoured Irish clergy and anglicisation. The controversy surrounding the use of English at the 1910 Eucharistic Congress in Montréal was indicative of such linguistic tensions.[49] The evolution of the Vatican's attitudes under Benedict XV (1914–1922) noted by Jérôme aan de Wiel, towards increasing of the Irish rather than the English hierarchy was perhaps also influenced by this North American context; in any case, the French Canadian hierarchy believed themselves neglected by the Vatican until the pontificate of Pius XII (1939–1958).[50]

This Franco-Irish clash is perhaps epitomised by Irish Catholic Mgr Michael Francis Fallon, who, as soon as he was ordained Bishop of London, Ontario, in 1909, became a *de facto* ally of the Orange Order on the Ontario Schools Question.[51] Typically, Mgr Fallon asked the Apostolic Delegate, Mgr Sbaretti: "Shall the Catholic Church ally itself with the certain and visible destiny of that New World, or shall its policy be decided by those who stand first for nationality and only afterwards for Catholicity?"[52] Also embodying the "waning of the Green," Fallon, an imperialist, visited Ireland in 1918 and was taken aback by the revolutionary mood, fearing "grave dangers for Ireland in the Sinn Fein movement. It is not unfair to say that it has bred a sort of insanity in many of its adherents," deploring the "exaggerated conscience of nationality."[53]

In contrast, the Irish Revolution enthralled French Canadian nationalists. Following Sinn Féin's electoral victory in 1918, the Self-Determination for Ireland League of Canada (SDILC) wrought a (temporary) *rapprochement* between French Canadian nationalists and Irish Canadian Catholics with large input from Irish Quebeckers; such leading *nationalistes* as Armand Lavergne (a close associate of Bourassa's) spoke at a SDILC convention in 1920 (which adopted resolutions recognising Canada's bilingualism).[54] At this convention, Lavergne declared: "we'll stick by you. [...]." If the Irish Canadian nationalists' support was subdued in tone compared to that of Irish Americans, Lavergne's was not: "If I were an Irishman [...] I would take my rifle and fight to the last drop of my blood [...] I would try a Black and Tan first."[55] Even though *nationalistes* of the 1920s presented the (implicitly Catholic) "assimilated Irish" as a stereotypical adversary of the rights of the French in Canada, nonetheless the Irish Free State continued to be a source of inspiration in Quebec.[56] The main separatist newspaper in the 1930s, *La Nation*, which agitated for an *État libre du Québec*, would state: "Nous voulons un *French Canadian Free State* comme il y a un *Irish Free State.*"[57]

French Canadian papers were mostly partisan, Whig or Tory, with a significant minority, either Catholic or nationalist, termed "independent." Liberal papers had the largest circulation. Most conservative-leaning papers refused to follow their party's suicide in Quebec. The only exception was *L'Événement*, which defended conscription until the end of the war. *L'Action catholique*, although non-partisan, was among the very few papers defending the government. The Montréal daily *Le Devoir* (1910–present) was edited by Bourassa. Joseph Bégin edited the Montréal weekly *La Croix* (1903–1918). Both were staunchly ultramontane Catholics and nationalists but of differing opinions on Quebec separatism.

Le Devoir was one of the most influential French Canadian papers. Showing interest in Ireland since its first publication, many of its journalists followed events with considerable rigour compared to most of the press.[58] Henri Bourassa, who considered himself a friend of Redmond and his IPP in 1914, fully backed the IPP's non-separatist views but, after the Rising, his position evolved very quickly, perhaps more rapidly and boldly than that of the Irish Canadian Catholic press.[59] In 1919 *Le Devoir*'s weekly supplement *Le Nationaliste* published weekly bulletins on the Irish situation, often in English for the benefit of Irish Canadians, because the English language press in Canada, with its British point of view, offered biased reports.[60]

In the weeks before the Easter Rising, Bourassa was still praising Redmond and attributing Ireland's exemption from conscription to the merits of the IPP.[61] He wrote in an editorial that Ireland should inspire Canada and that Redmond had been mispresented by the jingoes in Canada.

(In reality, Redmond had demanded and obtained concessions in exchange for supporting recruitment.) The implicit parallel is with Regulation XVII. Canada's participation, according to *Le Devoir*, alone stood out in its foolishness in the Empire, purely for the Empire's prestige in the final victory, not the usually invoked reasons, such as solidarity with Belgium. "*Tout pour l'Empire!*" was the real slogan of politicians in Ottawa, no matter the consequences for Canada, an "odious and ridiculous" attitude, as shown by the contrast with British policy in the United Kingdom itself which took into account the particular situation and sentiments of Ireland.[62]

Le Devoir's first article on the Rising, published on 26 April 1916, interestingly provided no detail on the actual events, but instead contextualised the insurgency by recalling the natural desire for self-determination, the delaying of Home Rule and the impact of the Gaelic Revival, a cultural movement which *Le Devoir* celebrated and represented as "unstoppable" and capturing "the heart of the country." *Le Devoir* saw in the Gaelic revival the promise of Ireland's future: "Whatever follows immediately upon the rising, this [...] movement will continue; it is the promise [...] of a new Ireland." This view is revealing: while *Le Devoir* conveniently avoided any embarrassing discussions over the appropriateness of revolt in view of Catholic theology, the paper stated optimistically that Ireland offered an example of successful resistance to English assimilation in the Empire.[63]

Le Devoir deplored the effects of censorship as Irish papers were censored in Canada and so were, partially, Irish-American papers, which it used to balance the wire stories of British sources.[64] In its next report on the Rising, again rather than detailing the events, the paper quickly turned to denouncing the severity of the British repression and to legitimising the rebels. Fundamentally, if the Germans could try to manipulate the revolt and if Irish-Americans were prepared to finance a rising, was this not because Ireland has suffered so greatly under British rule? the British authorities ought to realise the insurgents were not the only ones to be blamed; the contrast with Carson's Ulster rebels, also armed by Germany but who were rewarded, is blatant. *Le Devoir* recalled the clemency recently shown in South Africa after the Boer Rebellion of 1914–1915. If such clemency prevailed that would indeed make imperialists in Canada stand out for their rabidity.[65]

This positioning was not yet a clear break with *Le Devoir*'s support of the IPP. Such as break happened as soon as news of the executions came out. Bourassa himself denounced the bloody repression, whilst expressing sympathy for Redmond's and the IPP's despair, reminding his readers that he had backed the Irish constitutionalist movement for twenty years. He also showed understanding for the "Sinn Féiners," as the rebels were rapidly termed, as "believers in and martyrs for a Free Ireland" who had been irritated by Redmond's attitude and concessions to the English. Bourassa added: "before condemning the rebels, let us think of ... the unremitting torture of this people."[66] In order for his readers to understand, they only had to remember French Canada's history since the Conquest and the deportation of the Acadians. Bourassa compared Ireland to Lower Canada in 1841, Redmond to L.-H. Lafontaine and Sinn Féin to L.-J. Papineau. The Irish were right to be doubtful about England's willingness to concede autonomy. Bourassa denounced the hypocrisy of the English who wanted to mobilise Canadians against the peoples suffering from German oppression while themselves practising oppression. How could this bloody repression be justified when compared to the passive British response to the Ulster Unionist threat of rebellion in 1912? Strikers in Britain had also been shown clemency, Bourassa continued: bloody repression was once again reserved for Irish Catholics. The Dominions should protest. Bourassa also wondered how it was that no MP of Irish origin had yet denounced these executions. "Has colonialism and imperialism worn them [Irish MPs] down so much that they look on in silence at this bloodbath of their unfortunate countrymen?" he asked. This was an instance of French Canadian nationalists preceding many Irish Canadian Catholics in supporting the Irish Revolution. From that point on, *Le Devoir* attributed the surge in support for Sinn Féin to British government decisions, quoting Bishop O'Dwyer of Limerick's harsh words on the actions of the military governor of Ireland, General Sir John Maxwell, appointed to deal with the Rising.[67] In 1918 the paper gave extensive front-page coverage of resistance to conscription in Ireland, reproducing Cardinal Logue's denunciation of it, while also covering the shilly-shallying on Home Rule and the "*anti-papiste*" movement for partition in Ulster.[68]

La Croix remains a little studied paper.[69] Much smaller than *Le Devoir*, it represents another ultramontane tradition, sympathetic to separatism. It would begin to support separatism in early 1917, believing conscription to be imminent. In this it was a leader, preceding other groups, then close to Bourassa, that would begin to express open support for independence only at the end of the year.[70] *La Croix* proposed that Quebec become a separate Dominion within the Empire, perhaps in the hope of rendering the option more realistic. Republicanism was more common amongst radicals than ultramontanes but *La Croix*, sympathetic to the Irish Revolution, never demonstrated any unease with Irish republicanism. On the contrary, *La Croix* was likely unique amongst French Canadian newspapers in publishing the French version of the Proclamation of the Irish Republic.[71] This accompanied its first report of the events, saying little of victims and nothing about German help. Part of its bulletin of events is summarised from British wires, although sympathy for the Easter Rising surfaced in the choice of news, titles and occasional comments. Perhaps even more pointed were its silences. *La Croix* did not enter into considerations of Catholic theology on the legitimacy of rebellion, nor did it allude to German designs. In a later melancholy dispatch, *La Croix* announced that "The Irish revolution is dying under the English boot."[72] Their news was largely taken from Irish American news sources whose admiration for the courage of the insurgents echoed their own, perhaps thus circumventing censorship. Like *Le Devoir*, it also followed the situation closely, deploring the bloody repression and the double standards that applied to Ulster in 1912 and South Africa in 1914–1915.

Interestingly, in 1918 *La Croix*, focusing on Irish resistance to conscription, uses the Irish clergy's pronouncements to defend their own rejection of conscription in terms compatible with Catholic theology.[73] Elaborating on the resistance to conscription in Ireland might have been a smart way of circumventing the wrath of official censorship for some time, though the paper was eventually suppressed in September 1918. *La Croix* was positively enthused by the Irish hierarchy and clergy's opposition to conscription and credited the Church, even more than the IPP or Sinn Féin, for success in this matter.[74] It repeatedly published articles on this theme in 1918, using one particularly expressive headline: "The energetic attitude of the Irish clergy will save Ireland."[75] At this point the paper believed that conscription would be avoided and Home Rule adopted. Tellingly, though *La Croix* followed the war closely and expressed solidarity with war-torn France, articles on conscription in Ireland often took precedence over articles on France in the paper.[76]

L'Action catholique (1912–1973) was a Québec City daily controlled by the archdiocese, seat of the primate of Canada, then occupied by Cardinal Bégin. It reflected the thinking of the Quebec hierarchy, with some nuances when their positions were not unanimous and because some degree of autonomy was allowed to the paper. During World War I, the most famous debate in the French-language press pitted Bourassa against Father Joseph-Arthur d'Amours, editor of *L'Action catholique*. D'Amours wrote in his own paper and also contributed more outspoken articles in others under the pseudonym "Le Patriote." The cleric stood down from his position on foot of his polemic with Bourassa in early 1917.[77] *L'Action catholique* in these times followed a line that was very friendly to the Conservative government's positions on the war (even though Cardinal Bégin spoke out against Regulation XVII).

L'Action catholique's immediate reaction to the Rising was very telling. It was a total condemnation, with an editorial denouncing "*Une faute et un crime*."[78] The conclusion, it felt, was unavoidable for any Catholic and patriot. Whatever the past grievances of Ireland, nothing in the current situation could justify or even excuse such sedition against established authority, especially in cooperation with England's enemies, even if the Rising could have claimed a chance of success (as required by Catholic theology).[79] Of course, the "real" leaders of the Irish race (implicitly the IPP) condemned the rising; so had the pope and Irish bishops. Reminding the Irish of their "duty" towards "established authority," the paper trusted the Irish not to commit the folly of ignoring their pastors. We can infer that the newspaper saw Home Rule as akin to the existing order in the Dominion and its writers feared that the status quo was at risk due to growing tensions

in Canada and nationalist agitation, much like in Ireland. The partially legitimate aspirations were used by Germans, oppressors of Danes, Poles, Al-
satians, to fool revolutionary simpletons who failed to see how this would
only justify the strengthening of Britain's hold on Ireland. A second editorial
repeated this excoriation during the first days of the Rising, as "a senseless
rebellion against established authority."[80] It blamed German manipulation
and modern revolutionary ideals which were contrary to Catholic theology
and which had their origins in the Protestant Reformation. One should not
confuse natural liberty with independence nor believe monarchies cannot
be freer than many republics, such as those of Portugal or France, where
there is less liberty than in the days of Saint-Louis or in the present-day
Dominion of Canada.

Interestingly, in 1918 *L'Action catholique* was diametrically opposed to
La Croix's coverage, in that it preferred to emphasise Cardinal Logue's condemnation of Sinn Féin on the basis of the hopelessness of attaining an Irish
Republic in the face of British military power rather than his condemnation
of conscription.[81] *L'Action catholique* reiterated the legitimate conditions
for revolt for Catholics, instead permissible only when constitutional means
did not exist, notably by summarising a sermon by the bishop of Clonfert,
a western Irish diocese, on this topic.

L'Événement (1867–1967) was a daily paper belonging to Tory interests. Its first report on the Rising appeared at the top of its front-page col-
umn dedicated to the events of the war, on 29 April. The "situation" was
presented as "serious" and the paper highlighted Redmond's declaration
on the insurrection reproduced on inside pages, in which he expressed his
"horror" and "discouragement," views that chimed with the paper's own
position. When more details of the events appeared on 1 May, the presentation was not sympathetic: the rebellion was inspired and armed by
Germany, the rebels killed loyal civilians while the government forces were
doing their best to minimise the bloodshed.[82] This coverage was based on
British and American news sources and even the "Cologne Gazette [*Köl-
nische Zeitung*]," which apparently admitted that the situation now offered
little hope of advantage to Germany.

In 1918 *L'Événement* valiantly attempted to deny any basis for
comparison with rejection of conscription in "the sister island" and Quebec, dismissed as "odious" given the demand for Home Rule.[83] It is not
surprising that *L'Événement* would not approve of revolutionary resistance to conscription in 1918, but it is surprising that it dared to criticise
the Irish Catholic clergy and hierarchy for not condemning a revolt which
it saw as tantamount to a revolt against God and his Church.[84] This is all
the more striking given that it reiterated its support for Home Rule and the
IPP's argument that Home Rule should precede conscription.[85]

In sum, the reaction to the Rising in the French Canadian press is revealing. French Canadians of all strands supported Home Rule, with some
degree of natural sympathy due to similarities with their situation within

the British Empire. Yet as news of the Rising arrived, the nascent Irish Revolution generated two opposite reactions. The first rejected Sinn Féin and defended the existing order both in Ireland as in Canada and continued to support the IPP until the end of the War. *L'Action catholique* and *L'Événement* clearly feared potential ideological "contamination" from the example of the Irish Revolution in Quebec. This was made explicit in 1918, when a conscription crisis engulfed Quebec and Ireland, but this fear of contamination was already present in 1916.

On the other hand, French Canadian nationalists immediately supported the Rising, even before the Irish Canadian press did so. They followed events in Ireland closely and used them to comment on Canadian politics and to criticise imperialists and assimilationists at home, including Irish Canadian Catholics, and even as veiled criticism of the Quebec Church in comparison with the Irish Church, especially in 1918. In 1916, the separatist *La Croix* showed special interest in the Proclamation of the Irish Republic. *Le Devoir* emphasised the Gaelic Revival as context for the Rising, denounced the bloody repression and would consistently support Sinn Féin during the Irish Revolution. This show of support was not only useful in the context of ongoing debates in Canada, but the Irish Revolution itself would also provide inspiration for new and growing separatist movements themselves. In conclusion, the fact that the Easter Rising resonated so strongly and lastingly with French Canadians attests to the significance of the Easter Rising in the development of anti-imperialism across the British Empire.

Notes

1 Charles Townshend, *The Republic: The Fight for Irish Independence* (London, 2013) and *Easter 1916. The Irish Rebellion* (London, 2015); Diarmaid Ferriter, *A Nation and Not a Rabble: The Irish Revolution, 1913–1923* (London, 2015); Jérôme aan de Wiel, *The Catholic Church in Ireland, 1914–1918* (Dublin, 2003).

2 Linda Cardinal and Simon Jolivet, "Nationalisme, langue et éducation: les relations entre Irlandais catholiques et Canadiens français du Québec et de l'Ontario," in Linda Cardinal, Simon Jolivet, and Isabelle Matte, eds., *Le Québec et l'Irlande. Culture, histoire, identité* (Québec, 2014), 83.

3 From Grosse Île, Québec's quarantine station: www.bac-lac.gc.ca/eng/discover/immigration/immigration-records/immigrants-grosse-ile-1832-1937/Pages/immigrants-grosse-ile.aspx.

4 Simon Jolivet, "Le Québec, les Irlandais et la politique au début du XXᵉ siècle," *Histoire Québec* 17.1 (2011), 18 and "French Canadians and the Irish Question, 1900–1921," in R. J. Blyth and K. Jeffery, eds., *The British Empire and Its Contested Pasts* (Dublin, 2009), 222.

5 Ferriter, *A Nation and not a Rabble.*

6 Robert McLaughlin, *Irish Canadian Conflict and the Struggle for Irish Independence, 1912–1925* (Toronto, 2013), 30.

7 Montreal's *Irish Vindicator* became one of the main *Patriote* papers; see Gérard Filteau, *Histoire des Patriotes* (Québec, 2003); Garth Stevenson, *Parallel Paths. The Devlopment of Nationalism in Ireland and Quebec* (Montreal, 2006);

Julie Guyot, *Les insoumis de l'empire. Le refus de la domination coloniale au Bas-Canada et en Irlande, 1790–1840* (Québec, 2016).

8   The only monograph on the Conscription Crisis in Quebec is dated and tends to explain it by a supposed "parochialism": E. H. Armstrong, *The Crisis in Quebec, 1914–1918* (New York, 1937). The most authoritative treatise on the conscription crises of the twentieth century in Canada did not have the space to insert these debates in their imperial context: J. L. Granatstein and J. M. Hitsman, *Broken Promises. A History of Conscription in Canada* (Toronto, 1985).

9   Patrick Bouvier, *Déserteurs et insoumis. Les Canadiens français et la justice militaire (1914–1918)* (Montréal, 2003); Béatrice Richardm, "1er avril 1918. Émeute à Québec contre la conscription: résistance politique ou culturelle?," in Pierre Graveline, ed., *Les dix journées qui ont fait le Québec* (Montréal, 2013), 137–59. One exception stands out: Carl Pépin, "Du *Military Service Act* aux émeutes de Québec: l'effort de guerre canadien-français vu de France (1914–1918)," *Bulletin d'histoire politique* 17.2 (2009), 89–110.

10 To compare coverage in the first days of the Rising we have consulted, besides the four papers analysed here, liberal *La Presse* of Montréal, conservative-leaning *La Patrie* of Montréal, "independent," Catholic and nationalist *Le Droit* of Ottawa. I wish to thank the following M.A. students who helped in the perusal of the newspapers: Pierre-Yves Renaud, Sarah Lapré and Francis Bergeron. Linda Cardinal, Simon Jolivet and Isabelle Matte, "Les études irlando-québécoises, un nouvel objet d'étude?," in Jolivet and Matte, eds., *Le Québec et l'Irlande*, 3–12. See also Simon Jolivet, *Le vert et le bleu. Identité québécoise et identité irlandaise au tournant du XXe siècle* (Montréal, 2011). Simon Jolivet is the exception although his studies actually focus more on the 1918–1922 period: "La presse nationaliste et la question irlandaise, 1914–1918," in J. Lamarre and M. Deleuze, eds., *L'Envers de la médaille. Guerres, témoignages et representations* (Québec, 2007), 93–109 and "French Canadians," 217–34.

11 Frederick J. McEvoy, "Canadian Catholic Press reaction to the Irish Crisis, 1916–1921," in David A. Wilson, ed., *Irish Nationalism in Canada* (Montréal, 2009), 122.

12 The term *Québécois* only gained currency in the 1960s.

13 Site for Language Management in Canada, "The Linguistic Policies of the Founding Provinces," University of Ottawa: https://slmc.uottawa.ca/?q= policies_founding_provinces.

14 Tim Cook, *Warlords. Borden, Mackenzie King, and Canada's World Wars* (Toronto, 2012), 62.

15 R. Borden to Sir C. H. Tupper, 2 January 1916, quoted in R. C. Brown and Ramsay Cook, *Canada 1896–1921* (Toronto, 1974), 264.

16 Granatstein and Hitsman, *Broken Promises*, 45.

17 Olivar Asselin, "Sur un discours de Mgr Bruchési," *L'Action*, 16 September 1914, quoted in H. Pelletier-Baillargeon, *Olivar Asselin et son temps*, vol. 1 (Montréal, 1996), 641.

18 See Jean Hamelin and Nicole Gagnon, *Histoire du catholicisme québécois. Le XXe siècle 1898–1940*, vol. 1, (Montréal, 1984), 305; Lionel Groulx, *Mes Mémoires*, vol. 1 (Montréal, 1971), 285; René Durocher, "Henri Bourassa, les évêques et la guerre de 1914–1918," *Historical Papers* 6.1 (1971), 248–75; Mgr Paul Bruchési's biography on the Montréal diocese website: http://diocesemontreal.org/leglise-a-montreal/notre-histoire/nos-eveques/ mgr-paul-bruchesi/articles/periode-1921-1939-maladie-reclusion-mort.html.

19 See Desmond Morton, "French Canada and War, 1868–1917: The Military Background to the Conscription Crisis of 1917," in Jack L. Granatstein and

Robert D. Cuff, eds., *War and Society in North America* (Toronto, 1971), 84–103.

20 Granatstein and Hitsman, *Broken Promises*; Desmond Morton, *A Military History of Canada* (Toronto, 2007), 151–53.

21 Jean Provencher, *1918. Québec sous la loi des mesures de guerre* (Montréal, 2014, orig. 1971); Martin F. Auger, "On the Brink of Civil War: The Canadian Government and the Suppression of the 1918 Quebec Easter Riots," *The Canadian Historical Review* 89.4 (2008), 503–40.

22 Granatstein and Hitsman, *Broken Promises*, 78.

23 See the posters in "World War I," *Canadian Encyclopedia*: http://the canadianencyclopedia.ca/en/article/first-world-war-wwi/.

24 Réal Bélanger, *Henri Bourassa. Le fascinant destin d'un homme libre, 1868–1914* (Québec, 2013); Sylvie Lacombe, *La rencontre de deux peuples élus. Comparaison des ambitions nationales et impériales au Canada entre 1896 et 1920* (Québec, 2002).

25 Jolivet, "French Canadians," 223.

26 Omer Héroux, "La conscription en Irlande," *Le Devoir*, 21 September 1916, which also addresses the debates in Australia.

27 Jean-Philippe Warren, "L'opposition d'Henri Bourassa à l'effort de guerre canadien," in C.-P. Courtois and L. Veyssière, eds., *Le Québec dans la Grande Guerre* (Québec, 2015), 94–112.

28 C.-P. Courtois, "La Première Guerre mondiale et la naissance d'un nouvel indépendantisme québécois," in Courtois and Veyssière, eds., *Le Québec*, 160–79.

29 See Jacques Ferron, *Le salut de l'Irlande* (Montréal, 1970) and Victor-Lévy Beaulieu, *James Joyce, l'Irlande, le Québec, les mots* (Montréal, 2006). See also Marc Chevrier, "Victor-Lévy Beaulieu, James Joyce, les langues et le Québec hibernien," in Jolivet and Matte, eds., *Le Québec et l'Irlande*, 203–25.

30 Hamelin and Gagnon, *Histoire du catholicisme*, 308.

31 Aan de Wiel, *The Catholic Church*, 112–4.

32 Aan de Wiel, *The Catholic Church*, 247. Secretary to Bishop Cohalan of Cork, quoted in Ferriter, *A Nation and Not a Rabble*, 161. Townshend, *Easter 1916*, 309–10.

33 McLaughlin, *Irish Canadian Conflict*, 34–60. See also Garth Stevenson, "Irish Canadians and the National Question," in Wilson, ed., *Irish Nationalism in Canada*, 165.

34 "Orange Order," *Canadian Encyclopedia*: www.thecanadianencyclopedia.ca/en/article/orange-order/.

35 Cecil J. Houston and William J. Smyth, *Irish Emigration and Canadian Settlement. Patterns, Links and Letters* (Toronto, 1990), 3.

36 Brian Clarke, "Religious Riots as Pastime. Orange Young Britons, Parades and Public Life in Victorian Toronto," in David Wilson, ed., *The Orange Order in Canada* (Dublin, 2007), 110.

37 Cecil J. Houston and William J. Smyth, *The Sash Canada Wore: A Historical Geography of the Orange Order in Canada* (Toronto, 1980).

38 Typically, D'Alton McCarthy, Conservative Member of the Provincial Parliament of Ontario and Grand Master of the Ontario West Orange Lodge, proclaimed in 1888: "Who should rule over Canada, the queen or the pope? Will this country be English or French? [...] This is a British country [...] Now is when the ballot box must deliver a solution to this grave problem; if it finds no remedy in this generation, the next generation will have to take up the bayonet." Quoted in "The Linguistic Policies of the Founding Provinces," Site for

Language Management in Canada, University of Ottawa: https://slmc.uottawa. ca/?q=policies_founding_provinces.

39 "Ontario Schools Question," *Canadian Encyclopedia*, http://thecanadianency-clopedia.ca/en/article/ontario-schools-question/.

40 Larry A. Glassford, "Meighen, Arthur," in *Dictionary of Canadian Biography*, University of Toronto/Université Laval, 2003–, www.biographi.ca/en/bio/meighen_arthur_18F.html.

41 Rosalyn Trigger, "Clerical Containment of Diasporic Irish Nationalism: A Canadian Example from the Parnell Era," in Wilson, ed., *Irish Nationalism in Canada*, 83–96; see Robin B. Burns, "McGee, Thomas D'Arcy," in *Dictionary of Canadian Biography*, www.biographi.ca/en/bio/mcgee_thomas_d_arcy_9E. html.

42 For instance, Terence J. Fay, *A History of Canadian Catholics* (Montréal, 2002), 175, asserts that "English-speaking Catholics supported National Registration and conscription and pursued the British vision of democracy." Mark McGowan, *The Waning of the Green: Catholics, the Irish and Identity in Toronto, 1887–1922* (Montreal, 1999).

43 McLaughlin, *Irish Canadian Conflict*, 34–60.

44 McLaughlin, *Irish Canadian Conflict*, 26–28; Simon Jolivet, "Entre nationalismes canadien-français et irlandais: les intrigues québécoises de la Self-Determination for Ireland League of Canada and Newfoundland," *Canadian Historical Review* 92.1 (2011), 47.

45 Jolivet, "Entre nationalismes," 43–68.

46 McLaughlin, *Irish Canadian Conflict*, 118.

47 Matteo Sanfilippo, "Les relations des Irlandais et des Canadiens français à l'aune des archives vaticanes," in Jolivet and Matte, eds., *Le Québec*, 42–81; Yves Roby, *Les Franco-Américains de la Nouvelle-Angleterre* (Sillery, 1990).

48 Archbishop Louis-Nazaire Bégin of Québec complained to the Vatican Secretariat of State in 1909: "les Irlandais sont envahisseurs à outrance". Quoted in Sanfilippo, "Les relations," 47. Roberto Perin, *Rome in Canada: The Vatican and Canadian Affairs in the Late Victorian Age* (Toronto, 1990).

49 Roberto Perin, "Bégin, Louis-Nazaire," in *Dictionary of Canadian Biography*, www.biographi.ca/en/bio/begin_louis_nazaire_15E.html. See "Controversy Surrounding the Use of the French Language at the Eucharistic Congress of Montreal," in Claude Bélanger, *Documents in Quebec History*, http://faculty. marianopolis.edu/c.belanger/quebechistory/docs/1910/index.htm.

50 The rector of the Canadian College, future Cardinal Paul-Émile Léger, developed a privileged relationship with Pius XII: Gilles Routhier, "Léger, Paul-Émile," in *Dictionary of Canadian Biography*, www.biographi.ca/en/bio/leger_paul_emile_22E.html. See also Groulx, *Mes Mémoires*, vol. 4, "Déposition de Mgr Joseph Charbonneau", 247.

51 "Michael Francis Fallon", *Canadian Encyclopedia*: www.thecanadianencyclopedia. ca/en/article/michael-francis-fallon/.

52 Mgr M. Fallon to Mgr Sbaretti, 14 December 1910, quoted in Sanfilippo, "Les relations," 53.

53 See Adrian Ciani, "An Imperialist Irishman: Bishop Michael Fallon, The Diocese of London and the Great War," *Historical Studies* 74 (2008), 73–94. See also "Michael Francis Fallon," *Quebec History Encyclopedia*: http://faculty. marianopolis.edu/c.belanger/quebechistory/encyclopedia/MichaelFrancisFallon. html. Mgr Michael Francis Fallon's diary, quoted in Cardinal and Jolivet, " Nationalisme, langue et éducation," 91.

54 See Hermas Bastien, "Les Irlandais et nous," *L'Action française* 107 (1927), 327–28.

55 McLaughlin, *Irish Canadian Conflict*, 117, 144–45.

56 See Lionel Groulx, *The Iron Wedge* (Eng. Trans. Ottawa, 1986, orig. 1922), a nationalist novel set in World War I and centered on Regulation XVII, in which one of the protagonists is one of the "assimilated Irish"; nevertheless Groulx would continue to show solidarity with the SDILC and find the independence of Ireland and De Valera inspiring. On Ireland as an inspiration to Canadians, see Antonio Perrault, "Le Canada et le Commonwealth, aspect juridique," *L'Action nationale* (March 1939), 241 and André Laurendeau, "Fête de l'indépendance, quand même," *L'Action nationale* (December 1940), 335.

57 P. Bouchard, "Le vieux sur la colline," *La Nation* 1.12 (30 April 1936), 1. See also "L'exemple de l'Irlande," *La Nation* 2.13 (5 May 1937). On Paul Bouchard, editor of *La Nation*, see Robert Comeau, "Paul Bouchard et les séparatistes de *La Nation*," in R. Comeau, Denis Monière, and C.-P. Courtois, eds., *Histoire intellectuelle de l'indépendantisme québécois*, vol. 1, *1834–1968*, (Montréal, 2010), 102–14.

58 Jolivet, "La presse nationaliste."

59 Henri Bourassa, *Ireland and Canada Address Delivered in Hamilton* (Montréal, 1914).

60 Jolivet, "French Canadians," 227.

61 "Solidarité impériale," *Le Devoir*, 15 January 1916.

62 See also G. Pelletier, "Another Scrap of Paper," *Le Devoir*, 29 July 1916.

63 Omer Héroux, "En marge de la question irlandaise," *Le Devoir*, 26 April 1916.

64 Omer Héroux, "La conscription en Irlande," *Le Devoir*, 21 September 1916.

65 Omer Héroux, "La révolte irlandaise," *Le Devoir*, 2 May 1916.

66 H. Bourassa, "La vengeance de l'Angleterre," *Le Devoir*, 10 May 1916.

67 Omer Héroux, "La Question du Home Rule," *Le Devoir*, 12 July 1916 and "La conscription en Irlande," *Le Devoir*, 21 September 1916.

68 "La conscription en Irlande," *Le Devoir*, 10 April 1918; "Un projet de Home rule à l'étude," *Le Devoir*, 15 April 1918, "Un plaidoyer pour l'Ulster," *Le Devoir*, 7 May 1918.

69 See Pierre Trépanier, "Introduction," in Lionel Groulx, ed., *Correspondance*, vol. 4, *1915–1920*, (Montréal, 2013), 94–99.

70 See D. Monière, "Jules-Paul Tardivel" and C.-P. Courtois, "Lionel Groulx," in Comeau, Courtois and Monière, *Histoire intellectuelle*; Susan Mann Trofimenkoff, *Action Française: French Canadian Nationalism in the Twenties* (Toronto, 1975).

71 "La République irlandaise," *La Croix*, 6 May 1916.

72 *La Croix*, 3 June 1916.

73 Joseph Bégin, "Le service militaire obligatoire considéré du point de vue moral," *La Croix*, 11 May 1918,

> Ils ont éminemment raison le cardinal Logue, les archevêques et les évêques de la Verte Erin de s'opposer ouvertement et fortement à l'application du service militaire obligatoire en Irlande […] Ils ont préféré obéir à Dieu plutôt qu'aux hommes. Cet acte de courage catholique les honore grandement. Il fera pardonner bien des fautes au peuple irlandais.

74 "Le clergé en Irlande repousse la conscription," *La Croix*, 20 April 1918, 2; "La conscription en Irlande," *La Croix*, 6 July 1918, 3.

75 *La Croix*, 1 June 1918.

76 For example, " Sur le champ de bataille," *La Croix*, 18 May 1918, is presented after an article on " La situation en Irlande" where Cardinal Logue's message against conscription is highlighted.

77 Dominique Marquis, "Être journaliste catholique au XXe siècle, un apostolat: les exemples de Jules Dorion et Eugène L'Heureux," *Études d'histoire religieuse* 73 (2007), 40.

78 *L'Action catholique*, 28 April 1916.
79 J. aan de Wiel, *The Catholic Church*; "War," *Catholic Encyclopedia* (1914).
80 "L'indépendance politique," *L'Action catholique*, 29 April 1916.
81 "Le Cardinal Logue et les Sinn Feiners," *L'Action catholique*, 7 January 1918, an article reproduced from *La Croix* of Paris.
82 "Les insurgés irlandais résistent désespérément aux troupes anglaises," *L'Événement*, 1 May 1916.
83 "En Irlande," *L'Événement*, 12 April 1918.
84 "La crise d'Irlande," *L'Événement*, 22 May 1918.
85 "En Irlande," *L'Événement*, 12 April 1918.

4   The Great American Protest
African Americans and the Great Migration

Cecelia Hartsell

As in many political situations across the world in 1916, by participating in the Great Migration, African Americans were reacting against a social and economic structure not of their choosing, which affected them adversely.[1] The Great Migration is broadly periodised from 1916 to 1970 and defined by historians as the voluntary relocation of approximately 6 million African Americans from the rural South to cities in the North, Midwest and West. It is often analysed as separate periods, with the two largest migrations surrounding the world wars. This essay will focus on the details of the First Great Migration, which began in earnest in 1916 and continued until 1930. Most historians agree that approximately 450,000–500,000 southern African Americans relocated to northern cities between 1916 and 1918 and at least another 700,000 made their way north during the 1920s, with the majority traveling primarily to Chicago, Illinois; Cleveland, Ohio; Detroit, Michigan; and New York City.[2]

The First Great Migration is routinely discussed as occurring as the result of several damaging agricultural occurrences in the South and a series of war-related events: a severe agricultural depression in the South, brought on by restricted access to European markets and a labour shortage in the industrial centres of the North, caused by the disruption of European immigration.[3] Those were the causes, but an analysis of the larger story of this migration reveals that it consisted of four stages, during each of which African Americans took action against segregation and racial violence in the South and governmental policies that nurtured structural racism in the North. During the decision-making process to leave the South, potential migrants utilised specific communication and information networks in determining the opportunities for economic and social equality in the North; after those decisions were completed, individuals and organisations helped facilitate the migration process. Once the migrants arrived at their destinations, progressive reform groups aided their transitions from the rural South. Lastly, synthesising revolutionary influences from other cultures, with their population numbers augmented by the Great Migration, people of colour in the North began to develop a new type of protest politics, changing the level of influence they could bring to bear on the American political system.

This essay will argue that the migrants were not mere bystanders, buffeted by forces beyond their control, but active participants who, in 1916, made conscious decisions to resist the discriminatory policies of the Wilson Administration. They chose to leave the South, and, in the North, they actively pursued specific employment opportunities to which they were best suited; and they availed themselves of aid and counsel offered to them by various African American self-help organisations in the cities where they made their new homes. In turn, their reactions to new dimensions of employment, political, educational and cultural dynamics created an environment that changed the manner in which African Americans and other people of colour agitated against structural racism in the United States.

President Woodrow Wilson's presidency was characterised by two agendas that were diametrically opposed: the promotion of liberal internationalism and the maintenance of racial segregation in the United States. Wilson believed that America's foreign policy would be most effective if underpinned by a substantial amount of international trade and investment and that those efforts would also be effective in facilitating political progress globally. His belief in the strength of the principles of American democracy shaped his vision of a post-war international community inspired by those values. In fact, in his "Fourteen Points" address to the United States Congress, President Wilson made the case that it was possible for the Great War to be "the war to end all wars":

> We entered this war because violations of right had occurred which touched us to the quick and made the life of our own people impossible unless they were corrected and the world secure once and for all against their recurrence. What we demand in this war, therefore, is nothing peculiar to ourselves. It is that the world be made fit and safe to live in; and particularly that it be made safe for every peace-loving nation which, like our own, wishes to live its own life, determine its own institutions, (and) be assured of justice and fair dealing by the other peoples of the world...[4]

From an international perspective then, President Wilson was dedicated to the idea of American democracy as an unimpeachable force for freedom across the world. However, he presided over a nation in which African Americans were severely limited in their access to civic inclusion. In the United States, during the two decades before the outbreak of the Great War, political identity had become a tinderbox for African Americans. The period of the 1880s through the 1890s was characterised by civil rights crises resulting from the Compromise of 1877, which ended the Reconstruction Era and dictated the removal of federal troops from the South. The South was essentially left to its own devices to deal with the race question and did so with physical violence, with lynching being the most notorious example; economic restriction through the large-scale enforcement of tenant farming among African Americans; and the use of intimidation, poll taxes, and literacy tests to prevent African American men from exercising their rights to vote. The 1896 Supreme Court ruling on the *Plessy v. Ferguson* case upheld the concept of "Separate but Equal" in education, housing, public transportation and public space, and thus legalised the southern segregation system known as Jim Crow.[5]

In 1913, during his first term in office, President Woodrow Wilson supported congressional southern democrats in restricting federal intervention to protect African American voting rights in the South and his administration re-segregated all federal offices in Washington D.C., which had been integrated during Reconstruction. Wilson's decisions were not entirely separate from politics – every American President has endeavoured to create political partnerships that might expedite the progression of his legislative agenda through Congress. Wilson was no different and the passage of his "New Freedom" domestic programme was dependent upon the cooperation of southern congressmen. Wilson maintained that he viewed segregation not as an instrument of humiliation, but as a means to "ease racial tensions" and thus, authorised members of his cabinet to resegregate federal agencies as they saw fit. Applications for Civil Service jobs also required a photograph, causing the number of those positions available to African Americans to plummet. At the White House in 1915, the President also screened the film, *The Birth of a Nation*, which glorified the efforts of the Ku Klux Klan to reassert its authority after the end of Reconstruction. Thomas Dixon, author of the novel *The Clansman*, upon which the film was based, was a former classmate, friend and political supporter of President Wilson's. The President's decision to screen *The Birth of a Nation* at the White House implied his tacit approval of the film's perspective on race in the United States.[6]

Therefore, by the eve of the Great War in Europe, civic inclusion for African Americans had not only been limited by actions across the South, but notably across the executive, judicial and legislative branches of the federal government as well. While African American migrants would find that opportunities available to them outside of the South were not without complications, the Wilson Administration's domestic policies regarding race made it imperative that action be taken against them, in any way possible.

James R. Grossman and Steven Hahn offer perspectives on the issues that influenced the African American migrants' decisions to leave the South, as well as the strategies they implemented to facilitate the migration process. Grossman makes the case that the concept of migration was a familiar one for African Americans, that "from emancipation onward, as a symbolic theme and social process, migration – forced and unforced – has epitomised the place of African Americans in American society." Spatial mobility had always been a crucial component of African Americans' conception of freedom, thereby making it a viable protest option during the years of the Wilson administration.[7] Steven Hahn maintains that the migrants constructed communication channels composed of churches, benevolent societies, lodges and local associations, as well as kinship networks of relatives, neighbours and friends who had already left the South themselves, or knew people who had. He argues that the information flowing through those channels aided potential migrants in making informed decisions.[8] Those communication networks were buttressed by the black church and the black press, both of which undergirded African American communities and focused on racial pride and addressing circumstances that contributed to oppression. The black press played an especially active role in the Great Migration.

By 1910, African American national newspaper circulation was approximately 500,000 across 288 newspapers, with the most radical papers published primarily in the urban centres outside of the South. However, those numbers do not adequately reflect the scope of their circulation, as they were often shared at barbershops, beauty parlours and churches and had a readership across the rural South, due in part to distribution by African American railroad porters. *The Chicago Defender* was one of the market leaders, selling 230,000 copies per week by 1920.[9] After mid-1916, the paper and its editor, Robert Abbott, wielded a great deal of influence in the decisions of African Americans to leave the South.[10] Abbott established *The Chicago Defender* in 1905 and fashioned the paper into what he referred to as an "advocacy press" on behalf of African Americans, using editorials and political cartoons to agitate against lynching, disenfranchisement and segregation while publishing articles highlighting positive events within Chicago's African American communities. As he also believed in the capacity of the individual to change his or her circumstances, he campaigned for African Americans to participate in what he referred to as the "Great Northern Drive".

Toward that end, Abbott organised migration clubs and arranged discounted rates with the Illinois Central Railroad, as well as trips scheduled to coincide with potential migrants' payroll dates. Once the migrants relocated, they could refer to *Defender* articles regarding acculturation, designed to ease their transition from southern culture to an urban one. Abbott's beliefs ran counter to many African Americans involved in reform through uplift organisations, as he was convinced that a large number of migrants in the northern cities would serve to reduce racial prejudice there. In addition to urban acculturation, *The Chicago Defender* and other metropolitan papers advised recent southern migrants regarding potential access to employment. A number of those newspapers' editors were former Southerners themselves, forced to leave the region in order to effectively campaign against discriminatory practices.

Robert Abbott was part of a group of African American reform leaders who, during that period, were fashioning civil rights advocacy strategies in response to the Wilson administration's policies regarding race. Some of its most well-known members included W.E.B. Du Bois, scholar, social scientist and co-founder of the National Association for the Advancement of Colored People (NAACP); Mary Church Terrell, the first president of the National Association of Colored Women (NACW), one of the most prestigious organisations of the clubwomen movement; and Eugene K. Jones, the First Executive Secretary of the National Urban League. Those three organisations were instrumental in providing assistance to African American migrants and in facilitating their transition to the realities of urban life. Those efforts were viewed by the organisations as "self-help," which had a long tradition in the African American community. However, the Great Migration took place during the Progressive Era in America, causing African American reformers to fuse "self-help" with progressive principles of protecting the poor and the working class from negative consequences of industrialisation and urbanisation, creating the concept of "racial uplift." Aid societies, church-based outreach, temperance organisations and education initiatives were some ways in which African American reformers implemented racial uplift strategies. The National Urban League, founded in New York City, was one of the most prominent institutions established during that era, actively working to aid migrants in their transition to new lives in the North.[11]

The National Urban League developed out of three interracial organisations, founded between 1905 and 1906, which addressed issues surrounding urban African American "settlers" – those who had lived in larger cities for a number of years – and newly arrived migrants. These were the National League for the Protection of Colored Women, the Committee for Improving Industrial Conditions of Negroes in New York City, and the Committee on Urban Conditions Among Negroes. Each of those organisations confronted urban crime, delinquency and overcrowded housing. Once founded, the National Urban League would go on to play a decisive role in implementing those strategies, as the numbers of migrants in the North swelled after 1916. The organisation placed an early focus on housing and employment discrimination, as the minutes of its first meeting in 1910 demonstrate[12]:

> Improving of housing ... higher rents are usually charged to coloured people than to white for similar accommodations. The causes and remedies, if any, need attention. The employment problem needs attention. It is the crux of the situation. Negroes are ill prepared to grapple with an intensive industrial competition, and, except in domestic and personal service, meet a race prejudice which is often insurmountable.[13]

By 1916, the National Urban League was working from the viewpoint that while there was a risk that overwhelming numbers of migrants might aggravate the types of issues addressed in that first meeting, successful uplift strategies had the potential to mitigate those situations. One of the hallmarks of the organisation's strategies was a vocational exchange that organised classes with participating technical and vocational schools, in the belief that the competence African Americans built in those classes might reduce the role race played in employer hiring decisions. The Urban League's activities during the Great War period were grounded in specific self-help strategies of vocational training, housing assistance and advice on adherence to the Victorian moral values of thrift, monogamy and industry, which reformers believed would neutralise racial prejudice. That dedication to the power of acculturation was one shared by W.E.B. Du Bois, although he and the NAACP favoured the use of agitation tactics in tandem with racial uplift".[14]

The clubwomen movement was also active in addressing issues of concern to the migrants. It had its roots in relief work that African American women did through their churches during the Reconstruction era, using education and moral training as their tools. By 1916, middle-class African American women were working through their women's groups to help uplift the black working class, using those same approaches and claiming their authority in those matters from their authority in the domestic sphere. The women's clubs, particularly the NACW, went on to coordinate a number of activities that benefitted black working-class communities, especially the migrants from the South. The NACW, whose slogan, "lifting as we climb", was emblematic of its mission, was established in 1895 as the National Federation of Afro American Women (NFAAW). Its local clubs focused on a broad spectrum of community services, including nutrition and childcare classes; the establishment of orphanages; procurement of lodging for domestic workers; and raising funds for legal representation.[15]

While newly arrived migrants certainly availed themselves of resources available from African American reform institutions, they also chose to pursue specific types of employment of their own accord and ultimately organised themselves within their new communities in a manner duplicating the type of kinship ties they would have relied upon in the South. Peter Gottlieb argues that, despite the fact that industrial work proceeded at a faster pace, there were certain factors present in their experience in southern agricultural labour, (such as their familiarity with hard labour in the heat), that made migrants uniquely qualified for certain industrial jobs. Gottlieb maintains that they recognised that fact and used it in their quest for employment:

> Southern blacks in Pittsburgh clearly sought certain jobs in preference to others. The southerner who first tried work in a Detroit laundry and tired of the rapid pace and dust might apply for an open-hearth job in a Pittsburgh steel mill. Black coal miners in the same fashion could exchange their pit tools for the wheelbarrows and shovels of a Pittsburgh factory field gang. The heat and fumes of forges, furnaces, and rolling mills could also propel other migrants to try cleaner and quieter domestic service jobs. The significance of this experience with

northern jobs was that it made the shaping of a black industrial working class a process that the migrants as well as the mill managers could
manipulate.[16]

Thus, the migrants blended their labour experiences in the rural South with
attitudes and behaviour patterns they had developed in their new industrial environments, once again making decisions informed by their experience and forging their own paths. However, while the circumstances of
the Great Migration provided migrants with those opportunities, they also
created challenges such as housing discrimination and segregation in the
workplace. Over the two decades immediately following 1916, they realised
that a transfer of location would not necessarily be enough to guarantee the
economic, social and educational opportunities they sought by leaving the
South. The migrants would continue to reinvent themselves, as they became
aware of the importance of grassroots organisation and political action in
attaining civic inclusion.

A new urban black coalition was forming during the decade following
the end of the Great War, as a result of the Great Migration and new waves
of immigration from the Caribbean to the East Coast of the United States,
as well as the transformation of the Democratic Party through the consolidation of the "Roosevelt Coalition" in the mid-1930s.

Bruce Nelson makes the case for a substantial Anglophone Caribbean role in that process, arguing that while those immigrants made up
approximately 20 per cent of the black population of New York City, they
made significant cultural and political contributions to the movement
beyond what their numbers would suggest. He maintains that it was not
only superior education and a majority perspective undergirding the radical position of the Anglophone Caribbean immigrants, but the breadth of
their travels and their exposure to other forms of radical nationalist strategies across the diaspora and across Europe, especially those in Ireland.
Nelson considers the influence of Irish nationalist thought on Marcus Gar-
vey's Universal Negro Improvement Association (UNIA), as well as on his
choice of Liberty Hall as the name of the UNIA's Harlem headquarters;
and examines Cyril Briggs' use of the Irish Republican Brotherhood (IRB)
as a template in the founding of his African Blood Brotherhood for African
Liberation and Redemption (ABB) organisation in New York City. Nelson
raises these examples in support of his contention that the combined effect of the Anglophone Caribbean immigrants' global nationalist influences
and their experiences with the American racial climate created a particular brand of radicalism, which left a distinct imprint on black radicalism
in Harlem. That radicalism would manifest itself in new political action
strategies as that new urban black coalition became of interest to the Democratic Party in the 1930s.[17]

By 1932, when Franklin D. Roosevelt was elected president, African
Americans were still voting for the Republican Party, (the party associated
with Abraham Lincoln and the end of slavery). However, by the midterm

congressional elections in 1934, there was a noticeable shift in their party affiliation to the Democratic Party. By 1936, voter polls estimated that 76 per cent of northern blacks voted for President Roosevelt. It was twenty years on from 1916, when the Great Migration had begun in earnest and not only had the populations of Chicago, New York City, Detroit and other large cities swelled, those migrants had become acculturated to life outside of the South, which included civic responsibility and political agitation. As mentioned earlier, 450,000–500,000 southern African Americans relocated primarily to the North between 1916 and 1918; and at least another 700,000 made their way there during the 1920s. Because of those population numbers, black voters in those cities became crucial to the Democratic Party's electoral strategies.[18]

But how did the Democratic Party achieve that transformation? Franklin Roosevelt's New Deal, designed to pull America out of the Great Depression with large-scale federal work projects, such as the Civilian Conservation Corps (CCC) and the Works Progress Administration (WPA); and the creation of social programmes such as Social Security, created the "Roosevelt Coalition" of working class and immigrant voters, particularly in large cities. However, the structure of the New Deal did not favour African Americans. Like Wilson's New Freedom, Roosevelt's New Deal programmes had to be approved by southerners in Congress and they did not proceed through the legislative and administrative processes unscathed. As a result, agricultural workers and domestic workers were excluded from Roosevelt's National Recovery Act, as well as the Social Security programme and legislation governing minimum wages, which affected approximately 70 per cent of African American workers. In the South, most New Deal agencies were constrained by the prevalence of localism.[19]

Despite that poor record, Anthony Badger makes the case that the New Deal ultimately was beneficial to African Americans, due to greater assistance provided to them by New Deal agencies within state and local governments in the North. In addition, the WPA which put approximately 8 million people to work on public works projects over seven years, was directed by Harry Hopkins, who worked to ensure that African Americans were not excluded from the benefits of the WPA. Badger argues that as the 1930s wore on, New Deal politicians, anxious to retain African Americans within the "Roosevelt Coalition", realised they had to make themselves available to those members of the public and often brought representatives into the Roosevelt Administration to act in an advisory capacity regarding issues of concern to African Americans and facilitated the appointment of African Americans into Civil Service jobs. Lastly, many of those progressive politicians in the Roosevelt administration, ("New Deal liberals" as they came to be referred to), would become valuable allies in the ongoing struggle for civil rights.[20]

The population shifts caused by the Great Migration provided a base for the development of northern, urban protest strategies that were particularly relevant to the issues facing those new arrivals. One campaign launched in New York City in the 1930s, was the movement to promote neighbourhood employment in Harlem. Often carrying placards reading, "don't buy where you can't work," the activists were protesting the fact that while the majority of businesses in Harlem were not owned by African Americans, but still patronised by them, the majority of those businesses did not employ people of colour. The Harlem Housewives League, founded in 1930, vigorously lobbied chain retail stores with branches in Harlem, requesting that those stores hire blacks as workers in proportion to the amount of trade those stores received from Harlem residents. In the tradition of the NACW, the Harlem Housewives League was composed of middle-class African American housewives from politically active families. Mrs. A. Philip Randolph was the vice president of the league, which also coordinated its activities with Harlem's Citizen's Committee on More and Better Jobs, and the NAACP's "New Economic Programme," all prioritising lobbying local businesses to hire people of colour.[21]

When World War II broke out across Europe, African American political leaders made a decision to employ political agitation tactics similar to those employed during the Great War. However, at that point they had northern, urban population numbers augmented by the Great Migration in their arsenal, as those numbers had translated into political influence within the Democratic Party. That made it possible to exert pressure directly on the President of the United States in a manner that would not have been feasible during World War I. The 1941 March on Washington Movement is an illustration of the scope of that strategy.

In the spring of 1941, months away from America's entry into World War II in December of that year, the American defence industry was booming, as a result of President Franklin D. Roosevelt's "arsenal of democracy" initiative. In his "fireside chat" on 29 December 1940, Roosevelt outlined his plan for making the United States the "arsenal of democracy" that Britain and France would need to defeat the Axis powers. Presented to the public, as an alternative to American military intervention in the war, his strategy included enormous increases in industrial production targets, which translated into a corresponding increase in defence industry contracts.[22]

However, more than 50 per cent of defence industry employers refused to hire African American workers. In response, leaders of the national African American civil rights organisations attempted to persuade President Roosevelt to intervene. When they were unsuccessful, it was decided that a march on the White House should be planned. A. Philip Randolph, a veteran union organiser and head of the Brotherhood of Sleeping Car Porters Union, seized upon the suggestion and instead called for a massive demonstration in Washington D.C., on 1 July 1941. The expectation was that this March on Washington Movement (MOWM) could potentially rally 100,000 African Americans to descend upon the nation's capital. This was not a conflict that President Roosevelt wished to present on the international stage, where certain parameters of American freedom and democracy could be called into question against the backdrop of fascism in Europe. However, with the numbers of protestors potentially involved, international attention would have been unavoidable. Roosevelt ultimately prevented the march by compromising and issuing Executive Order 8802 on 25 June 1942, which desegregated the defence industry and established a Fair Employment Practices Committee (FEPC) to monitor the process. He did not desegregate the United States military, which had also been a demand of the movement's organisers.

Over the interwar period, African Americans had progressed from utilising democratic language and the black press to protest the racial climate in the United States, to the tactics Randolph utilised in the MOWM. African Americans had never been in a position to demand rights from the federal government. The population numbers and political organisation facilitated by the Great Migration created that leverage. A precedent was set: A. Philip Randolph would use the march template again on a smaller scale in New York City in 1943; and would serve on the organizing committee using that protest format with great success in 1963, during the Civil Rights Movement. The circumstances of the Great Migration created political clout for northern African Americans and gave rise to comprehensive protest strategies that brought new pressure to bear on business and government sectors in ways that would been unimaginable two decades earlier.[23]

This essay has placed the Great Migration within the global revolutionary climate of 1916, through the analysis of actions taken by African Americans to alter adverse political situations that were not of their choosing. Isabel Wilkerson describes the Great Migration in the following terms:

> They did what humans have done for centuries when life became untenable ... what the Irish did when there was nothing to eat, what the European Jews did during the spread of Nazism... They did what human beings looking for freedom throughout history have often done. They left.[24]

African American migrants did leave the South, but leaving was only the first step. They did not just look for freedom, they took action to make it a reality, by utilising communication and kinship networks to strike out from the South. After they relocated, they came to understand that freedom was not confined to place, but also entailed making choices regarding types of employment and negotiating boundaries between urban acculturation and retention of southern culture and values. However, the Great Migration was also composed of two additional groups of African Americans, who were instrumental during different segments of the migration process. As the migrants were preparing to leave the South, one of the most robust sources of information and assistance originated with the black press, particularly *The Chicago Defender*, whose publisher Robert Abbott, organised the "Great Northern Drive" campaign. Once the migrants arrived in the North, African American progressive reform groups such as the National Urban League and the NACW provided support in securing appropriate housing and creating a sense of community among the migrants.

Along with that process of acculturation, the migrants also referred back to their work experience in the South, using it to inform their decisions regarding appropriate industrial employment. However, they still experienced discrimination in housing and employment, which led them to interact with racial uplift organisations in a different capacity, developing political protest strategies in order to achieve a higher degree of civic inclusion. They gained inspiration from other groups across the world that were making revolutionary choices against political systems they found untenable, including the Irish nationalists and Anglophone Caribbean immigrants to the United States. Indeed W.E.B. Du Bois had remarked in August 1916 on the similarities between the political situations of the Irish and African Americans,

> We must remember that the white slums of Dublin represent more bitter depths of human degradation than the black slums of Charleston and New Orleans, and where human oppression exists, there the sympathy of all black hearts must go. The recent Irish revolt may have been foolish, but would to God some of us had sense enough to be fools.[25]

The resulting blend of political advocacy flowered during the interwar period and into the World War II era, as a result of the new political clout wielded by people of colour in the North, enhanced by the population shifts of the Great Migration. Alain Locke wrote of the Great Migration in 1920:

> The wash and rush of this human tide on the beach line of the northern city centers is to be explained primarily in terms of a new vision of opportunity ... of a spirit to seize ... a chance for the improvement of conditions.[26]

Locke was writing in the context of his analysis of the "New Negro," whom he argued had undergone a political and cultural transformation, due to the scope of the migration experience. That activist ethos of the Great Migration, which began in earnest during the same year of the Easter Rising in Ireland, sustained its transformation into the Great American Protest, placing it securely in the revolutionary tradition of 1916.[27]

In an analysis placing African Americans in the anti-imperial tradition of 1916, it is imperative to include a discussion regarding their outlook on World War I. The Great Migration, like the Easter Rising in Ireland and other seminal events of 1916, was also shaped by the war, which in turn influenced the perspectives and protest strategies of African American political and community leaders. W.E.B. Du Bois and other African American reform activists utilised the Wilson administration's wartime democratic language to lobby for full citizenship for African Americans, as well as recognition of the political and human rights of coloured people abroad. It became an article of faith among the black reform class that the country's mission to end oppression overseas was inseparable from the cause to end oppression at home. Not unlike John Redmond's National Volunteers, African Americans did ultimately "close ranks" and serve in the First World War, in the hopes that their service would advance their political goals. In his 16 July 1918 editorial in *The Crisis* encouraging them to do so, Du Bois wrote:

> That which the German power represents today spells death to the aspirations of Negroes and all darker races for equality, freedom and democracy. Let us not hesitate. Let us, while this war lasts, forget our special grievances and close our ranks shoulder to shoulder with our own white fellow citizens and the allied nations that are fighting for democracy.

Notes

1 In her book on the Great Migration, Isabel Wilkerson describes the decision to migrate as, "a response to an economic and social structure not of their own making." Isabel Wilkerson, *The Warmth of Other Suns: The Epic Story of America's Great Migration* (New York, 2010), 14.
2 Although Great Migration destinations encompassed cities outside of the Midwest region and northern East Coast of the United States, significant numbers of migrants relocated to these cities. For ease of reference, this grouping of cities is referred to as "the North" in this essay.
3 Steven Hahn, *A Nation Under Our Feet: Black Political Struggles in the Rural South from Slavery to the Great Migration* (Cambridge, MA, 2003), 466.
4 President Woodrow Wilson, Fourteen Points Speech (8 January 1918), U.S. Government Documents, www.ourdocuments.gov, accessed 2 February 2017.
5 See Leon F. Litwack, *Troubled in Mind: Black Southerners in the Age of Jim Crow* (New York, 1998).
6 A. Scott Berg, *Wilson* (New York, 2013), 311–12; "Wilson Would Aid Negroes," *The New York Times*, 16 December 1914, n.p.; Henry Blumenthal, "Woodrow Wilson and the Race Question," *The Journal of Negro History* 48.1 (1963), 1–21.
7 James R. Grossman, *Chicago, Black Southerners, and the Great Migration* (Chicago, IL, 1989), 19, 36.
8 Hahn, *A Nation Under Our Feet*, 467–68.
9 William G. Jordan, *Black Newspapers & America's War for Democracy, 1914–1920* (Chapel Hill, NC, 2001), 32.
10 Patrick S. Washburn, *The African American Newspaper: Voices of Freedom* (Evanston, IL, 2006), 73–83.
11 Washburn, *African American Newspaper*, 84–89.
12 Touré F. Reed, *Not Alms but Opportunity: The Urban League & The Politics of Racial Uplift, 1910–1950.* (Chapel Hill, NC, 2008), 12.

13 Minutes of the First Meeting of the National Urban League, 29 September 1910, www.pbs.org/wnet/jimcrow/stories_org_urban.html.

14 Reed, *Not Alms*, 26.

15 Jacqueline M. Moore, *Booker T. Washington, W.E.B. DuBois and the Struggle for Racial Uplift* (Lanham, MD, 2003), 106–9; Wilson Jeremiah Moses, *The Golden Age of Black Nationalism, 1850–1925* (New York, 1978), 130–31.

16 Peter Gottlieb, *Making Their Own Way: Southern Blacks' Migration to Pittsburgh, 1916–1930* (Urbana, IL, 1987), 141.

17 Bruce Nelson, *Irish Nationalists and the Making of the Irish Race* (Princeton, NJ, 2012), 191–206.

18 Anthony J. Badger, *The New Deal: The Depression Years, 1933–1940* (New York, 1989), 251.

19 Badger, *The New Deal*, 306–7.

20 Letter, Harry L. Hopkins to Stephen Early regarding Prohibiting Discrimination in the WPA. President's Master Speech File, WPA Administration, 17 June 1935, (Box 22), Franklin D. Roosevelt Presidential Library, www.fdrlibrary.marist.edu, accessed 22 January 2017; Badger, *The New Deal*, 252–54.

21 Cheryl Lynn Greenberg, *Or Does It Explode? Black Harlem in the Great Depression* (New York, 1991), 116–17.

22 Franklin D. Roosevelt, Fireside Chat on National Security (Arsenal of Democracy Speech), 29 December1940, Library and Museum, www.fdrlibrary.marist.edu/_resources/images/tully/5_20.pdf, accessed 16 March 2017.

23 A. Philip Randolph, "Call to Negro America to March in Washington for Jobs and Equal Participation in National Defense," *Black Worker* 14 (1941), n.p.

24 Wilkerson, *The Warmth of Other Suns*, 14–15.

25 W.E.B. Du Bois, *The Crisis* (1916), 166–67.

26 Alain Locke, "The New Negro," in Locke, ed., *The New Negro* (New York, 1925), 6.

27 W.E.B. Du Bois, "Close Ranks," *The Crisis* 16 (1918), 111. See also, W.E.B. Du Bois, "We Return Fighting," *The Crisis* 18 (1919), 13; "The First Biennial Meeting of the Association for the Study of Negro Life and History at Washington," *The Journal of Negro History* 2.4 (1917), 442–48. In the American Army, with the exception of the short-lived 92nd Division, African Americans served in non-combatant, service and supply roles. The 93rd Division was sent to serve with the French Army, did so with distinction and returned home to a nation anxious to uphold the segregated racial order. Dashed expectations regarding political rights in return for military service was a familiar scenario for African Americans, one they might have shared with many colonial troops who served in the war. W.E.B. Du Bois, "The African Roots of the War," *Atlantic Monthly* (1915), 707–11; Jonathan Rosenberg, *How Far the Promised Land? World Affairs and the American Civil Rights Movement, From the First World War to Vietnam* (Princeton, NJ, 2006), 18–23.

5 Lala Lajpat Rai, Indian Nationalism, and the Irish Revolution

The View from New York, 1914–1920

David Brundage

The myriad connections between Indian and Irish nationalist movements are finally beginning to receive the scholarly attention that they deserve. Recent work by Kate O'Malley, Michael Silvestri and others has shed light on links going back to the Irish "New Departure", if not before. The impact that the 1916 Easter Rising had on the Indian struggle for independence has garnered particular attention, with even recent popular accounts mentioning, for instance, the influence that the Rising exerted on the Bengali Jugantar Party militants who carried out the 1930 Chittagong armoury raid.[1]

This chapter builds on this work but approaches the topic from a somewhat different perspective. The following pages consider the political activities of the Indian nationalist Lala Lajpat Rai not in India but in New York, where he resided for most of the period from November 1914 to February 1920. Lajpat Rai was a towering figure in the history of Indian nationalism, both an important political leader of the Indian National Congress and an intellectual who wrote prolifically on a wide range of subjects. As this chapter will show, he was also a key figure in the construction of a vibrant multinational anticolonial movement that took shape in the United States – with its centre in New York City – in the years during and immediately following World War I.

This American anticolonial movement was influenced in profound ways by events in Ireland. The Irish revolution that began with the 1916 Easter Rising inspired a diverse group of New Yorkers by providing them with a potent example of the ability of a handful of militants to challenge a great empire, a revolutionary dynamic that could sweep aside compromises and halfway measures (such as Home Rule) almost overnight, and a deeply inspiring willingness of dedicated rebels to sacrifice their own lives for the sake of a larger cause. For Lala Lajpat Rai, there was another factor at work: in linking the Indian independence struggle to that of the Irish, he was fastening onto the national cause with by far the most favourable publicity and popular enthusiasm in the United States. In addition, as the Irish revolution unfolded, some Irish American nationalists, seeking to build an ever-stronger movement in its support, began reaching out to activists representing other nationalities with a presence in the city. In this context, Lajpat Rai discarded his initial scepticism about the Irish revolution and took a leading role in two important New York-based anticolonial organisations (the League of Small and Subject Nationalities and the League of Oppressed Peoples) in which its supporters were central.[2]

Lala Lajpat Rai's earliest commitments were not to Indian independence, but to the Arya Samja, one of the most important of the socio-religious reform movements that swept through British India in the last quarter of the nineteenth century. He was born on 28 January 1865 in Dhudike, a village in the Firozpur district of Punjab, the eldest son of a learned (if poorly remunerated) District Board teacher of Persian and Urdu. Lajpat Rai's father provided the youth with his first education at home, stimulating a lifelong interest in history and religion in particular. Although suffering near constant ill health, he was an accomplished student, completing his secondary education on a scholarship and passing the entrance examination for the Punjab University College in Lahore, where he matriculated in 1881. Given how few Indians received formal education in this period, this put Lajpat Rai on an elite track, despite his relatively humble birth, and his decision to pursue the study of law cemented this upward trajectory.[3]

But even as he pursued this career, larger cultural and political issues began to intrude. In the spring of 1882, Lajpat Rai embraced the cause of the Hindi language in the Urdu-Hindi controversy that rocked Punjab that year. Around the same time, a college friend introduced him to the writings of John Stuart Mill and Jeremy Bentham, which, together with newspapers that he now regularly consumed, began to have an impact on his thinking. But, as he later recalled, "the thing that made the deepest impression on my character was the Hindi movement, [which] generated within me the national feeling". He was particularly influenced by the ideas of Babu Navin Chandra Roy, who "looked upon Hindi as the national language of India, and wanted it to be the foundation for the edifice of Indian nationality".[4]

Even more important for the young Lajpat Rai was the Hindu religious reform organisation, the Arya Samaj, which he joined at the end of 1882, an event he later described as "a turning point in my life". Founded in 1875 by Swami Dayanand Saraswati, the Arya Samaj was one of the most successful of the socio-religious reform movements that emerged in India in the last quarter of the nineteenth century, and it had particular strength in the north of the country, in the United Provinces and Punjab. The Samaj pursued an ambitious social reform agenda, opposing child marriage, supporting education for girls and favouring a diminution of statuses based on birth. But at the same time, it was fiercely Hindu, harkening back to the Vedas as the essential guide for worship and behaviour in the contemporary world and vehemently opposing Muslim and Christian conversion efforts. The strongest supporters of the Arya Samaj were upwardly mobile professionals and merchants, who saw the movement as a way of building community and strengthening Hinduism, while simultaneously embracing "modernity". By 1884, Lajpat Rai was secretary of his local Arya Samaj and was regarded as among the organisation's "front-rank speakers".[5]

Though his ever-deepening involvement in the Arya Samaj slowed his academic progress, Lajpat Rai finally passed his law examination in 1885, and from 1886 to 1892 he practiced law in Hissar, a district town of about 15,000, quickly becoming one of its most successful lawyers. While in Hissar, he helped establish an active Arya Samaj and managed to "read a good many books on social and political problems, and on religion, besides general literature". In 1892, he moved back to Lahore, the administrative centre of the Punjab and a centre of social, educational and religious ferment as well. As his legal practice grew, he was able to contribute substantial funds to Lahore's Dayananda Anglo-Vedic School, established to honour the founder of the Arya Samaj, Swami Dayananda. He became a prominent member of the "College" faction of the Samaj, which increasingly moved into the area of social services, particularly orphan support and famine relief. In the terrible famines that struck India at the end of the 1890s, Lajpat Rai threw himself into the work of relief and, in 1898, he cut back drastically on his legal practice to devote more of his energies to the Arya Samaj.[6]

But even as he deepened his commitment to this Hindu (albeit modernising) movement, Lajpat Rai began to espouse a set of ideas that could best be called "liberal nationalism". This began as early as 1881 with his exposure (through the published speeches of the pioneering Indian nationalist Surendranath Banerjee) to the ideas of the Italian revolutionary Giuseppe Mazzini. Banerjee's speech on Mazzini, which Lajpat Rai later claimed brought him to tears, led him to read biographies of Mazzini and histories of Young Italy and other European nationalist movements, and he later translated Mazzini's *Duties of Man* into Urdu. "I made Mazzini my Guru", Lajpat Rai wrote in 1915, "and so he continues to this day". Not surprisingly, his evolving outlook eventually drew him to the Indian National Congress, founded in 1885 and propounding the view that the interests of individual, caste and community all be subordinated to the that of the "nation". In its first two decades, however, Congress was relatively dormant and though Lajpat Rai attended his first session in 1888, he did not take an active part in its work until after the turn of the century. He did, however, continue to produce a steady stream of nationalist writings, including Urdu-language biographies of Mazzini and Giuseppe Garibaldi.[7]

At the 1904 session of Congress, Lajpat Rai was selected as one of the members of its deputation to London, led by future Congress President Gopal Krishna Gokhale. In the summer of 1905, he toured a number of British cities, making contact with sympathetic British socialists and Labour Party leaders and attending the opening ceremony of India House, a nationalist-inspired residence for Indian students in London. In September 1905, he made his first trip to the United States. It was only after his return to India in November 1905 that Lajpat Rai was thrust into the vortex of

accelerated nationalist agitation, agitation triggered by what is now recognised as a defining moment in modern Indian history, the partition of
Bengal.[8]

George Nathaniel Curzon, who had assumed the position of Viceroy in
1899, acted on a long-held British view that the province of Bengal was
simply too large to govern effectively. But his decision to divide it into two
provinces, making Muslims the majority in eastern Bengal, deeply angered
the English-educated Hindu middle class of the province, who saw it as an
effort to dilute their influence. They opposed partition with a campaign of
"swadeshi", a boycott of British imports which they sought to replace with
increased use of local products. Huge demonstrations took place across
India, including in Lahore, where Lajpat Rai gave a powerful speech in support of swadeshi in December. He extended this militancy later that month
when he opposed a Congress resolution welcoming the Prince of Wales to
India, defended the "manly and vigorous policy" of swadeshi and called for
a sweeping "political regeneration of the country". The ringing concluding
words of his speech at this 1905 session of Congress laid the foundation for
the militant (if mainly nonviolent) nationalist activism of the next decade:
"If you show, in a few years, to our rulers that we are steadfast in our devo-
tion to our cause, I assure you that there is no power in the world that can
prevent you from going forward".[9]

Such rhetoric drew the attention of the British authorities to Lajpat Rai
and, following an explosion of agrarian unrest in the Punjab, they arrested
and deported him without trial to Mandalay, Burma, in May 1907. As
the victim of what was widely regarded as an unjust and illegal action,
Lajpat Rai's imprisonment, which lasted six months, ended up increasing
his already considerable stature, but upon his return he found the Indian
National Congress in the midst of a debilitating split between so-called
Moderate and Extremist factions. Though generally identified with the
latter, Lajpat Rai continued to participate in the Moderate-dominated
Congress, and in December 1913 he set off for London again as part of
a Congress delegation to lobby Parliament for a relatively minor political
reform, the introduction of an element of democracy in selecting the Indian
members of the Council of the Secretary of State for India. He was still
in Britain when war broke out in August 1914. Fearing arrest or deportation under the government's new emergency powers if he returned to India,
Lajpat Rai decided instead to travel to America. He arrived in New York
City on 21 November 1914.[10]

The metropolis of New York was home to a wide variety of immigrant
and descent groups in 1914, but its South Asian population was extremely
small. Although some Indian merchants could be found in the city as early as
the eighteenth century, substantial migration from the Indian subcontinent
to North America began only in the early twentieth century and was then
composed largely of Punjabi Sikh agricultural and lumber workers, who
settled primarily in the states of the West Coast and in British Columbia.

Among these migrants, whose total number never exceeded 10,000 before World War I, was an even smaller group of business people, students, intellectuals and professionals who gravitated toward western cities like San Francisco and Seattle. Some also made their way to New York, where, as early as 1906, a growing number of Indian university students could be found. Lajpat Rai's first New York speech, given about three weeks after his arrival in the city, was hosted by the New York branch of the Hindustan Association of the United States, a recently organised body of Indian students receiving their education in America.[11]

But New York, above all, was an Irish city. As the twentieth century opened, decades of substantial Irish emigration had led to a situation in which nearly as many Irish people lived outside of Ireland as within its borders and no city illustrated the growing importance of the Irish diaspora better than New York. Over 250,000 Irish-born people resided in the metropolis in 1900, making it (after Dublin and Belfast) the largest centre of Irish population in world. But a focus on the Irish-born understates the Irish character of the city, for by 1900 the real demographic weight lay with the second- and increasingly even third-generation American-born Irish. Irish immigrants and their descendants were still overwhelmingly working class, with particularly strong representation in New York's important trade and transportation sectors, but they were also heavily represented in the skilled trades and in municipal employment. Many by this time were small business owners, operating neighbourhood stores and saloons, while several very wealthy Irish Americans, like the corporate attorney John Quinn, the lawyer and politician Bourke Cockran and the construction magnate John D. Crimmins, had found a secure place within New York's increasingly cohesive bourgeoisie.[12]

Irish nationalism was a very powerful force in the city, but it was mainly of the constitutional variety. Though the "physical force" revolutionary republicans of the Clan na Gael maintained a presence in New York in the early years of the twentieth century, the nationalist movement was dominated there, as elsewhere in the United States, by the United Irish League of America (UILA), the US-based fundraising arm of the Irish Parliamentary Party. By 1912 the Irish Party, led by John Redmond, seemed on the verge of winning its long-term goal of Home Rule, a greater degree of political autonomy for Ireland within the larger framework of the British Empire. However, the balance of forces was already changing by the time of Lajpat Rai's arrival in November 1914. The precipitating factor was the outbreak of World War I in August and Redmond's decision to support the British war effort and accept a postponement of Home Rule. Even more than in Ireland itself, these events transformed the Irish nationalist movement in America, undermining support for the UILA and leading to a sharp rise in the fortunes of its revolutionary wing.[13]

Over the course of Lajpat Rai's time in New York, the power of revolutionary Irish nationalism grew significantly. In March 1916, a new organisation, the Friends of Irish Freedom (FOIF), was established at a so-called Irish Race Convention in New York, attended by over two thousand American men and women. In the wake of the Easter Rising the following month and the subsequent execution of its leaders and of the internationally renowned Sir Roger Casement in August, and the onset of the Irish War of Independence in 1919, the ranks of Irish revolutionary nationalists in America expanded even further. The FOIF claimed nearly 300,000 members by 1919, and its later rival, the American Association for the Recognition of the Irish Republic (AARIR), founded by Éamon de Valera during his eighteen-month organising campaign in the United States, had 700,000 members and had raised over ten million dollars for the proclaimed Irish Republic by 1921. Both organisations had significant strength in New York, while smaller (and sometimes more radical) Irish organisations could be found there as well. The Irish Progressive League, which was active from the fall of 1917 until its merger with the AARIR in November 1920, for example, brought together anti-war liberals, left-wing progressives, women suffragists and socialists in its campaign for Irish independence.[14]

Lajpat Rai was initially unenthusiastic about Irish America's new turn toward revolution. He was no stranger to Irish nationalism of course. He had met leaders of the Irish Parliamentary Party on his first trip to England in 1905 and his long reading list while imprisoned in Mandalay had included the five-volume work, *A History of Our Own Times*, by Justin McCarthy, leader of the Irish Party from 1890 to 1896. But McCarthy was a moderate constitutional nationalist, not a revolutionary, and had even sent British Prime Minister William Gladstone the first two volumes of his *History* as a "tribute of admiration and respect". In New York, as in London, Lajpat Rai seemed to be most happy in the company of Irish Home Rulers like the vehemently anti-republican John Quinn, who gave him moral support (and apparently even some investment advice) and whom he gratefully acknowledged in the Preface to his 1916 book, *The United States of America: A Hindu's Impression and Study*.[15]

Equally important, Lajpat Rai was fighting his own ideological battles with Indian revolutionaries in the United States, which had become the base for a strong diasporic wing of Indian nationalism. On the West Coast, a militant organisation called the Ghadar Party had emerged in 1913, shaped in equal measures by opposition to British rule at home and to the often-violent expressions of anti-Asian racism in America. New York was an important centre for revolutionary activism as well. As Lajpat Rai later recalled, summarising his interactions with other Indian activists in America during World War I, "most of them were extremists, only a few moderates". Like the Clan na Gael, which served as an American conduit for secret wartime contacts between the German government and the Dublin rebels planning the Easter Rising, many Indian nationalists in New York and other US cities were also, as he noted disapprovingly, "in alliance with Germany and were being supplied with money by German government agents". The fact that Indian revolutionaries in America had welcomed the Rising – San Francisco's *Ghadar* newspaper had lauded its leaders, proclaiming that "the blood of martyrs is not wasted" for "every drop was as seed sown which has produced many harvests" – would have simply cemented Lajpat Rai's antipathy to the Rising's Irish American supporters.[16]

To be sure, Lajpat Rai himself had been generally identified with the "Extremist" wing of the Indian National Congress, which, as he noted in a February 1915 article that he wrote for the *New York Times*, did indeed seek "complete independence" for India in the long run – as against the Congress "Moderates", who were "contented to remain within the British empire on the same footing as Canada or Australia or South Africa". But this ambitious long-term goal did not lead him to embrace revolutionary violence or to conspire with German agents. Indeed, in the same article, Lajpat Rai celebrated the wartime "loyalty of India [which] has been warmly acknowledged by the English people in Parliament, in the press, and on the platform". It was in this sprit that, in October 1917, he established the India Home Rule League of America, with himself as President and an American missionary, J. T. Sunderland, as Vice President. The goal of this New York-based organisation was to make the Indian question an international one and, in particular, to reach out to potentially sympathetic Americans. Three months later, the group began publishing what soon became an influential monthly magazine, *Young India*, in order to further this goal.[17]

Part of the inspiration for Lajpat Rai's efforts came from new political initiatives back in India, especially the 1916–1917 emergence of Annie Besant's Home Rule Leagues, whose name and goals were in turn influenced by the Irish Home Rule movement. Like its Irish counterpart, the India Home Rule League of America expressed support for the British and American war effort, announcing "its entire and unqualified repudiation of any sympathy for Germany and her war aims". In an Irish (and Irish American) context, this position constituted at least an implicit repudiation of the 1916 Easter rebels, whose Proclamation of an Irish Republic famously acknowledged our "gallant allies in Europe", and a rejection of Sinn Féin, the Irish political party that subsequently took up the rebels' mantle. Lajpat Rai, it appeared, would have no dealings with the many Americans who were now filling the ranks of Irish republican organisations like the Clan na Gael or the FOIF.[18]

Nonetheless, pragmatically appreciating the rising tide of popular support for the Irish revolution in New York, and throughout the nation, Lajpat Rai slowly began to develop cooperative relationships with Irish and Irish American republicans. A key event in this turn was his support for a new body called the Friends of Freedom for India (FFI), founded in March 1919, in which such Irish American republicans played a central role. The FFI's national council boasted a number of eminent Americans, including Columbia University anthropologist Franz Boas and social reformer Upton Sinclair, but it was New York's Irish republicans who provided the most vigorous support for its efforts. Frank P. Walsh, a well-known labour law-yer who had served as part of an Irish American delegation to the Paris Peace Conference styling itself the American Commission on Irish Independence and who would go on to serve as Éamon de Valera's main US legal advisor, became a Vice President of the FFI, while the (similarly named) FOIF provided a good deal of moral and financial support.[19]

Lajpat Rai also worked with Irish and Irish American republicans in two important New York-based anticolonial organisations that he helped to build during and after the war. The first of these was a body called the League of Small and Subject Nationalities, led by Frederic C. Howe, a well-known reformer and President Woodrow Wilson's Commissioner of Immigration. Howe established the League in May 1917 as "a permanent congress of the small, subject and oppressed nationalities of the world", which he hoped would "assert the right of each nationality to direct representation at the peace conference following this war [and] present the case of these nationalities to the world". The objectives of the League reflected Howe's view that the United States' entry into the war could be justified – and he was, like Lajpat Rai, a war supporter – only if Wilson's idealistic wartime rhetoric about national "self-determination" was taken at face value and made the basis for a sweeping transformation of the world's balance of power. He argued forcefully for "the right of self-government as an indispensable condition for world peace".[20]

Though sympathetic to the Irish cause, Howe was not an Irish nationalist and did not privilege the Irish case for independence in his overall political outlook. Nonetheless, the post-1916 Irish question had an important (and sometimes disruptive) effect on the new organisation almost immediately. At its first large public meeting in October 1917, fallout from the Easter Rising – or more specifically the presence of the Irish republican and feminist Hanna Sheehy-Skeffington as the only speaker representing Ireland – nearly tore the infant organisation apart. Sheehy-Skeffington (widow of Francis Sheehy-Skeffington, a well-known Irish pacifist, who had been arrested and shot by British troops while trying to prevent looting during the Rising) was one of the most famous of the Irish republican émigrés working to generate American public support for independence after 1916. Her presence – and, equally important, the *absence* of representatives from such pro-ally "small and subject" nations as Armenia, Belgium or Poland – led no fewer than eight other speakers to back out of their commitments at the last minute. "Mrs. Sheehy-Skeffington is the sole representative of Ireland", the eight noted in an angry statement they released to the press. "Does she represent the Irish people or only the pro-German wing of the Sinn Fein?" The League weathered this initial storm, and as the war came to an end in November 1918 it boasted representatives from no fewer that twenty-two national groups, ranging from Poland, Denmark and Ireland (now represented by New York's well-known Irish American nationalist leader Dr. Gertrude B. Kelly) to Korea and the Transvaal. "Hebrews" were represented by Columbia University's Dr. Samuel Joseph and the Zionist activist Bernard G. Richards, while the African American civil rights activist and intellectual W.E.B. Du Bois spoke for sub-Saharan Africa. India was represented by Lajpat Rai.[21]

The Irish question erupted again the following month, however, when a British Labour Party representative named P. W. Wilson, who had been invited to speak at the League's second public meeting on 14 December 1918, made what a correspondent for *Young India* characterised as "certain remarks against Ireland which were resented by the audience". Wilson "assumed an attitude of hostility toward the League and towards Ireland", and as a result his speech was interrupted with boos and hisses. Lajpat Rai, who was presiding over the session, responded directly to the British visitor in a speech of his own, correcting what he regarded as Wilson's numerous mischaracterisations of both Indian and Irish positions. Nevertheless, the Irish question and the voicing of what the *New York Times* called "attacks on England" by Indian nationalists and Irish republicans again proved disruptive.[22]

Frederic Howe himself attended the Paris Peace Conference as a consultant on the Mediterranean, but the failure of the talks to take up anything resembling global self-determination led to his disillusionment with prospects for decolonization, and he moved on to other reform issues. Absent his leadership, the League of Small and Subject Nationalities was dead by November 1919. Taking up the same project, however, was a new organisation, the League of Oppressed Peoples, which held its inaugural public meeting the same month at New York's Lexington Theatre, with representatives of Ireland, India and Korea in attendance. This time, though, it was a leading New York Irish American republican who was the dominant figure: a lawyer and political activist by the name of Dudley Field Malone. With an executive committee that included Lajpat Rai, the group began reaching out to notable figures involved in anticolonial activities. At Malone's behest, for example, the organisation's secretary contacted Du Bois, who agreed to participate, as did some of the others who had been involved in the earlier association.[23]

Unlike Howe's organisation, Irish revolutionary nationalists figured prominently at every stage in the development of this new one. In fact, the original idea for the League of Oppressed Peoples apparently came from Frank Walsh, with financial support from yet another anticolonial activist, Sa'd Zaghlul, who had led the Egyptian delegation to the Paris Peace Conference. Walsh later told an acquaintance that Zaghlul had approached him at the Paris talks and asked him to serve as "Egyptian Counsel" in the United States, a role similar to that he would later play for Ireland's Éamon de Valera. An arrangement worked out by Seán T. O'Kelly and George Gavin Duffy (who were also in Paris, representing the proclaimed Irish Republic) provided Walsh with $90,000 in expenses and fees. Once back in New York, according to Maloney, Walsh used some of this money to pay journalists to "throw open their columns to Egyptian affairs" and some of it to pay the expenses of his old friend and political ally, the former governor of Missouri, Joseph W. Folk, to present the Egyptian case before the Senate Committee on Foreign Relations. But Walsh used $2,000 of the Egyptian money to found the League of Oppressed Peoples. The Friends of Irish Freedom supplemented the Egyptian funds with a pledge of $2,500.[24]

Ireland's Seán T. O'Kelly became a particularly strong advocate of such broad-based anticolonial efforts after the disappointing Paris Peace Conference, believing that

> if we had a closely knit, well organised delegation representative of even the oppressed peoples of the British Empire, not to talk of the oppressed peoples of all the great nations represented at that Conference, we could certainly have made ourselves felt as well as heard.

Three of the Irish Republic's envoys in New York – Harry Boland, Liam Mellows and Patrick McCartan – agreed, serving as the official representatives of "Ireland" on the central committee of the League of Oppressed Peoples. But it was Irish *Americans*, especially those on the left of the US political spectrum, who played the most important role. John Fitzpatrick, the long-time president of the Chicago Federation of Labor, served as an officer of the League and Peter Golden, a leader of New York's Irish Progressive League, worked to distribute its informational materials to potentially sympathetic newspapers such as the *Jewish Daily Forward* and the socialist *New York Call*.[25]

In the end, however, the most important individual in the League was Dudley Field Malone. Born to a prosperous Irish American family on Manhattan's West Side in 1882, Malone attended St. Francis Xavier's College (where he majored in French) and received a law degree from Fordham University in 1905. By the second decade of the century, he was active in anti-Tammany Democratic reform circles, drawing positive attention from then-New Jersey governor Woodrow Wilson. In return for Malone's tireless work in his 1912 election campaign, Wilson appointed him to the important position of Collector of the Port of New York. But Malone resigned his post in the summer of 1917, in a dramatic protest of the administration's failure to endorse women's suffrage and its arrest of militant suffragists picketing in Washington. This principled action drew much criticism and cost Malone some old friends, but it gained him a host of new ones, including the suffragist leader Carrie Chapman Catt, who called it "the noblest act that any man ever did on behalf of our cause". Frederic Howe, who would resign his own position as US Immigration Commissioner in September 1919 to protest Wilson's deportation of alien radicals, described Malone as "a magnetic personality in any group", noting that "he was gifted with extraordinary ability as a public speaker, a richly endowed personality, and a generosity that went out to causes only less whole-heartedly than it went out to personal friends".[26]

One of the closest of Malone's "personal friends" was Lala Lajpat Rai. Lajpat Rai arranged for Malone to present the Indian case for independence to the Senate Foreign Relations Committee and it was almost certainly Malone who arranged for Lajpat Rai to give a speech at the FOIF's February 1919 Irish Race Convention in Philadelphia. That speech, which Lajpat Rai noted afterwards, "was a great success and was applauded for several minutes", reflected the profound changes that had occurred in his thinking on questions such as British and US war aims, Irish republicanism, and the situation now facing "small and subject nations" more generally:

> During this war we fought for the Allies. We were told that the Allies stood for the right of all nations, big or small, to self-determination. But while now the principle is held applicable to the case of the German colonies, to the conquered part of the Turkish empire, to the Balkans, which are far, far behind India and Ireland in civilization and culture, it is being denied in the case of the latter. Is this honesty? Is this justice? If modern civilization stands for hypocritical dealings, for double-mindedness, for the right of might and of force, then God save us from this civilization. The diplomats and statesmen of the world are patching up a peace in Europe which does not recognise the fundamental rights of small and subject nations to rule themselves and to decide their own future. There can be no peace in the world as long as there are subject nations; as long as large blocks of humanity are held in subjection by small but powerful nations.[27]

Lajpat Rai's newfound support for the Irish revolution was epitomised by the welcome that he gave to Éamon de Valera when the Irish leader arrived in New York in June. As Lajpat Rai's secretary, N. S. Hardikar, recalled years later, "the two patriots embraced each other out of love and gave expression to their feelings that their countries would surely achieve their independence". As late as the 1960s, Hardikar still treasured his memory of "how their boundless joy overflowed when the two great patriotic heroes, who had to face a common enemy, came together".[28]

Nevertheless, unlike de Valera, Lajpat Rai continued to oppose revolutionary violence in the Indian context. He was, instead, inspired by the new strategy of satyagraha (passive resistance) and by the emergence of Mahatma Gandhi, whom he hailed in the October 1919 issue of *Young India* as the "one man who knows his mind, believes in his principles, refuses to equivocate or compromise and dares to act accordingly". When Lajpat Rai finally returned to India in February 1920 he threw himself into the non-cooperation movement that Gandhi had initiated, enduring another period of imprisonment from December 1921 to August 1923 for his activities. After his release, he made two more trips to Britain and one to Geneva, where he attended the 1926 conference of the International

Labour Organization. He never again travelled to the United States. None-theless, his political work in New York during and after the war had altered his view of the Irish revolution while simultaneously cementing his under-standing of the fight for Indian independence as part of a larger project for the liberation of *all* "subject nations" from the fetters of colonialism.[29]

Lala Lajpat Rai died on 17 November 1928, in part because of injuries he had suffered in Lahore three weeks earlier when baton-wielding police had charged into a procession of peaceful protesters that he had been leading. Gandhi was just one of many Indian independence leaders who eulogised him, noting that "men like Lalaji cannot die so long as the sun shines in the Indian sky". He was eulogised in New York City as well, but there it was Irish American veterans of the broad anticolonial movement that he had helped construct who took the lead. Dudley Field Malone undoubtedly spoke for many in that movement when he recalled his "abiding friendship" with Lajpat Rai and hailed him as "the most inspiring patriot I have ever known".[30]

Notes

1 Kate O'Malley, *Ireland, India and Empire: Indo-Irish Radical Connec-tions, 1919–64* (Manchester, 2008); Michael Silvestri, *Ireland and India: Nationalism, Empire and Memory* (Basingstoke, UK, 2009); Bríona Nic Dhiarmada, *The 1916 Irish Rebellion* (Notre Dame, IN, 2016), 159; Fintan O'Toole, "The Easter Rising: Powerful and Useless," *New York Review of Books*, 29 September 2016, 68. Recent scholarship on wider currents of anti-imperialism also provides insights on Indo-Irish connections. See Antoinette M. Burton, *The Trouble with Empire: Challenges to Modern British Impe-rialism* (New York, 2015); Jill C. Bender, *The 1857 Indian Uprising and the British Empire* (Cambridge, UK, 2016); and Paul A. Townend, *The Road to Home Rule: Anti-Imperialism and the Irish National Movement* (Madison, WI, 2016).
2 For a fuller elaboration of some of these themes, see David Brundage, "The Easter Rising and New York's Anticolonial Nationalists," in Miriam Nyhan Grey, ed., *Ireland's Allies: America and the 1916 Easter Rising* (Dublin, 2016), 247–59.
3 Though little of it focuses on his New York experiences, there is a substantial body of scholarship on Lajpat Rai. See Purushottam Nagar, *Lala Lajpat Rai: The Man and His Ideas* (New Delhi, 1977), Feroz Chand, *Lajpat Rai: Life and Work* (New Delhi, 1978), Shyamnandan Shahi, *Lala Lajpat Rai, His Life and Thought* (Delhi, 1986), Joginder Singh Dhanki, *Lala Lajpat Rai and Indian Nationalism* (Jalandhar, 1990), V. P. Gupta and Mohini Gupta, *The Life and Legacy of Lala Lajpat Rai* (New Delhi, 2000), and J. S. Grewal and Indu Bangu, eds., *Lala Lajpat Rai in Retrospect: Political, Economic, Social, and Cultural Concerns* (Chandigarh, 2000). For the low percentage of formally educated Indians – just 3 per cent as late as 1921 – and for the importance of the legal profession as an avenue of upward mobility, see Barbara D. Metcalf and Thomas R. Metcalf, *A Concise History of Modern India*, 3rd ed. (New York, 2012), 135.
4 Lala Lajpat Rai, *Autobiographical Writings*, edited by Vijaya Chandra Joshi (Delhi, 1984, orig. 1914), 26–27.
5 Lajpat Rai, *Autobiographical Writings*, 29, 32–33. For the Arya Samaj, see Kenneth W. Jones, *Arya Dharm: Hindu Consciousness in 19th-Century Pun-jab* (Berkeley, CA, 1976).

6 Lajpat Rai, *Autobiographical Writings*, 42; Jones, *Arya Dharm*, 80–86, 236–41.

7 Lajpat Rai, *Autobiographical Writings*, 81, 93. Banerjee's speech on Mazzini had a similar effect on some of the other key figures in the Indian National Congress, See, for instance, Bipin Chandra Pal, *Memories of My Life and Times* (Calcutta, 1973), 198–99. For Mazzini's influence among the first generation of Indian liberal nationalists more generally, see C. A. Bayly, "Liberalism at Large: Mazzini and Nineteenth-Century Indian Thought," in C. A. Bayly and Eugenio F. Biagini, eds., *Giuseppe Mazzini and the Globalization of Democratic Nationalism, 1830–1920* (New York, 2008), 355–74.

8 Lajpat Rai, *Autobiographical Writings*, 104–7; Gupta and Gupta, *Lala Lajpat Rai*, 54–55.

9 Lajpat Rai, quoted in Gupta and Gupta, *Lala Lajpat Rai*, 55–56. For the complex class and religious politics of the Bengali movement, which ended up intensifying Hindu-Muslim tensions even as it furthered the nationalist movement, see Sumit Sarkar, *The Swadeshi Movement in Bengal, 1903–1908* (New Delhi, 1973).

10 Lala Lajpat Rai, *The Collected Works of Lala Lajpat Rai*, 15 vols., ed. B. R. Nanda, vol. 5 (New Delhi, 2003), 63. For the details of his arrest and deportation, see Lajpat Rai, "The Story of My Deportation," in his *Autobiographical Writings*, 129–94.

11 Seema Sohi, *Echoes of Mutiny: Race, Surveillance, and Indian Anticolonialism in North America* (New York, 2014), 35; Joan M. Jensen, *Passage from India: Asian Indian Immigrants in North America* (New Haven, CT, 1988), 24–41; Lajpat Rai, *Collected Works*, vol. 5, 66; *Bulletin of the Hindustan Association of U. S. A.* (1913), 6.

12 Fearghal McGarry, "'A Land Beyond the Wave': Transnational Perspectives on Easter 1916," in Niall Whelehan, ed., *Transnational Perspectives on Modern Irish History* (New York, 2015), 167; Sven Beckert, *The Moneyed Metropolis: New York City and the Consolidation of the American Bourgeoisie, 1850–1896* (New York, 2001), 166–67. For a good overview of Irish New York in this period, see Chris McNickle, "When New York Was Irish, and after," in Ronald H. Bayor and Timothy J. Meagher, eds., *The New York Irish* (Baltimore, MD, 1996), 337–56.

13 For the long history of Irish nationalism in New York, as well as in other US locales, see David Brundage, *Irish Nationalists in America: The Politics of Exile, 1798–1998* (New York, 2016). The most detailed treatment of Irish American nationalism in the early twentieth century remains Francis M. Carroll, *American Opinion and the Irish Question, 1910–23: A Study in Opinion and Policy* (New York, 1978).

14 See Michael Doorley, *Irish-American Diaspora Nationalism: The Friends of Irish Freedom, 1916–1935* (Dublin, 2005), 21–137.

15 Lajpat Rai, "The Story of My Deportation," 169; Eugene J. Doyle, *Justin McCarthy*, rev. ed. (Dublin, 2012), 25; Lajpat Rai, *Collected Works*, vol. 5, p. 96. For Quinn, see Úna Ní Bhroiméil, "An American Opinion: John Quinn and the Easter Rising," in Grey ed., *Ireland's Allies*, 201–13.

16 Lala Lajpat Rai, *The Story of My Life: An Unknown Fragment* (New Delhi, 1978, orig. 1928), 70; Sohi, *Echoes of Mutiny*, 45–67; *Ghadar*, 10 May 1916, translated and quoted in Silvestri, *Ireland and India*, 27. See also Maia Ramnath, *Haj to Utopia: How the Ghadar Movement Charted Global Radicalism and Attempted to Overthrow the British Empire* (Berkeley, CA, 2011).

17 Lajpat Rai, *Collected Works*, vol. 5, 76–77.

18 Ibid., vol. 7, 91.

19 Erez Manela, *The Wilsonian Moment: Self-Determination and the International Origins of Anticolonial Nationalism* (New York, 2007), 171–72; "Report of Friends of Freedom for India, 12 August 1919," and Tarak Nath Das to Diarmuid Lynch, 16 December 1921, both in Daniel Cohalan Papers, American Irish Historical Society, New York. See also Doorley, *Irish-American Diaspora Nationalism*, 59, 155.

20 "Small Nations Leagued Together," *The Survey*, 5 May 1917, 120; Frederic C. Howe, *Confessions of a Reformer* (Chicago, IL, 1967, orig. 1925), 9–10.

21 *New York Times*, 29 October 1917; Marion A. Smith to Frank Walsh, 7 December 1918, Frank Walsh Collection, New York Public Library (hereafter NYPL); *American Jewish Chronicle*, 13 April 1917, 761; "Bernard G. Richards, Veteran Zionist, Honored on his 75th Birthday," *Jewish Telegraphic Agency*, 26 March 1952. The controversy that swirled around Sheehy-Skeffington during her time in the United States is a central theme of Joanne Mooney Eichacker, *Irish Republican Women in America: Lecture Tours, 1916–1925* (Dublin, 2003), 58–91. See also Margaret Ward, *Hanna Sheehy Skeffington: A Life* (Dublin, 1997), 184–210. For Kelly's activities in this period, see Miriam Nyhan Grey, "Dr. Gertrude B. Kelly and the Founding of New York's Cumann na mBan," in Grey, ed., *Ireland's Allies*, 75–89.

22 "The Small and Subject Nations League and the *New York Times*," *Young India*, January 1919, 23; *New York Times*, 20 December 1918.

23 "A New League," *Young India*, November 1919, 248; Arthur Upham Pope to W. E. B. Du Bois, 10 November 1919, W. E. B. Du Bois Papers, Special Collections and University Archives, University of Massachusetts Amherst Libraries.

24 W. J. M. A. Maloney, untitled typescript, 30 December 1921, W. J. M. A. Maloney Collection, NYPL; Dudley Field Malone to Frank Walsh, 8 October 1919, Walsh Collection, NYPL; Manela, *The Wilsonian Moment*, 153–55.

25 Seán T. O'Kelly, *India and Ireland* (New York, 1924), 3; David Fitzpatrick, *Harry Boland's Irish Revolution* (Cork, 2003), 370; Spofford to Frank Walsh, 21 September 1919, Peter Golden to Frank Walsh, 3 October 1919, Walsh Collection, NYPL.

26 Carrie Chapman Catt to Malone, 15 September 1917, quoted in Dudley Field Malone, *"Unaccustomed as I Am—": Miscellaneous Speeches* (New York, 1929), 50; Howe, *Confessions of a Reformer*, 249.

27 Lajpat Rai, *Collected Works*, vol. 8, 109, 127.

28 N. S. Hardikar, *Lala Lajpat Rai in America* (New Delhi, 1966), 2. For the meeting between the two men, see also Dhanki, *Lala Lajpat Rai*, 189–90, and Manela, *The Wilsonian Moment*, 172.

29 Lajpat Rai, *Collected Works*, vol. 8, 96.

30 Gandhi quoted in Gupta and Gupta, *Lala Lajpat Rai*, vii; Malone, *"Unaccustomed as I Am—,"* 176, 178.

6 Johannesburg's Green Flag

The Contemporaneity of the Easter Rising and the 1922 Rand Rebellion

Jonathan Hyslop

On 15 March 1922, South African troops stormed the headquarters of the Johannesburg area's striking miners in the working-class suburb of Fordsburg. Two months earlier, in January, the white workers of the Rand mining region, mainly British immigrants and recently urbanised Afrikaners, had entered into a confrontation with the Chamber of Mines over threatened mass redundancies. As the confrontation intensified, the miners formed militias, known in the Boer tradition as commandos. This situation required the engagement of the then South African Prime Minister, Jan Christiaan Smuts, who had in recent years attained imperial renown as commander in East Africa, member of the British War Cabinet and a key initiator of the League of Nations. Rather than seeking a solution, Smuts had backed the mine owners, and, in his notorious phrase, "let things develop", hoping to break the miners' union once and for all. The miners turned to violent methods and embraced the leadership of leftists and Afrikaner republicans. By the end of February, they were engaged in an insurrectionary conflict with Smuts's forces. Smuts declared martial law. In the March assault on the strikers, the government deployed bomber aircraft, artillery and about 15,000 soldiers, militia men and police to crush the labour strongholds.[1]

When the Durban Light Infantry took Fordsburg, amongst their trophies was a large green flag.[2] The banner belonged to a unit known amongst the strikers as the "Irish Brigade" or the 'Sinn Fein Commando'. Not all the members of the group were from Ireland, but they clearly found inspiration in the recent events there. They wore green rosettes.[3] One of their number, Louis Ryan proclaimed himself "a Sinn Feiner" and the rising to be "a second Ireland".[4] The Brigaders knew what they were about – typically, they had seen service in the British or South African armies during the First World War.[5] It is likely too, that some of them had connections with the vigorous, if short-lived, Irish Republican Association of South Africa, which then had nine branches across the Rand and was publishing a regular newspaper.[6]

The main difference between the South African and Irish events was of course the salience of race in the former case.[7] The Rand Revolt is often dismissed simply with a reference to the image of the notorious banner raised by the strikers, which read "Workers of the World, Unite and Fight for a White South Africa". The invocation of this sign then makes the revolt into an illustration of the doomed racist stupidity of South Africa's white miners. And the strike was indeed accompanied by serious white violence in working class areas against black workers, resulting in multiple fatalities. But the uprising also contained elements of revolutionary anti-capitalism: egalitarian and racist ideologies combined in complex ways. The racial attacks were not approved of by the main group of strike leaders, the Council of Action. The chief grievance of the strikers was that the employers were planning to introduce low-paid black workers into the jobs which had previously, by agreement, been reserved for white workers. The white miners viewed this as an attack of their relatively high living standards and strong union organisation. A significant portion of the leadership saw the strike as part of a global struggle for a new social and economic order, while many of the rank and file thought of what they were doing in far more racial or nationalistic terms.

The presence of the Irish Brigade suggests that there may be some complex links to be made between the Rand Revolt and the Easter Rising. The adoption of the name "Irish Brigade" alluded back to the Boer War and implicitly thence to 1916. In 1899, a group of a few hundred mainly Irish volunteers had banded together under that name and fought for Paul Kruger's Transvaal against the British Empire. Their commander had been the future 1916 martyr John MacBride. And they too had flown a green flag, donated on the initiative of Maud Gonne. In 1921 that banner had been displayed, impressively bullet-holed, at a public meeting in Pretoria addressed by Eamonn Brugha, the brother of the then "Minister of Defence" of the Irish insurgents and 1916 veteran, Cathal Brugha.[8]

There are two major modes in which the study of global history has been conducted: a long tradition of comparison and a more recent trend toward the exploration of connections. Both are employed in this chapter. From the point of view of the older comparative approach, there are at least some similarities that indicate 1916 and 1922 might usefully be placed alongside each other. Both were urban armed insurrections against British imperial authority. Both combined republican nationalist with labour elements, though in different proportions and ways. They were on a similar scale; the numbers of security forces deployed, and the numbers of fatalities amongst both insurrectionists and soldiery were of similar levels. They dwarfed other insurgent moments within the white empire of the time in their level of violence. Though there was a wave of strikes in Canada, Australia and New Zealand, often involving returning servicemen, from around 1916 to the early 1920s, they are hardly comparable in scale. The Winnipeg General strike of 1919, for example, is still regarded as the most apocalyptic event in Canadian labour history, yet its handful of casualties look minor in comparison to either the Irish or South African upheavals.[9] In terms of newer study of "transnational" connections, the links between the Boer War and the Easter Rising are relatively well known. The battles fought by the Irish Brigade in South Africa in 1899 and 1900 were an ideological boost for the nationalist movement at home.[10] Arthur Griffith's 1890s sojourn in the Transvaal formed the background to his rise to prominence as a nationalist leader, initially through pro-Boer agitation, on his return home.[11] And scholars have become aware of the South African role in Ireland in the 1916 aftermath as well. Smuts played a part in British negotiations with De Valera in 1921, and in the politics of partition. More significantly, South Africa's Prime Minister after 1924, General J.B.M. Hertzog, and Irish President W.T. Cosgrave forged a close alliance in the politics leading up to the formal transformation of constitutional basis of the British Empire in the Statute of Westminster in 1931.[12] This chapter will seek to extend this web of South African-Irish connections to the 1922 Revolt. In doing so, it will especially argue that there is a neglected labour political dimension which linked South Africa and Ireland.

However, there may be a third mode of analytical linkage between events, other than comparison and connection, which one might name as the study of contemporaneity.[13] This consists in the identification of ways in which spatially separated events are the products of a shared global conjuncture of social forces, political cultures and institutions. Distinct events manifest common characteristics which are part of a much wider, structural global pattern. And in turn, these commonalities enable participants in events in different parts of the world to recognise, or creatively misrecognise, each other as representing similar political projects. This then enables events across the globe to become an ideological reference point for local actors. Easter 1916 and the Rand in 1922 can both be usefully read in the context of a particular global concatenation of forms of warfare, labour movement and nationalism that prevailed from roughly 1911 to 1923. And Ireland and South Africa were significant reference points on each other's' mental political maps.

Robert Gerwarth and Erez Manela have persuasively argued for reconceptualising the Great War as truly a world war, and for shifting the focus of attention in studying it away from the Western Front. From this perspective, what most importantly characterised the war was the decomposition of Empires. This in turn implies a re-periodisation of the First World War as a conflict that started in 1911 and lasted until 1923. The beginning of this period is signalled by the assaults on the Ottoman Empire by the Italians in the invasion of Libya in 1911 and the Balkan Wars of 1912–1913. Its end comes with the consolidation of the Turkish Republic and the Bolshevik regime, as well as the temporary stabilisation of post-imperial Germany.[14] Easter 1916 and the Rand 1922 can be better understood when placed in the context of this "long" world war. 1922 can then be thought of, like 1916, as a wartime event.

The second thing that links the two events is a moment of labour history, the peak of which roughly coincides with this longer war of 1911–1923, and that is the global wave of working-class radicalism known as Syndicalism.[15] The start of the second decade of the twentieth century saw an eruption of intense labour militancy in many countries. Syndicalism was a current of politics which repudiated the incremental change through parliamentary politics sought by the now substantial socialist parties, and instead emphasised the idea that the direct action of the workers themselves would change society. Craft unions, representing narrow sectional interests, would be replaced by broad industrial unionism, uniting workers of all kinds. These revolutionary unions would act autonomously from state, creating organisational structures for a future, worker-controlled economic order. Syndicalism did not fade away with the coming of the Russian Revolution. To their dismay, the Soviet leadership found that many of the parties recruited into the Communist International were deeply affected by syndicalist ideas, which were incompatible with Leninist centralism. It was not until about 1923 that Moscow started to make substantial progress in "Bolshevizing" the new Communist parties and driving out of this syndicalist legacy.

The 1913 Dublin Lockout labour insurgency led by Jim Larkin's Irish Transport and General Workers Union (ITGWU) was an archetypal syndicalist movement. And the Irish Citizen Army, which was to become an important section of the Easter insurgents, was an organisation initiated by the ITGWU during that strike.[16] The radical labour activism of the Rand from 1913 to 1922 was also deeply marked by syndicalism. In the South African case, a number of the key leaders of 1922 were broadly syndicalist, while others were drawn from the syndicalist-influenced wing of the small and newly created Communist Party of South Africa (CPSA). And as we shall see, there were direct, if limited, flows of people and ideas between Rand and Irish syndicalism.

The third factor which links the two events was a transformation in the legitimacy of the nationalism of small and colonised nations. The pivotal significance of 1916 in Irish nationalist history is hardly open to dispute. The 1922 Revolt not only mobilised Afrikaner nationalism, but showed clear signs of spreading a nationalist identity to previously loyal British-origin South Africans. It is clear that globally, 1911–1923 was a climacteric for more extensive and militant national claims, and this was a tendency was which preceded, although it was much energised by, the 1917–1918 declarations of Woodrow Wilson and V.I. Lenin. As Eric Hobsbawm convincingly argued, in the mid-nineteenth century, and even later, by no means all national movements necessarily envisaged their own future state, often simply calling for autonomy within larger units. The late nineteenth century saw an intensification of national claims, the multiplication of nationalist group leaderships with separatist ambitions and the infusion of nationalism with pseudo-scientific language deriving from Social Darwinism.[17] But it took the long world war for the new hardcore nationalists to win over broader support. While Irish nationalism had a significantly longer history than its Afrikaner counterpart, the form that Irish nationalism took at the turn of the century and the newly emerged Afrikaner nationalist movement, despite their differences of scale, can be seen as having at least at "family resemblance".

By 1895, the effectively independent Boer Republic of the Transvaal found itself in possession of the world's most productive goldfields, running east and west of Johannesburg, along the Witwatersrand. At the end of that year, the Jameson Raid, an attempted putsch, aimed to bring the country under British rule, was engineered by the mine-owner Cecil John Rhodes. It was completely crushed by Paul Kruger's government. The Boers' defiance of the empire inspired the conspiratorial Irish Republican Brotherhood, and a number of its members surfaced in the Transvaal in the subsequent period, amongst them Arthur Griffith and John MacBride. Griffith unsuccessfully edited a small-town newspaper in Middleburg, before moving to Johannesburg. MacBride took a job in the surface works of a mine, where Griffith later joined him. MacBride also propagandised, rather successfully, in the cause of physical force nationalism amongst Johannesburg's thousand-strong Irish community, organising through a fraternal organisation, the Irish National Foresters.[18]

When war broke out between the Boer republics of Transvaal and the Orange Free State and the British Empire in September 1899, MacBride took the opportunity to form an Irish Brigade, a unit of only a few hundred men, to fight on the side of the Boers. Contrary to all expectations, within weeks of the outbreak of war, the ragged, rural Afrikaner armies inflicted a series of devastating defeats on the British. At Ladysmith and Colenso, the Irish Brigade was to fore of the battle. (The fact that they were vastly outnumbered by the Irish rankers of the British army facing them was seldom dwelt on by their supporters.) These developments were to have a dramatic effect in revivifying the national movement in Ireland itself. Griffith, now back at home, trumpeted the Boer cause in his *United Irishman* newspaper, and initiated a Transvaal Committee in solidarity with them, which evoked a massive response, manifested in sometimes violent demonstrations. Michael Davitt, Maud Gonne, John O'Leary, James Connolly and W.B. Yeats were all involved in the movement. Davitt travelled to the Transvaal and produced a book glorifying the Boer struggle. The historian Alice Stopford Green played a major role in propagandising for the Boer cause, and became a close friend of Smuts, during the war a dashing guerrilla commander. The campaign seeped into popular culture, with street gangs adopting the names of Boer generals. For the Irish nationalists, the image of a nation of humble farmers defeating the historic enemy in the field was irresistible. And so was the idea of the Brigade, which in the minds of many, as Maude Gonne said of her future husband John MacBride, had saved the honour of Ireland. This ferment provided the context for a quadrupling of the size of nationalist cultural and sporting organisations and the reunification of the divided Irish parliamentary party. It also gave Griffith, in 1900, the political momentum to launch the organisation that would become Sinn Fein.[19]

Of course, the Boer success of the opening weeks of the war could not last. The British brought more than 400,000 troops to the region and by mid-1900, the Boer Republics' towns had been taken, although the war dragged on in guerrilla form for another two years. The Irish Brigade dispersed, but left behind it a considerable legacy of nationalist enthusiasm, as well as a political admiration of the Boers which was to be a significant factor in Irish political culture into the 1930s. And it was a reference point for the insurrectionaries of Easter. The Irish Citizen Army went into battle wearing slouch hats modelled on the Boers' broad-brimmed headgear, and variously named "Cronjé hats" or "De Wet hats" after the celebrated Boer generals.

The Irish nationalists of 1899 were almost entirely oblivious to the racial subordination of African people which formed the political bedrock of the Boer polities. Moreover, Gonne and others bought into discourses of African savagery as part of their support for the Boers.[20] It is almost impossible to overstate the pervasiveness of racial ideology in the United Kingdom, the British dominions and North America at the turn of the century. The assumption that white people were equipped for self-government and others were not was widely accepted. As Bruce Nelson has shown, important Irish nationalist figures frequently articulated the political injustices of Ireland in terms of it being the only "white" country not to have self-government.[21]

There was a complex relationship between the Irish Brigade, working class radicalism and the subsequent development of revolutionary syndicalism. First of all, the Irish Brigade came largely from a transnational radical Irish working-class milieu. Irish Brigade veteran and Easter Rising participant Commandant Thomas Byrne, who himself worked on the Rand mines, told of recruiting men for the Brigade from the among the miners, and after the fighting ended, going with a group of "fifty or sixty" Brigade veterans to the United States, where, according to him, most went to work on Western mines.[22] In the mining centre of Butte, Montana, where a strong local Irish enclave was extremely supportive of the Boers, no less than 19 veterans of the Irish Brigade found work after leaving southern Africa.[23] Butte was stronghold of labour militancy, which in the next two decades saw a series of spectacular strikes and syndicalist agitation.

There is also a skein of individual biographical intersections between the worlds of the Irish Transvaal, the syndicalist insurgencies of Johannesburg and Dublin and the Easter Rebellion. Political actors across the world were connected with, and politically legible to, actors elsewhere. The book that captured the moment of syndicalism in the then 'British' Isles, was Robert Tressell's *The Ragged Trousered Philanthropist*. A brilliant novel of socialist propaganda, the book achieved instant fame with the left in the English-speaking world when it was published in early 1914, at the height of the syndicalist wave. "Tressell" was the pseudonym of Robert Noonan, a

Dublin-born painter and decorator, who was Secretary of the Johannesburg Trades Council in the late 1890s. Noonan was present at the discussions which led to the formation of the Brigade, although he left the Transvaal at the outbreak of war and did not actually participate in the fighting.[24] A close associate of Noonan's in Johannesburg, a Scottish trade unionist (and secret agent for the Boers) by the name of James Thompson Bain, did fight in the ranks of the Irish Brigade. Narrowly escaping execution for treason, Bain was imprisoned on Ceylon, before returning to the Transvaal.[25] Back on the Rand, Bain became a dominant figure amongst the local syndicalist activists, and the key leader of general strikes in 1913 and 1914 and of a workers' occupation of Johannesburg municipality in 1919. The Irish syndicalist Tom Glynn established a branch of the Industrial Workers of the World (IWW) in Johannesburg and led a major tramway strike, before moving to Australia, where he became an important labour and anti-war militant. Bain collaborated with a small Johannesburg group led by John Campbell, who had been a member of the Socialist Labour Party in Glasgow, founded by syndicalist and 1916 martyr James Connolly. The most important syndicalist mouthpiece in the region was the newspaper, *The Voice of Labour*, edited by Mary Fitzgerald and her partner, the Scot, Archie Crawford.[26] Fitzgerald was the daughter of an Irish nationalist family from County Wexford, who had been radicalised into labour politics while working in the office of the Transvaal Miner's Association. Her militant role in disputes won her the sobriquet of "Pickhandle Mary".[27]

Bain, Fitzgerald and Crawford all played leading roles in the dramatic general strike of white workers on the Rand in early July 1913. Fitzgerald was widely believed to have instigated the burning of down of the offices of the local pro-mine-owner newspaper and the main railway station. Following a night of shooting between police and strikers, there was a confrontation between protestors and the Royal Dragoons, who had been mobilised to restore order. The British troops opened fire killing twenty people. Under massive political pressure because of the shootings, the government of Prime Minister Louis Botha and his right-hand man Jan Smuts backed down and forced the employers to concede the strikers demands.[28]

Just as the situation in Johannesburg calmed the dramatic Dublin Lockout dispute broke out in late August, catapulting Jim Larkin and James Connolly to international prominence as syndicalist leaders. They were certainly aware of what had just happened in South Africa. Connolly referred in one of his articles written during the strike to the "Johannesburg massacres".[29] A particular connection between the Lockout and the Rand syndicalists was provided by the remarkable figure of Dora Montefiore. Montefiore, a wealthy English widow, had become a prominent women's suffragist in England. During a sojourn in Australia she had come under the influence of a syndicalist group, and had also met Archie Crawford, then on a world tour, who persuaded her to visit South Africa. She gave a number of well-received speeches to the Rand leftists during 1912. Returning to the United Kingdom, she came up with the idea of supporting the Dublin strikers through billeting their children on sympathisers in England. Unfortunately, this well-intended notion proved a gift to the anti-labour movement clergy, who alleged a plot to expose impressionable children to anti-Catholic ideas. Many nationalists, including Gonne, joined in, in vitriolic terms. Montefiore was charged with abduction, though the case was eventually dropped.[30]

In South Africa, in January of 1914, Smuts deliberately precipitated a second strike and then unleashed martial law. Hundreds of trade unionists were arrested, and nine, including Bain and Crawford, were deported. Botha and Smuts's repression attracted considerable international criticism. In London, Jim Larkin spoke alongside English labour radicals George Lansbury and Tom Mann in the numerous meetings which attacked the South African government, and Larkin considered going to South Africa as an advisor to the labour movement.[31] Eventually, the South African government was forced, by political contingencies at the start of the First World War, to allow the strike leaders to return.

In 1915, a small number of leading supporters of the trade-union supported South African Labour Party (SALP) broke away to form the International Socialist League (ISL) over the SALP's support for the war. The ISL was syndicalist in orientation.[32] They worked to revive the white labour movement in the face of strong support for the war, but they also began to support initiatives to create militant black unions. The ISL's membership comprised largely British artisans and leftist East European Jewish immigrants. In 1921, the League transformed itself into the CPSA, but for several years would retain syndicalist tendencies, until these were wrung out of it by the Communist International, commonly known as Comintern. The CPSA was split between two factions however. While both were formally committed to racial egalitarianism, one, led by S.P. Bunting, believed the party should concentrate on organising black workers. The other was led by W.H. Andrews, who had been a close ally of Bain in the earlier struggles, and believed that practical politics dictated that the party focus of leading the already strong white unions. Andrews was to become a central leader of the 1922 strike, and probably only survived it because Smuts imprisoned him before the main fighting took place.

Thus both 1916 and 1922 had roots in earlier syndicalist moments. But in both countries, there were long running tensions between this form of social radicalism and nationalism, which were to be important later on. The Johannesburg strikes of 1913 and 1914, and the later workers' occupation of Johannesburg municipality led by Bain in 1919, all encountered the hostility of Afrikaner nationalist politicians toward anti-capitalist politics. In a similar way, the 1913 Dublin Lockout was a crucial moment in the pre-history of 1916.[33] But Arthur Griffith specifically understood the socially radical element of the labour movement of that time as syndicalist, and condemned it, presaging future strains between 'pure' nationalists and leftists over the objectives of Ireland's revolt.[34]

The outstanding scholar of the 1922 Revolt, Jeremy Krikler, has trenchantly made the point that although historians have given enormous attention to the militarization of politics on the European and international right as a consequence of the First World War, they have been much less willing to acknowledge that the left was almost equally affected by the pervasive culture of militarism. Krikler provides a detailed analysis of how the specific forms of organisation, military culture and combat knowledge were transferred by veterans to the Rand Commandos.[35] This at least prompts the question of whether the effect of global war in giving a militaristic tinge to progressive nationalisms, including that of Ireland, may not also repay further investigation.

Within the syndicalist strikes of 1913–1914, in both South Africa and Ireland there was a clear turn to the militarisation of labour activism. In the Dublin Lockout, there was the formation of the Irish Citizen Army. On the Rand, there was highly structured organisations of pickets, and a coordinated attempt to seize the New Kleinfontein Mine, which was the initial centre of dispute. South African strikers showed a willingness to take up the gun. They raided firearms shops, and exchanged fire with the security forces. During the Johannesburg upheavals, a prominent militant, George Mason, proposed that they organise themselves in groups of "six men and a corporal". In a speech in January 1914, Bain went one better than Mason, asking "Why not 10,000 men and a Commandant?", while threatening that the renewed general strike would bring down the government.[36] These statements were very closely echoed by Connolly's words at the time of the formation of the ICA:

> Listen to me, I am going to talk sedition. The next time we are out for a march, I want them to come with their corporals, sergeants and people to form fours. Why should we not drill and train our men as they are doing in Ulster?[37]

The ICA's formation in 1913 reflects the prestige of the military mode within syndicalism. This was manifested in the entrusting of its training to the anarchist-inclined but ideologically incoherent Captain Jack White, formerly a British Army Boer War hero and son of the General Commanding at the Siege of Ladysmith.[38]

In 1914, the South Africa's entry into the war unleashed an armed Afrikaner nationalist rebellion.[39] This upheaval was an important event in itself but it was also significant for what would happen in 1922. The revolt was engineered by a group of disaffected senior officers of the Defence Force, who were already, before the war, in touch with the German garrison in the colony of South West Africa. They gained support amongst impoverished farmers, tenants and labourers of the rural northwest. The

Boers mobilised in the traditional form of commandos. Prime Minister Botha and Minister of Defence Smuts mobilised their troops and the Rebellion was quickly crushed with relatively limited loss of life. One reason why Smuts and Botha were reasonably successful in stabilising the post-rebellion situation is that, more astutely than the British government in Ireland, they gave a clear and consistent message that they would not impose conscription on a reluctant population. The dominant parliamentary wing of Afrikaner nationalists under Hertzog sat on the fence and did not support the rising. But unlike their Irish parliamentary nationalist counterparts, the Hertzogites paid no price for turning their back on the insurrectionaries. This was a reflection both of Hertzog's political skills and the absence at that point of a set of more radical nationalist intellectuals able to challenge him.[40]

The year 1914 bequeathed to 1922 the idea of the Commando as a way of challenging the state. On the mines, it came together with the very advanced military skills of British and South African miners who had served in the war. The significant casualties the miners inflicted on the security forces spoke to the effectiveness of the fusion between these different groups. The level of militarisation in the 1922 Rand Strike was extraordinarily high. There were only about 20,000 strikers on the Rand, but the police estimated that 10,000–15,000 men participated in the Commandos. It is also significant that military drilling played a big part in the parades and demonstrations of the strikers before fighting broke out.[41] Though the Commando was a long-established tradition, it had a highly informal culture, and drill and saluting had never played a part in it. The fact that large numbers of Afrikaner strikers participated in such conventional military procedures suggests a cultural shift in the context of global war.[42] So does the fact that Afrikaners were willing to accept British Army veterans as trainers.

The years 1916 and 1922 then were contemporaneous in that they both emerged in a context which civilianised forms of protest seemed grotesquely inadequate – especially to the old soldiers within their ranks. In a world organised for war on an unprecedented scale, the taking up of the gun became the common sense of politics.

Although Irish nationalism was far older than Afrikaner nationalism and involved a far bigger population, the forms they took in the late nineteenth and early twentieth century closely converged. The themes of their ideologists bore a close resemblance, with the historic crimes of the British Empire and the notion of sturdy farming communities as the essence of the nation as central concerns. In both contexts, the rural world was celebrated and the degenerative effects of city life deplored. In both cases, intellectuals "discovered" the folk community through their research and cultural productions, and language movements played a crucial organisational role. As in the Ireland, the turn of the century saw a strengthening nationalism in the upper social strata, with Afrikaner notables, who, especially in the

Cape, had previously been quite Anglophile, undertaking a political and cultural re-fashioning in the mould of a new nationalism. Both nationalisms initiated modernist style social movements of youth and women, with great vigour and success.[43] In both cases the language of nation became imbricated with that of race.[44]

1916 in Dublin was a broadly-based nationalist, largely middle-class led, rising with a subordinate radical working class element in the form of the ICA. 1922 on the Rand was a labour rising led by British working class syndicalist radicals, in alliance with recently proletarianised Boer workers who identified strongly with the Afrikaner nationalist cause. Yet both events ultimately brought middle-class versions of nationalism to power. These long-term trajectories reflect a major feature of the world that emerged between 1911 and 1923. The war destabilised the existing political and social order, unleashing a vast range of oppositional political movements across the world. Such movements often manifested a militarization of politics, and sometimes took an insurrectionary form. But these movements were met by counter-revolutionary violence from the old order and the violence of competing political factions. Almost universally, except in the Soviet Union, by 1923 this contest resulted in the triumph of nationalism over the hopes of radical egalitarians. Not syndicalists or Leninists, but nationalists came out on top in the global conflict of 1911–1923.

There are striking similarities between Dublin 1916 and the Rand 1922 in the combination of a politics of nationalism in uneasy alliance with syndicalism. It was clear that many Afrikaner strikers hoped that the upheaval would take forward the republican cause. What was a more striking and unexpected feature of the events of 1922 was that British-origin workers, who had previously showed no sympathy for Afrikaner nationalism, began to discuss the possibility of moving in a republican direction. A key role in this was played by the Australian-born R.B. Waterston, a Labour politician, and one of the 1914 deportees. About a month after the 1922 strike began, in early February, a mass meeting of strikers gathered in Johannesburg Town Hall. Waterston proposed a resolution that it was time to call a halt to the "domination" of the country "financiers". It therefore called on a meeting of Labour Party and Afrikaner Nationalist Party MPs which was scheduled to meet in Pretoria the next day, "to proclaim a South African Republic and immediately to form a provisional Government for this Country".[45] The resolution received the overwhelming support of the meeting. Yet on the morrow it became clear that the strikers were far more radical than the leaders to whom they were appealing. The MPs would not touch the idea, and even Tielman Roos, the Afrikaner nationalist MP generally regarded as most radical on the question of the republic, backed away, scared by the strikers' anti-capitalist framing of the question.[46] The mainstream leaders of Afrikaner nationalism, like their Irish counterparts, proved averse to tampering with the fundamental forms of property ownership.

In both the Irish and South African cases, the legacy of intra-societal violence meant that there could be no easy consensus about national identity. As a consequence of his repression of the 1922 rising Smuts's leadership was destabilised. The South African Labour Party, which was supported by British working-class immigrants had backed the war effort. White working-class opinion was alienated through Smuts' blatant partisanship toward the mine owners, his extreme use of force, and the dispensing of hundreds of prison terms and eighteen death sentences to strikers (although unlike the British authorities in Dublin, Smuts reprieved all but four of the Death Row cases). In the 1924 election the SALP embraced an alliance with Hertzog's Nationalists, driven into their arms by the event of the strike period. Hertzog proved considerably more adept than Irish constitutionalist leaders, succeeding again, as in 1914, in harnessing the power of an insurrectionary movement in which he had not participated. The nationalist-labour alliance won, forming a "Pact" government, but Labour was very much the junior partner.

It has been claimed by Stephen Garton that nationalism was the ideological cement that unified the white-ruled dominions of Canada, Australia, New Zealand and South Africa after World War I.[47] According to Garton, this then differentiates the dominions from Ireland and India. But this political typology does not work, for precisely the reason that South Africa's experience of insurrection by white workers in 1913–1914, Afrikaner nationalists in 1914–1915, and both in 1922, created a far more profound set of fractures than in the other Dominions, making it extremely hard to reconcile Afrikaner and British factions in southern Africa. In this sense, the South African trajectory was much more like Ireland's. These countries politics were exponentially more violent than that of Canada and Australasia, and the divisions consequently far harder to heal. *Contra* Garton, white South Africans proved resistant to unification around a single nationalist vision of the kind Jan Smuts tried to create, just as in Ireland, Unionists and Republicans and, later, pro- and anti-Treaty nationalists could not find common ground.

In Ireland, there has been at least a debate about whether there was an Irish revolution, although the historical consensus seems to be that there was not.[48] Nobody today in South Africa would speak of the revolutionary nature of 1922, for it appears from the vantage of the present merely as a factional squabble within the dominant white minority.

Yet both 1916 and 1922 were revolutionary situations, both products of world war, both inflected with syndicalism, and both shaped by hypernationalism. This common conjuncture gave the two events a contemporaneity which enabled the Irish Commando of Fordsburg to look to Ireland's insurrectionaries for inspiration. Behind the adoption of their green flag lay more than two decades of transnational interaction in which political imaginations and actual biographical intersections had stretched across worlds of labour and national identity.

Notes

1 This chapter is heavily indebted to the brilliant Jeremy Krikler, *The Rand Revolt: The 1922 Insurrection and Racial Killing in South Africa* (Johannesburg, 2005). See also Norman Herd, *1922: Revolt on the Rand* (Johannesburg, 1966) and Ivan Walker and Ben Weinbren, *2000 Casualties: A History of the Trade Unions and the Labour Movement In the Union of South Africa* (Johannesburg, 1961), 91–167.

2 Donal P. McCracken, "Irish Identity in Twentieth Century South Africa," in D. P. McCracken, ed., *Ireland and South Africa in Modern Times* (Durban, 1996), 11.

3 Krikler, *Rand Revolt*, 58.

4 Ibid., 106.

5 Ibid., 58.

6 D. P. McCracken, "The Irish Republican Association of South Africa," in McCracken, ed., *Ireland and South Africa*, 46–66.

7 An attempt to compare the racial violence in South Africa in 1922 to sectarian violence in early twentieth century Belfast is however made in Niall Ó Murchú, "Split Labour Markets and Ethnic Violence after World War I: A Comparison of Belfast, Chicago and Johannesburg," *Comparative Politics* 39.4 (2007), 379–400.

8 McCracken, "Irish Republican Association," 56.

9 Daniel Francis, "1919: The Winnipeg General Strike," *History Today* 34.4 (1984), 4–8.

10 Donal P. McCracken, *MacBride's Brigade: Irish Commandos in the Anglo-Boer War* (Dublin, 1999).

11 P. A. McCracken, "Arthur Griffith's South African Sabbatical," in McCracken, ed., *Ireland and South Africa*, 227–62.

12 Donal Lowry, "Irish-South African Relations and the British Commonwealth, c. 1902–1961," in McCracken, *Ireland and South Africa*, 89–135.

13 I am indebted here to Sebastian Conrad's argument that we need a 'third' notion beyond comparison and connection, though the term 'contemporaneity' is my own suggestion: see Sebastian Conrad, *What is Global History?* (Princeton, NJ, 2016).

14 Robert Gerwarth and Erez Manela, "The Great War as a Global War: Imperial Conflict and the Refiguration of World Order, 1911–1923," *Diplomatic History* 38.4 (2014), 786–800.

15 Yann Beliard, "Revisiting the Great Labour Unrest, 1911–1914," *Labour History Review* 79.1 (2014), 1–17.

16 Richard English, "Socialist Intellectuals and the Irish Revolution," in Joost Augusteijn, ed., *The Irish Revolution* (London, 2002) 203–23; John Newsinger, "'In the Hunger-Cry of the Nation's Poor Heard the Voice of Ireland': Sean O'Casey and Politics 1908–1916," *Journal of Contemporary History* 20.2 (1985), 221–40.

17 E. J. Hobsbawm, *Nations and Nationalism since 1780: Programme, Myth, Reality* (Cambridge, 2012).

18 As well as McCracken, *MacBride's Brigade*, see Padraic Colum, *Arthur Griffith* (Dublin, 1959), 33–56; Douglas Blackburn and W. Waithman Caddell, *Secret Service in South Africa* (London, 1911); and the coverage of MacBride's activities in the *Transvaal Sentinel*, especially 23 March 1898.

19 Arthur Davey, *The British Pro-Boers 1877–1902* (Cape Town, 1978), 130–44; Donal P. McCracken, *The Irish Pro-Boers 1877–1902* (Johannesburg, 1989); R. F. Foster, *W.B. Yeats: A Life: Volume 1: The Apprentice Mage 1865–1914* (Oxford, 1997); Robert Kee, *The Green Flag: A History of Irish Nationalism* (London, 2000), 441–46.

20 Bruce Nelson, *Irish Nationalists and the Making of the Irish Race* (Princeton, NJ, 2012).

21 Nelson, *Irish Nationalists*.

22 Bureau of Military History, Deposition of Commandant Thomas Byrne, www.bureauofmilitaryhistory.ie/reels/bmh/BMH.WS0564.pdf#page=2 downloaded 8 June 2016.

23 David Emmons, *The Butte Irish: Class and Ethnicity in an American Mining Town 1875–1925* (Urbana, IL, 1990), 329–30.

24 Jonathan Hyslop, "A Ragged Trousered Philanthropist and the Empire: Robert Tressell in South Africa," *History Workshop Journal* 51 (2001), 64–86.

25 Jonathan Hyslop, "A Scottish Socialist Reads Carlyle in Johannesburg Prison, June 1900: Reflections on the Literary Culture of the Imperial Working Class," *Journal of Southern African Studies* 29.3 (2003), 639–55.

26 Jonathan Hyslop, "The British and Australian Leaders of the South African Labour Movement, 1902–1914," in P. Grimshaw, K. Darian-Smith, and S. MacIntyre, eds., *Britishness Abroad* (Melbourne, 2007), 90–108.

27 Louise Haysom, "Pickhandle Mary: Gender Battles and Public Protest on the Witwatersrand 1903–1916," MA thesis, University of Kwazulu-Natal, Durban (2009), and Lucien van der Walt and Wessel Visser, "Circumnavigator of the Industrial World': Archie Crawford, South African Labour, and Travels in the Global Public Sphere," unpublished paper given at "Political Travel in the British Empire 1850–1950: A History Workshop Colloquium," University of the Witwatersrand, Johannesburg, 2010.

28 Elaine N. Katz, *A Trade Union Aristocracy: A History of White Workers in the Transvaal and the General Strike of 1913* (Johannesburg, 1976).

29 James Connolly, "Glorious Dublin," *Forward*, 4 October 1913.

30 Pádraig Yeats, *Lockout: Dublin 1913* (Dublin, 2001), 245–79.

31 *The Advertiser*, 3 March 1914; Emmet O'Connor, *Big Jim Larkin: Hero or Wrecker* (Dublin, 2015), 157–59.

32 Lucien van der Walt, "'The Industrial Union is the Embryo of the Socialist Commonwealth': The International Socialist League and Revolutionary Syndicalism in South Africa, 1915–1919," *Comparative Studies of South Asia, Africa and the Middle East* 29.1 (1999), 5–28.

33 Lauren Arrington, "Socialist Republican Discourse and the 1916 Easter Rising: The Occupation of Jacob's Biscuit Factory and the South Dublin Union Explained," *Journal of British Studies* 53 (2014), 992–1010.

34 Diarmaid Ferriter, *A Nation and Not a Rabble* (London, 2015), 142.

35 Jeremy Krikler, "The Commandos: The Army of White Labour in South Africa," *Past and Present* 113.1 (1999), 202–44.

36 J. C. Smuts, *The Syndicalist Conspiracy in South Africa* (Cape Town, 1914), 22; *The Worker*, 15 January 1914.

37 Ferriter, *A Nation*, 141.

38 Leo Keohane, *Captain Jack White: Imperialism, Anarchism and the Irish Citizen Army* (Kildare, 2014).

39 Albert Grundlingh and Sandra Swart, *Radelose Rebellie?: Dinamika van die 1914–1915 Afrikanerrebellie* (Pretoria, 2009).

40 C. M. van den Heever, *General J.B.M. Hertzog* (Johannesburg, 1946).

41 Krikler, "Commandos," 213–14.

42 Ibid., 219–20.

43 Compare Joost Augusteijn, "Motivation: Why Did They Fight for Ireland: The Motivation of the Volunteers in the Revolution," in Augusteijn, ed., *Revolution*, 103–20, with T. Dunbar Moodie, *The Rise of Afrikanerdom: Power, Apartheid and the Afrikaner Civil Religion* (Berkeley, CA, 1975); Dan O'Meara, *Volkskapitalisme: Class, Capital and Ideology in the Development of Afrikaner*

Nationalism, 1934–1948 (Johannesburg, 1983); Herman Giliomee, *The Afrikaners: Biography of a People* (Charlottesville, VA, 2003).
44 Nelson, *Irish Nationalists.*
45 Krikler, *Rand Revolt*, 108.
46 Ibid.
47 Stephen Garton, "The Dominions, Ireland and India," in Robert Gerwarth and Erez Manela, eds., *Empires at War* (Cambridge, 2014), 172–73.
48 Augusteijn, ed., *Irish Revolution.*

Section III

North Africa, Asia and the Pacific

7 1916 in the Middle East and the Global War for Empire

Michael Provence

The year 1916 was the nadir in Britain's war for the Middle East. Desperation triggered by military disasters in France, Gallipoli and Iraq brought a range of initiatives with results that continue to affect the Middle East. This chapter is an overview of the war events up to and including 1916 in the Middle East and argues the crisis facing Britain's Empire was far more serious than commonly remembered. The reverberations of the Middle Eastern disasters of 1916 reached Ireland and around the world – making the Great War truly and catastrophically a World War.

In January 1916, the British army withdrew from the Gallipoli peninsula, bringing to a close a campaign to march on the Ottoman capital some 150 km away. British troops had advanced a few kilometres over the course of a year and suffered 200,000 casualties. Four months later, and five days after the Easter Rising in April, a British colonial army of 13,000 officers and men surrendered at Kut south of Baghdad after suffering about 30,000 dead and wounded. The next month, May 1916, British and French diplomats, Mark Sykes and Francois George-Picot, signed the Asia-Minor or Sykes-Picot Agreement, secretly negotiating the hoped-for, post-war partitioning of the Eastern Ottoman lands, and promising France colonial compensation for its war sacrifices. Middle East borders still resemble the agreement's lines. Nearly every conflict in the Middle East over the past century can be traced in some way to the decisions made between 1916 and 1920, and the attempts by British and French statesmen to wrest some redeeming prize from the waste of the war.

The war in the East in 1914, and the 1912–1913 Balkan Crisis from which it sprang, had roots in the Eastern Question of the nineteenth century. The Great Powers of Britain, France, and Russia engaged a century-long, mostly "cold war" conflict over their mutual, and mutually incompatible, goal to destroy the Ottoman Empire and dominate its lands ringing the Eastern Mediterranean and the Straits to the Black Sea. Like the Cold War of the twentieth century, the conflict was mostly fought by proxies, defined not by political ideologies of Marxism or Capitalism, but by religious identity. The Great Powers serially mobilised Ottoman Christians as clients and "national people in formation", starting with the

Greek Revolt of 1820, and including a shifting constellation of claims and interests including the Crimean War of the 1850s, the Turko-Russian War of 1877–1878, and the British invasion of Egypt in 1882, ostensibly to protect Eastern Christians claimed to be menaced by their Muslim overlords. Thus, the Great Powers expanded into the region accompanied by an array of racial, religious and civilisational oppositions that inevitably claimed to advance a well-armed Christian and European cultural supremacy that was, they claimed, locked in mortal combat with Islamic barbarism.[1]

The final Ottoman crisis of 1911 and the Italian invasion of Ottoman Tripoli, or today's Libya, fit exactly into the schema and inaugurated the ultimate scramble for Ottoman territory that brought the Balkan War the following year, and the Great War three years later. When, in 1911, the leaders of the independent Balkan League states of Bulgaria, Greece, Serbia and Montenegro witnessed the Italian invasion and annexation of Libya, they resolved, with tacit encouragement from the Great Powers, to invade the remaining Ottoman territory in the Balkans. Serbia was a Russian client and Greece a British client during this Balkan War of 1912 and each Great Power encouraged their proxy. The Balkan League defeated the Ottoman Army and forced an evacuation to the outskirts of Istanbul. There was also a major humanitarian crisis as Greek- and Slavic-speaking and Slavic speaking Muslims were made refugees and pursued both by their former neighbours and the devastating spectre of cholera and famine, foreshadowing the crop failure, famine and influenza pandemic that accompanied the Great War five years later. The Balkan League quickly split over

Figure 1 Italian postcard commemorating the invasion of 1911, reading "Dawn of Civilisation." Source: By kind permission of Dr. Wolf-Dieter Lemke.

FOUR des
BALKANS

TURQUIE

LES ALLIÉS :
On va donc partager le Croissant

Figure 2 French postcard from the period 1912–1913. Balkan War, reading 'The Balkan Oven, The Allies: So we are going to share the croissant (a metaphor for the Muslim crescent, identified here as Turkey)'. Source: By kind permission of Dr. Wolf-Dieter Lemke.

the territorial spoils, again encouraged by its Great Power patrons, and the Ottoman army counterattacked in 1913 and expelled Balkan League armies from the region around one-time Ottoman capital of Adrianople, or Edirne.[2]

In the eleven-month interval between the Balkan ceasefire and the assassination of Archduke Franz Ferdinand, the Great Powers prepared for confrontation. British Lord of the Admiralty Winston Churchill had become convinced the future of British naval supremacy depended on oil rather than on coal. Fuel oil meant faster ships and greater world-spanning range. England, Scotland and Wales lay atop vast coal beds, but there was no oil. In June 1914, he convinced Parliament to purchase a controlling 51 per cent share of the Anglo-Persian Oil Company, which owned the Persian oil concession, and the new oil refinery at Abadan at the head of the Persian Gulf, which was directly across the river from Ottoman territory and a few miles from the Ottoman provincial capital at Basra.[3]

Churchill delivered his parliamentary speech on 17 June 1914, eleven days before the fateful assassination at Sarajevo, another former Ottoman provincial capital. As the Great Powers marched to war in summer 1914, the Ottoman Empire stood back. Ottoman statesmen like their foreign counterparts, however, argued the looming war could offer an opportunity to right wrongs and regain lost territory. Churchill inadvertently helped the Ottoman war party to make the case for war in July. The Admiralty ordered the seizure of two completed and paid-for battle cruisers, built, and ready to enter service, at the Vickers shipyards at Barrow-in-Furnace.[4] The ships had been ordered and funded by popular subscription among Ottoman subjects. For Ottomans, the ships represented a patriotic expression of the modernity and power of the state and its place among the powers of Europe.

The German General Staff attempted to capitalise on the insult Churchill's seizure represented. The Ottoman-German military alliance had been in force since the 1880s, and successive generations of Ottoman military officers had received advanced training in Germany. The Ottoman State was not, however, part of the Central Powers' alliance, and the population, having experienced war since 1911, widely favoured neutrality. Militaristic Ottoman and German politicians colluded to bring the war to the Ottoman capital of Istanbul, but during the summer of 1914 German generals were more committed to hostilities than their Ottoman counterparts.

Early in August the Royal Navy, not yet at war with Germany, shadowed two German battle cruisers across the Mediterranean. On 4 August when hostilities commenced, Churchill ordered that the two German ships be intercepted, but the German command had ordered the ships to flee for Istanbul. The ships entered the Dardanelles Straits within view of British pursuers, which broke off, rather than engage Ottoman coastal defences. Upon entering the harbour at Istanbul, German officials presented the two ships to the Ottoman state in an official ceremony during which they were re-christened the *Yavuz Sultan Selim* and *Midilli*; their German flags were lowered and Ottoman flags raised.

The propaganda value of the contrast between German friendship and British insult was incalculable and there were rapturous public celebrations in Istanbul.[5] The ships stayed in Istanbul and the Ottoman High Command negotiated possible alliances with both Germany and Russia. Leading Ottoman statesmen, especially War Minister Enver and Naval Minister Cemal, tried to secure German support for the Ottoman position without entering the war as long as possible. Finally, at the end of October, German-crewed naval ships flying the Ottoman flag steamed into the Black

Sea and attacked and sank two Russian warships and also shelled the port of Sevastopol.[6] Russian recalled its ambassador. British, French and Russian forces attacked Ottoman positions and ships, and on 10 November the Ottoman State declared war against Russia, Britain and France. Britain had declared war five days before.

A British Indian Army Division had already anchored at the head of the Persian Gulf on 29 October to await orders to enter Ottoman territory and secure the Anglo-Persian Refinery at Abadan. On the morning of 6 November, British naval artillery bombarded and landed soldiers at the Ottoman fort at the mouth of the Shatt al-Arab. The British forces dug in at Abadan and waited for reinforcements before moving on to Basra only seven or eight miles up the river. The province of Basra and its port and oil resources were critically important to British war aims, but the region was remote and unimportant to the Ottoman State. By the time the British co-lonial troops had marched to Basra, its Ottoman garrison had withdrawn and taken position further up the river. Basra and the towns along the river were lightly garrisoned and defended, making the British advance decep-tively easy.[7]

As the war in the west became a bloody stalemate by September 1914, British war policy pivoted to keep the Russian Empire in the war. A naval attack on the Ottoman straits at the Dardanelles could help relieve Russia and seemed logical. Churchill was more ambitious and less worried than some among the Cabinet and General Staff about Ottoman defences; he dreamed of attacking the straits, and shelling and occupying the Ottoman capital from the sea. The Russian command was enthusiastic but sought to extract a promise from Britain and France "for the richest prize of the en-tire war". British and French statesmen secretly conceded Russian demands for the European side of Constantinople and all the remaining Ottoman territory west of the Bosphorus.[8] The resulting Constantinople Agreement of March 1915 was the first of several secret agreements between the En-tente Powers over their post-war claims on Ottoman territory. In overturn-ing a century of British and French efforts to keep Russia away from the Mediterranean, the agreement was emblematic of wartime desperation and short-sightedness.

The assault on the Dardanelles elicits general opprobrium even in a war that was full of waste and human stupidity. The campaign, originally en-visioned as a modest show of force to awe the Ottomans and perhaps provoke a capitulation, grew, until it comprised a massive naval assault on the Straits beginning in February 1915. British and French naval shelling destroyed the outer Ottoman forts and fixed guns, but when the flotilla advanced, Allied commanders discovered they could not sweep the thor-oughly mined waterway without encountering well-hidden and mobile shore artillery. The Allies spent a month attempting to clear mines from areas where none were to be found, yet when they finally steamed east, concentrated and newly laid Ottoman mines and the remaining shore batteries brought one of the most serious naval defeats of the war to the British and French forces. In the course of a few hours, the Ottoman defenders sank three major battleships, and disabled three others. Ottoman defenders suffered few losses, but more than 1,000 Allied sailors went down with their ships.[9]

The naval defeat decided the ensuing course. Retreat from the straits was unthinkable, but so too was the potential loss of additional valuable ships. In order to secure the straits, 75,000 ground troops would land on the peninsula. The landings, like the naval assault that preceded it, were rushed and began a month later, by which time the Ottoman and German command had carefully prepared with concealed fortifications, trench works, and gun emplacements on the high ground of the peninsula. The landings began badly as Ottoman positions commanded the beaches and destroyed boats and men before they could come ashore. The peninsula's geography massively favoured the defenders and British planners could only have stumbled into the campaign by a persistent inability to take Ottoman forces seriously. They paid for their miscalculation and hubris with hundreds of thousands of dead and wounded soldiers. The invaders finally evacuated during December and January 1915 and 1916. The defeat damaged Winston Churchill's reputation and contributed to the slow-motion collapse of the government of Prime Minister Herbert Asquith. Historian Eugene Rogan pointed out that rather than shortening the war, Gallipoli lengthened it and cemented the German-Ottoman alliance and determination to fight on.

The desperate war situation steadily worsened with the approach of 1916. After the landing at the head of the Persian Gulf in November 1914, British Indian Army General John Nixon ordered General Charles Townsend's 6th Poona Division to advance north along the Shatt al-Arab and Euphrates rivers. In July 1915 Townsend's forces besieged Nasiriyya, an important Ottoman town on the Euphrates in the central quarter of the Basra province. The British advance under the difficult conditions of heat and lack of healthy food and water was characterised by official neglect of the Indian soldiers making up the force, and pervasive faulty intelligence and disregard for the capabilities and quality of the Ottoman defenders. At Nasiriyya the British seemed lucky and Ottoman forces withdrew under cover of darkness to regroup in positions further north.[10]

Nixon wanted fervently to press his advantage and prove his superiority over the Ottoman forces, but London and Delhi were unable to provide reinforcements or meaningful resupply. Nixon convinced the command at Delhi that he could press on without reinforcements. Townsend, in the field, was more cautious, but proceeded to advance upon the town of Kut on the Tigris, up the al-Gharraf canal, or Shatt al-Hay, linking Nasiriyya and the Euphrates at Kut, and midway between Baghdad and Nasiriyya. Kut lay in a hook of the Euphrates and at the confluence of the canal and river. Townsend's division of 11,000 men moved into position south of the city in late September 1915.

British attackers found themselves pinned down and intensively fired upon by well-fortified Ottoman defenders, but after a difficult night and day, the exhausted British forces found the Ottomans had abandoned their positions and disappeared. The entire force had silently retreated and regrouped under cover of darkness to the northern outskirts of Kut. Townsend considered it a victory, but was evidently troubled with a slight sense of foreboding, and waited to continue his fateful pursuit, being drawn ever deeper into Ottoman territory, up the river, and away from supply lines. The decisive battle took place toward the end of November 1915 when the British forces reached entrenched and newly reinforced Ottoman forces south of Baghdad. Casualties were heavy and while Ottoman wounded were readily transported to hospital in Baghdad, wounded British Indian soldiers suffered in agony in their trenches. The British offensive lasted three days by which time General Townsend realised his impossible situation and ordered a retreat south back to Kut under fire.

Kut occupied a u-shaped bulge in the river, and was thus surrounded by water on three sides. Townsend knew his 15,000-man division and the town's civilian inhabitants faced a siege, but believed his two months of provisions would suffice. He expected reinforcement to arrive from the south and relieve his forces. He was wrong on both counts. The siege was terrible for soldiers and civilians alike. Ottoman forces shelled and fired on the town relentlessly. Food and clean water became scarce. Townspeople saw their food seized, their homes despoiled and ruined, and their possessions taken by force. Ottoman forces destroyed relief columns south of the town, and provoked ever more desperate measures on the part of the British command.

Captain T.E. Lawrence (of Arabia), meanwhile, was detailed to attempt to either raise a revolt in Iraq or pay a huge cash ransom to end the siege at Kut during April 1916. Both efforts failed and the entire force of 13,309 starving officers and men at Kut surrendered to Ottoman General Halil Pasha.[11] Halil Pasha had asked the British command to loan ships to transport the prisoners to Baghdad so that the starving army would not be forced to march. The British command could not make accommodations for its captured soldiers, and the captors were disinclined to treat them better, so they marched at gunpoint through the desert to captivity. Officers were treated well, but thousands of the common soldiers died on their march to prison camps in Anatolia. During the months that the Siege of Kut dragged on, Entente diplomats dealt with an increasingly dire situation.

Hundreds of thousands of French and German soldiers died on the Western Front in 1915. British soldiers perished too, but in smaller numbers. As the disaster at Gallipoli concluded and the disaster at Kut began to unfold, British and French diplomats worked to gain advantage while holding their unsteady alliance together. The British government had already, along with

France, promised Constantinople to Russia to help keep Russia in the alliance. Without consulting its Allies, the British government had promised Hussein bin Ali, Sharif of Mecca, an independent Arab kingdom in return for a revolt against the Ottomans. For British policymakers, Sharif Hussein of Mecca had the potential to dull the Ottoman Sultan's call to the world's Muslims to defend the last Muslim Empire. British planners feared a worldwide revolt of Muslims, and hatched a fantastical plan for a Muslim leader counterweight to the Ottoman Sultan/Caliph as leader of the Islamic world. The correspondence and promises between High Commissioner for Egypt Henry MacMahon and Hussein resulted in the famous, but strategically unimportant, Arab Revolt, and the fitful sponsorship by the Entente of the Hashimite family, which still rules Jordan, and once ruled Iraq, and also, briefly, Damascus.

In summer 1915 French diplomat François Georges-Picot travelled to London to negotiate French claims on the Ottoman realms. Georges-Picot was a hard-headed lawyer and diplomat who had been the pre-war French consul in the booming Ottoman port city of Beirut. And it was his carelessly hidden files that led the former Ottoman Naval Minister, and then military governor of Syria, Cemal Pasha, to accuse various Beirut and Damascus political figures of treason and hang them. Georges-Picot was thus well-versed in British-French rivalry in the Middle East and knew the Ottoman enemy. He knew also that an Entente victory was far from certain and he was armed with the knowledge that, even though Britain was more dominant in the Middle East, British goals were impossible without French sacrifices in Europe. At this moment, Britain needed France more than France needed Britain. He arrived in London aware a deal was afoot that could deny France its territorial claims in the Ottoman Arab lands. According to James Barr, Georges-Picot intimated French awareness that, at the same time as the staggering French losses on the Western front, Britain had made deals to allocate Ottoman territory behind the back of its ally. Georges-Picot's demands were more grandiose than what the French Government itself thought manageable, but Georges-Picot stuck to his position. British policy makers had put themselves in a difficult position since they could neither deny France nor acknowledge the extent of their pledges to Hussein. Georges-Picot perceived the corner into which his rivals had placed themselves and pressed his advantage. The discussion rapidly reached an impasse.[12]

While Georges-Picot made the rounds in London during summer 1915, Mark Sykes was in the midst of a six-month official tour and fact-finding mission of the Middle Eastern war theatre. Sykes was an aristocratic diplomat, army officer, adventurer, sometime writer, and Member of Parliament. When Sykes finally returned to London in December, by ship from Cairo, he had visited the Balkans, Dardanelles and the Hijaz. Sykes returned better aware than most of the disasters that loomed. He delivered his briefing directly to the cabinet and Prime Minister H.H. Asquith within days of his return. Unlike Georges-Picot, Sykes was flighty and erratic in his tastes, interests, and attention span. He had, however, seen first-hand the dire situation confronting Britain in the Middle East in late 1915.

Within days of his arrival, Mark Sykes became Georges-Picot's new interlocutor. They met in December in London and had broken the impasse by early January 1916 with an agreement on the Anglo-French partition of the Ottoman Arab lands. The map they marked in blue and red pencil in January 1916 has been the source of unending controversy and bitterness over the past century. Mark Sykes conceded much to France and agreed to most demands. They could not reach agreement over Palestine, which both wanted to control, and so blurred the difference, by colouring it brownish-yellow on the map and declaring it an "international zone". The agreement reflected the harsh realities of early 1916, but Sykes' superiors in the British government had difficulty accepting the desperate situation and attacked him and the agreement immediately. In May 1916, after secret consultations with Russian diplomats, the agreement was finally signed, and the coloured map initialled and deposited. The so-called Sykes-Picot Accord, or Asia Minor Agreement, briefly secret until Lenin released its details the following year, has been the object of a century of opprobrium. Georges-Picot and Sykes were empowered to ignore and supersede previous agreements and pledges for the purposes of achieving immediate concord. The British government and Sykes himself came to regret intensely the accommodations to French interests they had made in a moment of weakness and anxiety.

The Sykes-Picot Accord is the universal Middle East symbol of imperialist arrogance and has been variously, and with some justification, claimed to be the origin of most of the region's contemporary borders and all of its conflicts. Citizens of all ages in every Middle Eastern country know it as the root of suffering in their region. Such discussions usually lack specificity and the context of imperial crisis, impending defeat and collapse has usually been ignored.[13] In the Middle East it has been memorialised as the agreement that denied the people of the region their rights to their own destiny and wishes. Imperial historians have often noted that claims and criticisms notwithstanding, the agreement and its lines on the map do not correspond to the post-war borders. In the twenty-first century, as the Middle East and the zone between one-time French and British spheres of influence has again been in the headlines, French and Anglophone journalists have evoked the memory of the Sykes-Picot Accord to claim it is only a small part of the vexing problems of the region. But the borders and still- dominant arrangements surely resemble the Accord's outlines far more than any other single influence.

By the end of 1917, in contrast, the situation had vastly improved for the British Empire. The Easter Rising had been long since crushed, and, more recently, Ottoman Baghdad had fallen, America had entered the war, and by November 1917, the fall of Jerusalem was assured. In November 1917,

Foreign Secretary Arthur Balfour issued the Balfour Declaration, promising the British Government's support for the Zionist movement's aspirations to a Jewish state. The Balfour Declaration is universally acknowledged the decision that gave the world the conflict over Palestine. Recent historians, including James Barr and Eugene Rogan, have argued that Balfour's Declaration was, more than anything else, an effort to loosen the fetters of the Sykes-Picot Accord of the previous year, and stake a claim to more seized Ottoman territory than Mark Sykes had agreed to in the Empire's dark days of Winter and Spring 1916. The events of early 1916 provoked a range of desperate responses. The Anglo-French withdrawal from Gallipoli in January 1916, the Easter Rising in Ireland, and General Townsend's surrender at Kut in the same week nearly brought the British Empire to its knees. And while the results of the year 1916 reverberated throughout the world, they were perhaps felt most acutely, and most painfully, in the post-Ottoman and post-colonial Middle East.

Notes

1 Michael Reynolds, *Shattering Empires: The Clash and Collapse of the Ottoman and Russian Empires 1908–1918* (Cambridge, 2010).
2 Christopher Clark, *Sleepwalkers: How Europe Went to War in 1914* (London, 2013), 42–43.
3 Daniel Yergin, *The Prize: The Epic Quest for Oil, Money & Power* (New York, 1990), 145.
4 Mustafa Aksakal, *The Ottoman Road to War in 1914: The Ottoman Empire and the First World War* (Cambridge, 2008).
5 Aksakal, *The Ottoman Road*, 118.
6 Ibid., 179.
7 See Eugene Rogan, *The Fall of the Ottomans: The Great War in the Middle East* (New York, 2015), 81–86. Rogan's book is now the best treatment on the Ottoman Great War; this section is based on Rogan's work.
8 Quoted in Rogan, *The Fall of the Ottomans*, 133.
9 Ibid., 139–141.
10 Ibid., 223.
11 Ibid., 267.
12 James Barr, *A Line in the Sand: The Anglo-French Struggle for the Middle East* (New York, 2014), 16–18. Barr's book is now the best treatment of the negotiations and betrayals.
13 Barr, *A Line in the Sand*, 16–18.

8 "A Tempest in a British Tea Pot"

The Silk Letters and the Arab Question in Cairo and Delhi

Erin O'Halloran

In November 1916, an item appeared in the *Arab Bulletin*, a British intelligence brief compiled by the Arab Bureau, a recently established agency in Cairo. The heading read, "Intrigues in Afghanistan".[1] It began:

> Three pieces of yellow silk with fine Urdu writing on them came recently into the possession of a loyal Indian Mohammedan gentleman who handed them over to the British authorities in India... The two larger pieces form a valuable report, and some of the information which that report contains is of interest to those who are concerned with the Arab question.[2]

The *Bulletin* went on to recount the story of Maulana Ubaidullah, an Islamic scholar from Deoband, a seat of Islamic learning in the Punjab. His so-called "silk letters" – three in total – had been written from Kabul in the summer of 1916. They were addressed to Maulvi Mahmud Hasan, also a Deobandi scholar of Islam, now thought to be at Medina.

The *Arab Bulletin* continued:

> about the time of the pilgrimage in 1915, these two persons and some other Indian Mohammedans ... found themselves in the Hejaz ... some, at least, of the party conferred with the Turkish Governor, Ghalib Pasha, and at their request he signed a written message to Moslems in India and beyond.[3]

While the content of this message was not specified in the *Bulletin's* report, it was later determined to be a call to arms, exhorting Muslims living under British rule to rise up against their colonial masters in the name of Islam and assuring them of Ottoman support in their struggle for liberation.[4]

On the silk scarves, Obeidullah first recounted for Hasan what had happened to him since he had returned to India with the aforementioned incendiary message from the Turkish Governor in Medina. According to the Anglo-Indian[5] officer writing for the *Arab Bulletin*, Obeidullah was disappointed by the poor reception his message received in India; according to a different, Indian source who met Obeidullah in Delhi, he was not disappointed and succeeded in raising a considerable sum of money from prominent nationalist activists there.[6] He then ventured to Kabul, where anti-British sentiment was known to run high. Obeidullah arrived in the Afghan capital almost simultaneously with a delegation headed by German officers Werner Otto von Hentig and Oskar Niedermayer. Travelling with them were several Indian nationalists from remarkably diverse backgrounds. These included Mahendra Pratap Singh, a wealthy Hindu landowner with secular and socialist leanings; Har Dayal, a Dalit who had dropped out of Oxford to practice Buddhist austerities, before founding the revolutionary Ghadr party in the United States; Maulani Barakatullah, an Islamic scholar and previously a professor of Urdu in Tokyo, who also had links to the Ghadr party; and Chempakaraman Pillai, a Tamil who had become involved in Indian nationalist politics while studying engineering in Zurich. All of these men had found their way to Berlin after the start of the war, where they had been involved in anti-British pamphleteering and propaganda efforts as part of the Indian Committee of National Independence.[7]

The fomenting of uprisings among the Muslim subjects of the British, French and Russian empires was a key strategic goal of German war planners. Indeed, many in the German High Command felt that it was the Ottoman Sultan's status as Caliph (in theory, leader of the worldwide Sunni Muslim community), and not his army, which constituted the primary advantage of alliance with his empire.[8] Following the Ottomans' entry into the war in November 1914, the Sultan had duly declared a jihad, calling on Muslims to rise up against the Entente powers as a religious duty. Had the faithful heeded his appeal in any significant numbers, the results could have been devastating: in 1914, the French and Russian empires both contained sizeable Muslim minorities, which were in turn dwarfed by the Muslim population of the British Empire. In British India alone, Muslims accounted for a staggering 80 million souls, making King George V ruler of the largest Muslim empire on Earth; the Ottoman Empire placed a distant second.[9] However, despite the declaration of jihad (and undoubtedly to the great relief of war planners in Paris, London and Moscow), nothing really happened; at least, the wave of large scale internal revolts the Germans had envisioned failed to materialise. In many senses, this served simply to underscore the word 'theoretical' mitigating the Caliph's claim to authority among the faithful; too late in Berlin, it became clear that his role was not really analogous to that of a Muslim pope.[10] Of course, the Entente powers tried not to leave too much to chance: in the wake of the Ottoman entry into the war, Muslim notables in North Africa, the Near East and Asia were flattered, cajoled, threatened or simply bought off by their imperial patrons. Nevertheless, the Central Powers persisted throughout the war in attempts to stoke the fires of religious zealotry throughout much of the Muslim world – and the Entente powers continued to fear that they might succeed.

What were the British to make of these elaborate and interlocking conspiracies – pro-German, pan-Islamic, anti-imperialist, nationalist – to bring down its empire in the East? The rather cloak-and-dagger "silk handkerchiefs with fine Urdu writing" went on to become a celebrated symbol in India's and Pakistan's nationalist mythology (commemorated, for example, with an Indian postage stamp in 2013). But by the time of their discovery in late 1916, the Silk Letters had been undermined by the failure of the German-Indian mission to Afghanistan and the launch of the Arab Revolt by the British and their allies in Arabia. One of the men involved peripherally in the Silk Letters was Chaudhry Khaliquzzaman, who went on to become a founding father of Pakistan. He later wrote in his memoirs that "the whole scheme depended on so many uncertain factors that it could be dubbed a chimerical daydream, but we at the time refused to discern in it any flaws or insurmountable difficulties".[11] For wartime British officials, however, whether in India or Cairo, the prospect of a seditious plot encompassing Arabs and Indians was deeply alarming.

This chapter explores the reactions of British officials, in several agencies and imperial outposts, to nationalist and anti-imperialist movements in India and the Middle East during World War I. It seeks to challenge the perception of a politically unified British imperial administration, as well as complicate existing narratives of both the Arab Revolt and the Silk Letters Conspiracy. It is among the first attempts to discuss those movements – and British reactions to, and interactions with them – as connected phenomena. A 2013 article by Saul Kelly also discusses the links between the Silk Letters Conspiracy and the Arab Revolt, but Kelly sides with contemporary British officials in filing those links neatly under the heading of "pan-Islamic".[12] I argue that the nature of the anti-British conspiracies described in the Silk Letters were not as clear cut as most British (and indeed some nationalist and politically Islamic) accounts have asserted, then as now. Moreover, while the historical significance of the Silk Letters and their link to the Arab Revolt certainly have much to do with "Britain's encounter with pan-Islam", as Kelly asserts, they also transcend that heading.[13] This argument is influenced by scholars including Priya Satia and Noor-Aiman I. Khan, both of whom touch briefly on the Silk Letters in the context of broader works, and whose theoretical framings have been instructive in fashioning the account presented here.

Priya Satia's *Spies in Arabia* focuses on the peculiar evolution of British intelligence work in the Middle East during and after the First World War, resulting, in the 1920s, in an unprecedented aerial surveillance regime intended to erase the physical traces of British imperial control.[14] For my purposes, what is particularly compelling about Satia's analysis is the tendency she identifies of British agents in the Middle East to operate on the basis of unsubstantiated rumours, hunches, and assumptions, in an apparent attempt to replicate what they imagined to be the "intuitive knowledge" of the Oriental. To quote only the most entertaining example, here is Satia's account of Indian Army officer Norman Bray's "epiphany" in the Himalayas. Bray, who had deliberately done "very little reading" on the subject, emerged from the mountains to pen a widely circulated intelligence report suggesting that a broad, international pan-Islamic conspiracy lay behind the recently uncovered Silk Letters plot:

> In the intense solitude – the profound silence... I seemed to hear a whisper, to sense a feeling ... which had drifted, intangible as vapour ... over the thousands of miles of desert ... and ... left behind it a restlessness.' It came to him while he sat immersed in the magic information network. He sensed it, the way an Arabia agent could.[15]

Satia connects this intuitive mode of intelligence gathering, epitomised by and later modelled on romantic figures like T.E. Lawrence, to an equally stubborn reliance on ethnic and religious stereotypes in their attempts to explain the emerging nationalist, anti-imperial and pan-Islamic movements of the Middle East and India during the 1910s and 1920s. She identifies a strange confluence of condescension and paranoia, which permeated much of the British intelligence discourse surrounding Asiatics, and Muslims in particular. To wit:

> Officials attributed little agency to Middle Easterners themselves... In a sense, there could be no single 'mastermind' behind the conspiracies because Orientals did not possess individual minds as such. [...] To Charles Cleveland's query about the 'one brain' behind pre-war Indian agitation, [Bray] replied, 'Yes – but that brain is not a human one...!' This perception of a collective Asiatic mind derived both from an orientalist attitude incapable of recognizing the agency of 'Asiatics' and from agents' assumption that anything observed or observable, including an uncovered plot, was only an epiphenomenon of 'the underlying forces and organization'.[16]

A clear and concise expression of the dynamic which Satia describes is provided elsewhere by Sir Charles Cleveland himself, the fabled Director of the Indian Secret Service. In the aftermath of the Silk Letters' discovery, he painted a picture of the addled yet diabolical Maulvi (a Muslim doctor of the law) gathering to himself a collection of toothless elders and wayward children:

> ...his mind, the mind of a fanatical Indian maulvi to which war seems largely a judicious mixture of mutiny, riot and old-fashioned hill-fighting, endeavours to grapple with a vast situation. He tries to mould the Turks and Germans to his scheme by using ... an old Theological professor of seventy years of age, as a diplomat... He persuades a lot of fanatical schoolboys who have been maddened by the subtle

incitements of a learned, eloquent but hypocritical priest… It is all very pathetic and ineffective but nevertheless the danger of the cauldron of fanaticism boiling over is ever present.[17]

This "cauldron of fanaticism", imagined to extend from the deserts of the Hejaz to the mountains of Afghanistan and beyond, was sometimes thought to be Islamic in character, at other times nationalist, Bolshevik, anarchist, or something yet more sinister and ill-defined.[18] Together, these shadowy movements will here be referred to collectively as "Easternisms", a category that is only meaningful insofar as it mirrors the often muddled view of contemporary British agents, who sought variously to penetrate, contain, dismantle or utilise these inscrutable "forces" in India and the Middle East.

While Satia's work is more or less limited to British intelligence operations in Arabia, with only incidental forays beyond that desert's edge, Noor Aiman I. Khan's *Egyptian-Indian Nationalist Collaboration* takes these peripheries as her subject. Khan traces the development of connections between Indian and Egyptian nationalists throughout the first half of the twentieth century, from pre-war contacts among students in Paris and London, up until the outbreak of World War II.[19] Among the major contributions of her book is its contestation of the focus on pan-Islam – both in the British records and later in the secondary literature – as the key rubric for understanding international collaboration between Eastern peoples in the early twentieth century (and perhaps ever since). She argues that anti-imperialism informed by Enlightenment values and secular nationalism, became the overriding factors in the alliance between Egyptians and Indians, "who shared in a vision of a world community of sovereign nation-states".[20] She further asserts that this vision "lay at the heart of many of the connections forged between colonised peoples"[21]; certainly, the global response to Woodrow Wilson's Fourteen Points and the subsequent Paris Peace Conference of 1919 demonstrated that people from a staggering number of colonies and territories – including those in the Arab East – *did* aspire to membership of such a community. Satia's work on British officers' perceptions of the Middle East and its inhabitants, and Khan's research into the connections between Arabs and Indians, together inform my analysis of a specific encounter between British officials and nationalists in India and the Middle East in the midst of the Great War. Their story draws us back to Kabul, where Maulana Obeidullah had just encountered the Hentig-Niedermeyer delegation in 1916.

Upon enquiry, Obeidullah learned that the mission of this unlikely group of travellers was to win over Amir Habibullah, the ruler of Afghanistan, to the side of the Central Powers. In so doing, the Germans and their Indian allies hoped to unleash a 'holy war' against British interests in India and Central Asia.[22] This of course fit neatly with Obeidullah's own agenda, and he quickly made friends with the Indians travelling with Hentig and

Niedermeyer. Together, they conspired to form a Provisional Government of India. "After discussions for several days", wrote Obeidullah to Maulvi Mahmud Hassan,

> this [Provisional] Government [of India] agreed that if Afghanistan would join the war, they would be prepared to acknowledge her Prince as the permanent King of India... A request to this effect ... was laid before the Amir, but as the latter is not prepared as yet to join the war, the question has been postponed.[23]

Here it is interesting to note that the Anglo-Indian political officer, quoting this passage in his brief for the benefit of the *Arab Bulletin*, found the notion of Indians of different creeds organising in this fashion to be highly suspect, if not laughable. Referring to Mahendra Pratap, who was to be the head of the Provisional Government, he commented, "It would be interesting to know the mental reservations made by the Hindu President when he offered the Crown of India to a Moslem Prince".[24] Perhaps, he suggested, Pratap knew the Afghan king was not prepared to enter the war. "If so", he submitted, "he is not so mad as his friends in India would have us believe." This fits into a pattern: much, if not all, of the intelligence and analysis presented by the Government in Delhi to its colleagues in other parts of the Empire was couched in terms of communal identities. Hindu Indians were inevitably said to think one way, Muslims another. Any hint of a convergence of views between the communities tended to be dismissed, either as the work of a fringe minority, the short-term manoeuvring of an otherwise communally minded politician (as with Pratap), or as inauthentic in some other way. If it was inauthentic, the logic seemed to be, it must also be transient – and therefore there was nothing to worry about.

At this point, Obeidullah's letter itself moved on to discuss a second organisation, with which his correspondent, Mahmud Hassan, was to be more intimately connected. In its commentary, the *Bulletin* noted that, while this second organisation was purely Islamic in character, the link between it and the Provisional Government of India was that both were implacably hostile to Britain: "though apparently little more than conceived", states the *Bulletin*, this new organisation had "been given the name 'Al Janud Al Rabbania,' which Obeidullah himself translates as the 'Moslem Salvation Army'".[25] It was, according to Obeidullah,

> a special Islamic organisation based on military principles. Its first object is to create union between Muslim Kings. You [Mahmud Hasan] have been appointed President ... the chief centre being Medina. The idea therefore is, that you should, by living in Medina, try to have an alliance made by the great Caliphate, with Afghanistan and Persia ... please make the quickest possible arrangements to convey [the demands of Afghanistan] to the members of the Ottoman Government and the

Caliphate; because this is the only way of inflicting an effective blow on the infidels in India.[26]

Again, it is worth noting that, having transcribed this passage, the Anglo-Indian agent hastened to suggest that 'infidels' might here refer to Hindus as well as the British, regardless of the alliance the author, Obeidullah, had only just concluded with a Hindu, a Buddhist, and a Tamil in the common cause of overthrowing British rule. But perhaps that, too, was to be interpreted as a short-term manoeuvre.

The patrons of the fledgling Moslem Salvation Army were to be the three so-called 'Islamic Kings': the Ottoman Sultan, the Shah of Persia and the Amir of Afghanistan. Field Marshals were to include Ottoman General Enver Pasha; the Turkish heir apparent and Prime Minister; the Ex-Khedive of Egypt, Abbas Hilmi, who had been deposed by the British at the start of the War; the Prime Minister of Afghanistan; and Sharif Hussein of Mecca,[27] of whom more later.

The uncovering of the Silk Letters came at the end of an extraordinarily eventful year in the Middle Eastern theatres of World War I. 1916 opened with the failure of the Gallipoli Campaign in January, followed in April by the surrender of a British-Indian garrison at Kut in Mesopotamia. The surrender was the culmination of a brutal siege by Ottoman forces which had lasted over four months and decimated the Indian Army contingent stationed there. The combined effect of these two catastrophic setbacks for British forces in the Middle East was to be a complete overhaul of Imperial defence strategy in the region. This proved to be a particularly fraught task owing to the existence, in the lands between the Mediterranean and Indian Ocean, of overlapping and rival British jurisdictions. Specifically, it involved negotiation between two centres of the British Empire with remarkably different views of the world: Cairo and Delhi.

In the British Imperial imagination of the early twentieth century, the Middle East was perceived, in the excellent phrasing of Elizabeth Monroe, "as a desert with two edges, one belonging to the Mediterranean and the other to the Indian Ocean".[28] And for much of its history, British India enjoyed unfettered control over its half of the desert, which included southern Persia, the Arabian coast of the Persian Gulf, Aden, and parts of East Africa, with remarkably little interference from London. By 1916, however, the war had begun to interfere with British Indian prerogatives in these places, as the need for greater imperial oversight and a unified command structure meant that Cairo – closer to London by far and staffed by men with strong personal and professional ties to Whitehall and the Foreign Office – became increasingly the centre of British political and military operations in the Middle East.[29]

In the spring of 1916, as British strategic and military planners looked for ways to turn the tables on the Ottomans following the debacles in Gallipoli and Kut, they latched on to a correspondence with Hussein bin Ali, the

Sharif of Mecca, which had been initiated in 1915 by Lord Kitchener, and taken up by Sir Henry McMahon, the British High Commissioner in Egypt. In exchange for Sharif Hussein's commitment to launch a revolt against the Ottomans in the Arabian Peninsula, McMahon, with the approval of senior officials in London, pledged Britain's recognition of an independent Arab Kingdom to be ruled by Hussein's family, the Hashemites, after the war.

At around the same time as planning for an Arab revolt gained momentum in London and Cairo, Mark Sykes, a young MP who had implicated himself in Near Eastern policy circles, proposed to the British Cabinet the establishment of an "Islamic Bureau" for intelligence and propaganda coordination, to be based in Cairo. While the initiative garnered swift approval in London, it met with an icy reception in Delhi, which objected strenuously to this perceived interference in the Raj's privileged relationship with its own Muslim population. In deference to these objections, the name of the fledgling agency was changed to the "Arab Bureau", which sounded less like an encroachment on Delhi's Muslim prerogative. A telegramme from the Foreign Section of the Government of India addressed to the British Resident in Aden, which came under Delhi's formal supervision in early 1916, alerted him to the creation of the Arab Bureau, and was at pains to emphasise that, first, this new agency was only to concern itself with "non-Indian Muslims", and second, that the recipient still took his orders from the Government of India, and should keep them informed of anything he received from this new (and possibly suspect) agency in Cairo.[30]

Delhi bureaucrats had some justification for what Robert Blyth has called their prickly attitude toward their colleagues in Cairo. Ronald Storrs, the Oriental Secretary, was guilty on at least one occasion of musing about the possibility of a "Near Eastern Vice-Royalty" that "would surely compare in interest and complexity, if not in actual size, with India itself".[31] Beyond this sort of interdepartmental rivalry, however, were far more substantial differences over the direction of Britain's policy in the Arab region.

At the heart of the disagreement lay Cairo and Delhi's contrasting assessments of the viability of the Arab Revolt. Over the course of 1916, the Government of India advanced several reservations to what it saw as a Cairo-driven policy. First, it questioned the wisdom of promoting Arab unity, on the basis that this could present a threat to British, and especially Anglo-Indian, interests over the long term. "We have always regarded with much diffidence", warned a telegramme from the Government of India to its colleagues in the India Office in London in late 1915, "the creation of a strong Arab State lying astride our interests in the east and the Gulf as a not unlikely source of ultimate trouble."[32]

Delhi also took issue with the choice of Sharif Hussein (the aforementioned Sharif of Mecca) as Britain's key ally in Arabia, questioning his reliability, and, in a series of telegrammes, promoting his rival, Ibn Saud, as a much more reasonable and trustworthy friend of British interests. Indeed, the Government of India formalised its relationship with Ibn Saud in a treaty, ratified in 1916 – despite their awareness of the bad blood between him and Cairo's man, Hussein. Delhi was also implicated, through its political Resident in Aden, in the Kunfidah incident in 1916, when they supported the landing of Idrisi tribesmen in a contested port town on the Red Sea, almost resulting in open hostilities between the Idrisis and the forces of Sharif Hussein. British officers on the spot were forced to threaten Hussein in order to prevent an attack on the Idrisis, leaving the Arab Bureau fuming at this loss of face, which, they feared, might put their entire alliance with the Hashemites in jeopardy.

Throughout 1915 and 1916, officials in the Government of India wondered aloud at the effect of Britain appearing to back an indigenous revolt against an imperial power, especially under the banner of Islam, and especially given the strong sympathies many Indian Muslims still harboured for the Ottoman Caliphate. Prior to their being subject to censorship from late 1914, Indian Muslim newspapers such as *The Comrade* had given ample indication of the strongly pro-Ottoman sentiments of many within that community. In one of its final issues, the paper's editor lamented the "calamity" of war between Britain and the Ottomans:

> It would be a hypocrisy to disguise the fact that love of Turkey is to the Indian Mussalmans [*sic*] a deep and abiding sentiment and that millions of them reverence the Sultan as their Caliph. The unity of culture and faith has consecrated these feelings of sympathy and devotion and they have remained strong and vital forces through the ages.[33]

Further insight into the force of popular identification with the Ottoman Empire is offered by a notice in the back of almost every issue of *The Comrade* throughout 1914, advertising "Genuine Turkish Military Caps", made to "the same pattern as worn by Turk high officials like Enver Pasha".[34]

Of course, what the paper failed to acknowledge was the extent to which the Raj had encouraged these pro-Turkish sentiments among its Muslim populace. The propping up of the Ottoman Empire had been a pillar of British foreign policy for many decades prior to the outbreak of World War I, and even the central role of the Ottoman Caliph in the spiritual life of Indian Muslims was a notion revived and nurtured by Britain.[35] The awkward position this now created for authorities in Delhi was one reason why they were wary of promoting a new "Arab Champion" in Mecca as a rallying point for the Muslim faithful. The records of the India Office show that, throughout 1916, the Government of India and the India Office in London vehemently protested any attempt to package Hussein as a new defender of Islam or pretender to the Caliphate.[36]

Well after the Arab Revolt had gotten under way in June, the Government of India was at pains to emphasise to its counterparts in London and Cairo the extent of Indian antipathy towards it, noting that Muslim opinion remained "hostile" late into the year and underscoring the government's own role in the thankless task of quashing popular resistance to Britain's Arab policy.[37] This won it few friends in Cairo and Whitehall, where officials including Mark Sykes accused what he called "those idiot Sahib-landers, who are jealous and provincial", of "unconsciously or subconsciously" siding with Indian Muslim opinion in sympathy with the Ottomans.[38]

"As matters stand", seethed Sykes, "there is an Egyptian policy which is pro-Sharif, there is an Aden policy which is pro-Idrisi, a Gulf policy which is one difficult to define, and an Indian policy which is anti-Arab".[39]

A similar observation was made by Sharif Hussein himself, in a complaint made to Lt. Cl. C.E. Wilson, Britain's Resident Agent in Jeddah:

> You speak to me continually of the British Government and British policy... But I see five governments where you see one, and the same number of policies. There is a policy, first of your Foreign Office; second of your Army; third of your Navy; fourth of your protectorate in Egypt; fifth of your Government in India. Each of these British Governments seems to me to act upon an Arab policy of its own.[40]

The Sharif had a point, and increasingly, it threatened to hamper Britain's war effort in the Middle East. In the middle of the year, Gertrude Bell, a figure variously described in the literature as a "woman traveller" or "female explorer", who was then working as a political agent at the Arab Bureau, was dispatched to India in an attempt to improve relations. She wrote to her father at the time:

> There is a great deal of friction between India and Egypt over the Arab question which entails a serious want of cooperation between the Intelligence Departments of the two countries and the longer it goes on the worse it gets. It's absurd of course [...] but they don't realise what Arabia looks like from the West and I daresay we don't realise how it looks from the East.[41]

What many in Cairo failed to realise was that the dilemma faced by officials in Delhi was all too real. The Silk Letters Conspiracy was only one of the nationalist currents then organising itself in India in defiance of British Rule. The Christmas Day Plot, an ambitious German plan to smuggle arms to Indian revolutionaries across the Pacific from the United States, was intercepted by British authorities in the summer of 1915.[42] In December 1916, almost a year of negotiations led by political activists Muhammad Ali Jinnah and Annie Besant came to fruition, as Jinnah's party, the All-India Muslim League, held a joint session with the Indian National Congress, of which Besant was then president. The result was the signature of the Lucknow Pact, marking the first time that the two leading nationalist parties of India had united to demand self-rule. Lucknow was to serve as the fore-runner to the Khilafat Movement of the 1920s, when Congress again joined Indian Muslims in common cause against the British – this time to reject the break-up of the Ottoman Empire and the dissolution of the Caliphate.

If officials in Cairo, however, were somewhat insensitive to the threats British India perceived as emanating from "Easternisms", what perhaps was not sufficiently appreciated in Delhi was the complex role played by religious, and specifically Islamic, identities within the movements that sought to challenge it. Both the Silk Letters Conspiracy and the Lucknow Pact, as well as the secular revolutionaries involved in the Christmas Day Plot and the hostility of many Indian Muslims towards the Arab Revolt, indicated that nationalist and anti-imperialist sentiments were at least as important as communal or sectarian identities in driving political opinion – and anti-British action. It was the Europeans, and not necessarily the Indians or the Arabs, who saw pan-Islam as the crucial factor in mobilising "Asiatics".

For example, Khan recounts an episode in which Har Dayal, the founder of the (secular) Ghadr party, quit Berlin in 1915, frustrated by what he perceived as "the Germans putting Muslims in charge of everything". German officials involved in the efforts to promote revolt in the Middle East and India, notably the Director of Oriental Affairs, Baron Max von Oppenheim, tended to prioritise pan-Islamic movements ahead of secular nationalist organisations, like the one with which Dayal was affiliated. What is most intriguing about this episode is how it was resolved: "It was only the Muslim Barakatullah ... who could convince Har Dayal to go back to Germany. He convinced him to help in ... an upcoming plan to send a contingent of Indians, Ottomans, and Germans to Afghanistan".[43] Ultimately the Ottomans, logically the party with the largest stake in a pan-Islamic uprising, withdrew from the mission, leaving Hentig and Niedermeyer to cross the Persian desert with the Indian nationalists in tow.

As in the case of the Anglo-Indian agent writing in the *Arab Bulletin*, communal identities also remained of paramount importance for British officials, especially those in the Government of India. That Hindus and Muslims were incapable of cooperating, as too were Sunnis and Shias, for example, or for that matter the Arab tribes, was, in the intelligence briefings and personal telegrammes of the era, an immutable natural reality, much like gravitational force. Any and all accounts of cooperation between Hindus and Muslims against British rule, whether covert, as in the Silk Letters and the Christmas Day Plot, or public, as at Lucknow, were greeted with scepticism, if not outright dismissal. Within official circles, the Silk Letters were labelled a "pan-Islamic" conspiracy, a choice that required focusing on the fantastical and barely conceived Moslem Salvation Army, rather than the intercommunal Provisional Government of India. This was despite the fact that the Provisional Government was by far the more developed of the two plots and had enjoyed the backing of the Central Powers.

Similarly, and simultaneously, many in Cairo, including within the Arab Bureau, were dismissive of Delhi's concerns over the potential threat posed by a strong, unified Arab state. In a Cairo intelligence report penned by T.E. Lawrence for the benefit of skittish officials in London and Delhi,[44] the Arabs were to remain "in a state of political mosaic, a tissue of small jealous principalities, incapable of cohesion, and yet always ready to combine against an outside force. This is good for us."[45] In the words of Bruce Westrate, "Arab political potential was regarded with scorn": the tribes could be utilised to carry out the revolt, with minimum risk that they would actually coalesce into a viable Arab state.[46]

Despite the condescension apparent in official communications about Indian and Arab nationalists alike, during the same period, the Allied and Central Powers continued to vie for pro-Muslim credibility. British, French and German intelligence officers all spoke knowingly of the Arabs and the Muslim faith, and felt the urgency of winning this vast and supposedly uniform population over to their cause. There are numerous instances of European war planners on both sides of the conflict making reference to the almost magical powers of a call to jihad, if made by this or that Muslim notable of supposedly unimpeachable lineage, to rouse the faithful from the far corners of the earth. This, at least, was how Sharif Hussein was selected by the British as the most likely challenger to the Ottoman Sultan, and much ink was subsequently spilled in British outposts throughout Egypt, the Sudan, Iraq, Aden, and India as to whether or not he should be promoted as a potential Caliph, as if this was an office British endorsement could secure.

What emerges is the impression that all of these various Easternisms – Arab nationalism, Indian anti-colonialism, anti-imperialism, pan-Islamism – were thought to be pathetic, but also highly dangerous and indeed had the potential to be weaponised. Easternist movements were perceived as ideologically vapid enough to be manipulated, whether for or against British interests; but it was thought vital that they *be* manipulated, for they were believed to contain some secret power – perhaps even the power to determine the outcome of the War.

It is not difficult to see how certain aspects of this story resemble the threats, both real and imagined, confronting Western governments of our own era. The toxic combination of condescension and paranoia which characterise these historical depictions of Arabs, Indians and Muslims more broadly defined bear a striking resemblance to mainstream depictions of our own era. What is remarkable is not so much the dehumanising impact of these portrayals; they are repugnant, but far from uncommon, in this regard. What is remarkable, and echoes the approach of the British officials charged with understanding and confronting the Easternisms of the early twentieth century, is their stark inefficiency when translated into policy. From tourists pulled off of airplanes for "looking Arab", to Muslim women forced by police to disrobe on French beaches, to the Executive

Orders which have sought to bar Muslims of certain nationalities from entering the United States, the link between the problem of Islamist terror and the policies ostensibly designed to combat it, is increasingly questionable. When our adversaries become inhuman in the mind's eye, they also become impossible to fathom – and thus beyond the scope of rational action.

Notes

1 *Arab Bulletin*, 8 November 1916, 29. In *Arab Bulletin: Bulletin of the Arab Bureau in Cairo*, vol. 1, *1916–1919* (Oxford, 1986).
2 *Arab Bulletin*, 427.
3 Ibid.
4 FO 882/12 Vivian to Wilson, 7 December 1916; Maulana Muhammad Miyan (tr. Muhammadullah Qasmi). *Silken Letters Movement: Accounts of 'Silken Handkerchief Letters Conspiracy Case' from British Records* (Deoband, 2012), 54.
5 Throughout, the term "Anglo-Indian" is used to refer to the British Government of India, its agents and officials.
6 Choudhry Khaliquzzaman, *Pathway to Pakistan* (Lahore, 1961), 34.
7 Noor-Aiman I. Khan, *Egyptian-Indian Nationalist Collaboration and the British Empire* (New York, 2011), 77.
8 Eugene Rogan, *The Fall of the Ottomans* (London, 2015).
9 Scott Anderson, *Lawrence in Arabia* (Toronto, 2013), 161.
10 Khan, *Egyptian-Indian Nationalist Collaboration*, 60.
11 Khaliquzzaman, *Pathway*, 32.
12 Saul Kelly, "'Crazy in the Extreme'? The Silk Letters Conspiracy," *Middle Eastern Studies* 49.2 (2013), 167–78.
13 Kelly, "'Crazy'," 164.
14 Priya Satia, *Spies in Arabia* (Oxford, 2008).
15 Satia, *Spies*, 218.
16 Ibid., 223–24.
17 Quoted in Kelly, "'Crazy'," 169.
18 Satia, *Spies*, 224–25.
19 Khan, *Egyptian-Indian Nationalist Collaboration*.
20 Ibid., 5.
21 Ibid.
22 *Arab Bulletin*, 428.
23 Ibid.
24 Ibid.
25 *Arab Bulletin*, 429.
26 Ibid.
27 *Arab Bulletin*, 429–30.
28 Elizabeth Monroe, *Britain's Moment in the Middle East* (Oxford, 1963), 13.
29 Ronald Storrs, T. E. Lawrence, Mark Sykes, and Gertrude Bell were among the most prominent of the Arab Bureau's interconnected group of "intrusives," as they came to be known.
30 "A part of Cairo Intelligence Department is being formed and called 'The ARAB BUREAU' with the idea of collecting and circulating news favourable to GREAT BRITAIN and carrying on a Press Campaign among non Indian Moslems, without in any way upsetting the feelings of Entente Powers and Indian Moslems. ...When necessary you should refer to Government of India for orders and keep them posted with all important communications." India Office

Records, British Library, IOR/R/20/A/1569, Secret Paraphrase 19/2/1916: Foreign Delhi to British Resident, Aden.

31 Storrs to Fitzgerald, Cairo, 8 March 1915. Quoted in Robert J. Blyth, *The Empire of the Raj* (Basingstoke, 2003), 146.

32 IOR L/PS/10/586 Telegramme, Government of India to India Office, 4 November 1915.

33 "Indian Moslems and the War," *The Comrade*, 7 November 1914, 344.

34 *The Comrade*, 10 October 1914, 283.

35 In an appreciation of Indian domestic politics for the *Arab Bulletin* in 1916, an Indian political agent explained: "When we were pro-Turk and anti-Russian we, too, rallied Indian Moslems to the Prophet's Standard, filling their minds with novel ideas regarding the Ottoman Caliphate... Until a few years ago, Great Britain was regarded as the champion of Turkey and of the Ottoman Caliphate, but recent events outside India ... rendered her suspect before ever war was contemplated." *Arab Bulletin*, 522–23.

36 IOR/R/20/A/1570: 1916–1917 "Correspondence on Arabia."

37 *Arab Bulletin*, 521.

38 FO 882/2, ARB 15/3 Sykes to Clayton, 28 December 1915; Blyth, *Raj*, 150.

39 CAB 17/174 Memo by Sykes, 31 July 1916 enclosed in Sir Maurice Hankey (Committee for Imperial Defence) to Lloyd George, 31 July 1916.

40 Quoted in Bruce Westrate, *The Arab Bureau* (University Park, PA, 1992), 26.

41 Quoted in Blyth, *Raj*, 148.

42 Peter Hopkirk, *On Secret Service East of Constantinople: The Plot to Bring Down the British Empire* (London, 1994), 179–190.

43 Khan, *Egyptian-Indian Nationalist Collaboration*, 77–78.

44 Anderson, *Lawrence*, 164.

45 Quoted in Satia, *Spies*, 205.

46 Westrate, *Arab Bureau*, 94.

9 "Revolutionaries, Renegades and Refugees"

Anti-British Allegiances in the Context of World War I

Stephen McQuillan

Indo-Irish nationalist collaboration in America and Europe throughout World War I defied loyalty and allegiance at a time when such values were perceived as critical to the British war effort. For Britain, as for its adversaries, the war underlined the need for imperial patriotism among its own subjects. Anti-British fraternise was, therefore, a betrayal of imperial solidarity. Of course, nationalist connections should not obscure the deeper manifestations of allegiance professed to the British Empire upon the outbreak of War where 1.4 million Indian recruits served overseas, while in Ireland approximately 200,000 Irishmen served with the British armed forces.[1] The 1916 Easter Rising in Ireland was far from being the only rebellion against imperial rule during the First World War. In February 1915, an attempted Ghadar uprising in the Punjab in India was infiltrated and suppressed. The spectre of mass anti-imperial rebellion greatly troubled the British, who at the time ruled more Muslims than any other state. As graphically illustrated in John Buchan's 1916 novel, *Greenmantle*, politicians and soldiers worried about the ominous threat of a German-backed Islamic holy war against the Allies.[2] The occasion of World War I and the prevailing wartime mode of employing organised violence for national political ends provided for some separatists the most opportune moment to strike for freedom from the British Empire.[3] The following chapter will discuss the spatially disparate dynamics of wartime Indo-Irish fraternise. It will consider Irish involvement in the *Annie Larsen-Maverick* episode, an attempt to smuggle weapons into India from America. Relations between members of the Friends of Irish Freedom (FOIF) and the Berlin India Committee in Stockholm and Berlin relate to the narrative of wartime intrigue.

The Indo-Irish-German network was strongly represented in San Francisco, California. The Bay Area was home to Irish republican leaders Larry de Lacey, who had fled Ireland as a political exile in 1914, and Father Peter C. Yorke. As editor of the *Irish Leader* and owner of a publishing company, Yorke's political influence was matched by his financial power which he leveraged to support de Lacey in his subversive activities.[4] The West Coast was also home to Ram Chandra, leading member of the Ghadar Party and editor-in-chief of the *Ghadar* publication. Shortly after the outbreak of World War I, an Indo-Irish plot executed under the auspices of

German saboteurs was established to ship American weapons to India for a revolt against the Raj. Irish assistance with logistics was crucial to German and Indian efforts. German Embassy Military Attaché Franz von Papen, the notorious leader of conspiracies throughout the United States during World War I and later chancellor of the Weimar Republic, recalled in his memoirs that he had many connections with Irish and Indian revolutionary leaders and that it was he who instigated the Indo-German-Irish plots.[5]

In response to the concerted web of alliances, British intelligence operative Sir Robert Nathan arrived in America in March 1916 to assist in the establishment of a makeshift intelligence network in San Francisco to expose the intrigues of the Ghadar Party and, by extension, Irish republicans. Nathan was a retired officer of the Indian police and a member of the Security Service (MO5g, later MI5) between November 1914 and February 1916.[6] Nathan revealed the triadic leadership of the Indians, Irish and Germans in the *Maverick-Annie Larsen* conspiracy. He described the importance of Larry de Lacey, who had direct ties to republican leaders John Devoy and Joseph McGarrity in New York. According to Nathan, Indian infiltrators regularly attended conferences between Ram Chandra, Larry De Lacey and German agents. He reported that "The entire [Ghadar] movement is so co-related and connected with the German and Irish question that it cannot be considered separately and apart... Ram Chandra is the Indian brain; and De Lacey is the Irish brain." The Indians and Irish were to make no moves without the Germans.[7] The German General Staff approved Von Papen's Indo-German-Irish network and sent a message to Von Papen in January, during the arms purchase for the Indo-German conspiracy, which listed several Irish contacts who could assist him. Von Papen then called upon New York Irish republican Joseph McGarrity to make the necessary arrangements for shipping the *Annie Larsen* arms purchase from New York to Galveston, Texas, via an Irish-American shipping firm. From Galveston, the guns were sent by train to San Diego, where the *Annie Larsen* was waiting.[8] The *Annie Larsen* was to rendezvous with a larger steamship the *Maverick* off the Pacific coast of Mexico at Socorro Island. The *Maverick* was then supposed to take the arms shipment first to the Dutch East Indies and then to India. In the end the mission was aborted when the ships failed to rendezvous in the late spring of 1915 and a US Federal Investigation was launched to determine if US neutrality laws were violated.[9] The degree of Irish involvement in these events is captured by a Foreign Office report: "Even as late as February and March 1916, reports were received both from New York and the Pacific coast of activity among seditious Indians and Irish Americans in America directed towards the shipments of arms to India."[10] A retrospective account of these arms smuggling activities highlighted the parallels between Irish and Indian arms smuggling endeavours: "Arms were shipped, but captured. The method and fate of these Indian intrigues were very similar to those of the Germans dealing with Sinn Féin."[11]

The Irish involvement in the Indo-German arms smuggling efforts was relayed to US Attorney John W. Preston by Robert Nathan. Nathan revealed that Larry de Lacey constructed plans with the Ghadar Party to send two hundred of their followers to Mexico in the event that the United States declared war on Germany. These routes and contacts later proved useful when arresting some of the conspirators as they attempted to flee to Mexico. The Bureau of Investigation (BOI) arrested Ram Chandra and sixteen members of the Ghadar on 7 April 1917 the day after America entered the War. Along with the leading Indian revolutionaries, Larry de Lacey was also prosecuted for his involvement in the efforts to transport weapons into India.[12] These developments culminated in the longest and most expensive trial in US legal history to that date which took place in San Francisco between US attorneys, who were assisted by British secret agents, on the one side, and Irish American defence attorneys on the other.[13]

On 4 March 1916, leading members of the Clan na Gael gathered in New York to attend the Irish Race Convention. The Congress was convoked with the intention of "arranging means to enable Ireland to recover independence after the war".[14] The convention demanded the recognition of Ireland as an independent nation, and passed a resolution stating that

> Fighting for the success of the Allies would be fighting for the combined subjection of Ireland, India and Egypt to English rule. It would be a war against Ireland as well as Germany, and keep Ireland, whose sons fought for America in their war, under the heel of England.[15]

The FOIF was then established to advance and execute these aims. The organisational hierarchy comprised of John Devoy, Daniel Cohalan, Jeremiah O'Leary and Joseph McGarrity. A European branch of the FOIF was established in Stockholm, Sweden, to disseminate propaganda and create awareness of Irish demands for self-determination. Former US Consul General in Munich, Thomas St. John Gaffney, was appointed as the main European representative of the FOIF. Gaffney had been described by Mary Spring Rice as "an active antagonist of Great Britain".[16] In August 1914, as American consul in Dresden, he at once embraced the German cause in the war. A month later, he was recalled to the United States as his abrasive and unprofessional pro-German declarations had become a source of embarrassment to the Wilson administration.[17] Gaffney's second in command was George Chatterton-Hill, a retired Indian Civil Servant (ICS) official born in Madras (Chennai). Chatterton-Hill had been liberated from a prison camp in Ruhleben near Berlin by Roger Casement in March 1915. Before the war, he had written several books about philosophy, culture and sociology, lectured at the University of Geneva and had been dismissed as a "soi-disant Irishman" on one occasion by British government sources and "a little fop and pip-squeak" on another.[18]

Stockholm, in early 1917, was teeming with foreign political activists. Political exiles from an eclectic array of countries came together and fomented radicalism. Although technically a neutral power, Sweden was ideologically closer to Germany than to any of the Allied powers. Revolutionaries, renegades and political refugees could benefit from the relatively liberal atmosphere which prevailed. Although compulsory passport and visa regulations were introduced, foreigners were still granted great freedom to engage in political activity.[19] The Berlin India National Committee, also known as the Central European Committee of Indian Nationalists, had been established to represent the high volume of Indian political exiles based in Berlin and to coordinate the efforts of Hindu, Sikh and Muslim concomitant anti-British strategies with the German Foreign Office including plans for a German sponsored uprising in the Punjab in 1915.

In May 1917, the Berlin India National Committee sent several Indian representatives to Stockholm. The Indian National Committee was regarded by one intelligence official as "merely a high sounding name for the two well-known revolutionaries Virendra Nath Chattopadhyaya and Tirumah Achari [sic]".[20] Incidentally, Gaffney, Chatterton-Hill and the Indian representatives shared offices in Stockholm, demonstrating the close knit nature of their fraternise and the mutual reciprocation of their causes.[21] In relation to their presence in Stockholm a Department of Criminal Intelligence report described how the Indians had "rented two rooms on the back premises from a Swedish architect. On the door, they have put up a notice bearing the words "Indian National Committee", below which there is written in pencil "Friends of the Irish". There is also another notice to the effect that the Bureau is to be used by others amongst the "races oppressed by England".[22] An October 1917 DCI report observed that, "The India Bureau is going to co-operate with the other representatives or agents of the oppressed races; for example, the Irish, Egyptians, Georgians, etc. These nationalistic movements are represented in all neutral countries and even in the United States."[23] According to DCI records, between August and November 1907 Acharya was printer and publisher of the "seditious" nationalist weekly *India*, initially printed in Madras until it was moved to Pondicherry in July 1908. In November 1908, he moved to London where he became an active member of Shyamaji Krishnavarma's India House and was said to be "constantly in the company of V.D. Savarkar and V.V.S. Aiyar".[24] In October 1909 he went to Paris where he was associated with leading revolutionaries such as Bhikaji Cama. In November 1910 he went to Berlin, in April 1911 he was in Munich and in October of the same year went onto Constantinople.[25] According to intelligence records, he went to America in 1912 where he came into contact with George Freeman returning to Berlin in 1915 to meet up with a group of Indian revolutionaries residing there and collaborating with the Germans.[26] During the course of the war, he was reportedly among a group sent to the Suez Canal to assist the Germans in launching an invasion of British-controlled Egypt.

Subsequently, he was part of a group that went to Russia after the 1917 revolution in the hope of attaining Bolshevik support.[27]

According to Indian Political Intelligence (IPI) records, Virendranath Chattopadhyaya was first recorded as having become involved in sedition in 1908 during his residence in Shyamaji Krishnavarma's India House in London. Chattopadhyaya was believed to have been in Germany on the outbreak of war and became head of the Berlin India Committee. In early 1915, he went to Switzerland where he tried to initiate contact with Indian revolutionaries in England. During 1915, he twice visited Constantinople in relation to the business of the Berlin India Committee before ultimately settling in Stockholm.[28] Indeed these wartime intrigues had wider resonances in the popular and literary imagination. Chattopadhyaya was portrayed by author and IPI agent William Somerset Maugham as Chandra Lal in the short story *Giula Lazzari* from the Ashenden Spy Series.[29] Maugham was based in Switzerland during the war period monitoring the movements of Chattopadhyaya as well as a host of other Indian and Egyptian subversives. Maugham, the character "Ashenden", is informed by his chief, the cold blooded and aloof "W" (inspired by the head of IPI, Sir John Arnold Wallinger) that Chandra Lal (Virendranath Chattopadhyaya) from Berlin is "the most dangerous conspirator in or out of India" adding that "he's done more harm than all the rest of them put together".[30]

As further evidence of the close parallels between fiction and reality Somerset Maugham also used his wartime experiences in Switzerland as inspiration for the character Grantley Cayper in one of his other short stories, *Traitor*. The character Cayper was based on the life of an Irishman, Gerald Gifford, associated with Irish nationalist circles in Berlin. Gifford was Irish on his mother's side, having been born in India, where his father was an army general. He too joined the army before working as a journalist in Cairo. Gifford spent the war years in Switzerland, having sided with the Central Powers.[31] It was there that he met Gaffney, who put him in contact with the Sinn Féin delegation who would attend the Paris Peace Conference in the aftermath of the war. Gifford wrote to Paris in the summer regarding his desire to "be doing something practical on behalf of Ireland" and offering to undertake publicity work in Berlin. He had seemingly found it difficult to "put myself forward" in the past. "Surrounded as I have been hitherto by small people, who appear to me to place self before cause, I have not had any congenial opportunities and could not well work in harmony with them".[32] George Gavan Duffy favoured making use of him, but his advice was not acted upon.

The representatives of the FOIF and the Berlin Committee collaborated to disseminate anti-British propaganda, issue regular communications and to assert their claim to independent statehood in the context of any post war settlement that would derive out of projected peace negotiations. In April 1918, the Stockholm Indian delegation sent a telegramme to the British Labour Party conference stating that

If you desire world to believe you honest in talk about freedom and democracy, put an end to regime of brutal exploitation by which you yourselves have for centuries kept in misery, ignorance and degradation millions of human beings in India, Ireland, Egypt etc. You cannot honestly demand that other nations liberate their subject races until you have liberated yours... We therefore call on you to take determined action to enforce independence of India, Ireland and Egypt.[33]

In January 1917, a German organised Conference of Oppressed Nationalities took place in Lausanne, Switzerland. The purpose of the conference was to bring about cooperation among the various nationalities oppressed by England and Russia, but not Germany. An eclectic mix of Irishmen, Indians and Egyptians represented the peoples oppressed by England while Lithuanians, Poles and Ukrainians represented the people oppressed by Russia. The DCI reported that the conference was not very successful, as "according to some Egyptian nationalists who were present the proceedings were quite devoid of interest".[34] This was mirrored by the similarly inspired Conference of Oppressed and Dependent Nationalities which took place in New York in February 1917. The DCI reported that:

A number of malcontents of various nationalities held a meeting in New York for the purpose of securing co-operation among those subject nations which wish to demand political independence after the war. Among the 'oppressed nations' are Scotland, Ireland, Wales, South Africa and India.[35]

Well-known Indian nationalists Lala Lajpat Rai and Narendra Nath Bhattacharya (also known as M. N. Roy) were reported to have been amongst those who attended.

The inclination to display "ideological promiscuity" was only surpassed by a hopelessly deluded message on behalf of the Berlin Committee to the ex-Khedive of Egypt, Abbas Hilmi, "congratulating him on his arrival in Germany and expressing the hope that the victory of the Central Powers would soon liberate the enslaved peoples of Egypt, India and Ireland".[36] Egyptian nationalist Mansur Rifaat despatched a note to Pope Benedict XV claiming that "India, Ireland, Egypt and Persia must be liberated from the British yoke".[37] An October DCI surveillance report on subversion carried out by Indian revolutionaries in Europe observed the following:

the two Indians intended to carry on their propaganda here for the oppressed nations in secret. They are trying to disseminate news of Indian conditions partly through pamphlets and other writings, partly through newspaper articles and other notices in the Press, but more especially through some publication which is to be sent to the whole

World's press and in which information is to be given concerning Indian opinion and the events there.[38]

In 1917, Chattopadhyaya and Acharya published a propaganda brochure entitled *Roger Casement und Indien* (Roger Casement and India), a hagiographical account of Casement and his sympathy for the oppressed people of India. In February 1918, the Postal Censor in Bombay intercepted several packages containing anti-British literature, including the Casement brochure, sent by M.P.T. Acharya in Stockholm to the militant nationalist V.V.S. Aiyar, who was living as a political exile in French-ruled Pondicherry.[39] In September 1918, the Postal Censor again intercepted copies of a letter addressed by the Lord Mayor of Dublin, Laurence O'Neill, to President Wilson. The copies were posted from Dublin and sent to the editors of various newspapers in India. The letter was described as an appeal to the American people against the application of conscription in Ireland and was said to contain a "violent and rhetorical style ... which would find special favour with the Indian Home Ruler".[40] Wartime censorship measures were implemented to curb the dissemination of subversive propaganda, anti-British literature and anything deemed likely to distract the allegiances of a subject population. An April 1919 intelligence report highlighted the extensive nature of this censorship regime which had continued throughout the war. John Devoy's *Gaelic American* was proscribed in the North-West Frontier Province and the Punjab under the 1910 Press Act.[41] Indo-Irish partnership was evident in the publication of *A Book about England and her oppressed peoples* in Swedish including chapters on India, Ireland and Egypt.[42] The chapter on Ireland was contributed by Chatterton-Hill. The declared aim of the book was to expose the insincere motivations behind Britain's war aims and the hypocrisy of fighting on behalf of small nations.

These seditious activities prompted the British legation in Stockholm to take action. In January 1918, the Consul General in Stockholm, Sir Esme Howard, initiated counter-propaganda proceedings against the "energetic anti-British campaign carried on by Indians, Egyptians and Sinn Féiners".[43] Howard expressed concern that the barrage of "false and misleading statements and exaggerations" from the circle of agitators who made a habit of "continually inserting their malicious statements in the Press". Howard underlined that the campaign of propaganda was "having its effect upon public opinion here, and that some antidote is most urgently needed."[44] Howard suggested that the Foreign Office translate into Swedish and send one hundred copies of Horace Plunkett's book *Ireland in the Twentieth Century* for distribution in Stockholm in order to counteract this propaganda. In addition, it was recommended that pro-British books and pamphlets on British rule in India and Egypt should be sent to Stockholm for sale. Under-Secretary at the Foreign Office, Hubert Montgomery, an Ulster Unionist from County Tyrone, despatched a pro-British, retired

ICS official, A. Yusuf Ali, from the London School of Oriental Studies to carry out a series of counter-propaganda measures. Montgomery's Irish identity demonstrates that, although most senior civil-servants would claim to remain above party politics, many became actively involved in emotive domestic issues.[45] A. Yusuf Ali was politically moderate with a "warm appreciation of the British Empire", who was believed to be satisfied by the piecemeal reforms of the British governance in India.[46] He delivered a series of public lectures highlighting the allegedly benign realities of British imperialism and published some articles in an effort to discredit and undermine the campaign of sedition and political agitation undertaken by the Indian nationalists in Stockholm. Chattopadhyaya replied that the Indian National Committee in Stockholm was a revolutionary body, similar to the Irish Sinn Féin, striving for the independence of India. According to Chattopadhyaya, the Indian revolutionaries were not anarchists. On the contrary, "every Indian who believes that the English dominion in India is an oppressive and unjust regime of foreign exploitation which must be put an end to, is a nationalist."[47] It is evident that Chattopadhyaya perceived the Irish and Indian causes as belonging to the same historical emancipatory objective. Regarding the issue of German support and financing, Chattopadhyaya issued a strong riposte, declaring that:

> The insinuation has so often been made, not only against us but also against the Sinn Feiners, Finns, Ukrainians and even against the Russian Bolsheviks, that we consider it may be of general interest to touch upon the matter. In the present war there are not only two belligerent camps, but also two corresponding camps of oppressed and subject nationalists. Owing to an entirely natural combination of circumstances, the oppressed nationalities of the Entente desire the defeat of their oppressors, while the nationalities oppressed by the Central Powers desire the victory of the Entente. We hold that the interests of all the oppressed nationalities are identical, and it is our personal opinion that there is no prospect of world peace until not only aggressive imperialism has been crushed but also the power of the capitalist and militarist classes has been broken. But under present conditions and for the moment we Indians have only one fight to fight and that is the fight for our national liberty ... during this war we cooperate, like the Sinn Feiners and the Egyptian nationalists openly and intentionally with the enemies of England.[48]

Thomas St. John Gaffney echoed this perception at a later date when referring to the pro-Allied bias of the Dutch-Scandinavian committee presiding over the Stockholm Peace Conference:

> That the socialist committee has manifested great zeal in the interest of those nations which are oppressed by the Germans and their allies, for

instance, the Bohemians, Poles, and Armenians but very little concern in regard to Ireland, India and Egypt.[49]

In this regard, Chattopadhyaya and Gaffney touched upon the reality of *realpolitik*. The First World War had witnessed not only the opening of a tripartite nexus between Germany, India and Ireland but also a corresponding set of sponsored alliances between Britain and the nascent nationalist movements under the hegemony of the Central Powers. Ironically, while Germany had embraced the cause of Indian, Irish and Egyptian liberation, the British supported the independence of Poland, Bohemia and Armenia.

In June 1917, Gaffney and Chatterton-Hill decided to attend the International Socialist Peace Conference which had been summoned to meet in Stockholm. The impetus to hold this conference was heightened by outbreak of the February Revolution in Russia and the American entry into the War in early April. The Belgian Secretary of the International Socialist Congress Camille Huysmanns issued the call for the conference in April 1917, but proceedings were immediately beset with difficulties and obstacles. To begin with, all Entente governments refused to issue passports to delegates intending to travel to Stockholm while communication between Sweden and the belligerent countries was made extremely difficult owing to destruction of infrastructure and pervasive censorship measures. Since the Irish Labour Syndicates and representatives of the Irish Political Unions of America were prohibited from travelling to the conference there was, according to Gaffney, extra motivation to attend in order to provide a voice for the Irish cause. However, in dialogue with Camille Huysmanns, the Irish delegates only managed to secure a nebulous status at the conference. Nonetheless, this allowed them to interact with an assortment of political movements including:

> parties of socialists from all parts of the world made their way to Stockholm; there came Austrians, Italians, Croatians, Bulgarians, Finlanders, Hungarians, Turks, Germans of the majority and minority parties, natives of Ireland, Flanders, Georgia, Ukraine, Persia and India. There were also representatives of the United States of America, Jews and Tartars.[50]

Evidently, participation in conference circles exposed Gaffney and Chatterton-Hill to a diverse array of experiences and narratives. It appears the conference attracted a wide plethora of causes. In 1917 Stockholm was fertile ground for disenfranchised nationalist leaders, oppressed ethnicities and pacifists as well as socialist ideologues. The Irish representatives made it a priority to get to know these delegates and increase their awareness of the multiple causes which sought to gain the attention of the executive committee of the International. In addition to the Indian National Committee, Gaffney and Chatterton-Hill were on cordial terms with representatives of

Persia, Egypt and Ukrainian nationalist parties who had also established headquarters in the Swedish capital. They were on close terms with a group of Native Americans who had travelled to Stockholm to participate.

Participation in conference circles also allowed the Irish delegates to disseminate propaganda in order to amplify awareness of the Irish struggle for independence. A memorandum dealing with the Irish question was written by Chatterton-Hill in the liberal internationalist language which typified the era and subsequently translated into German and Russian. One thousand copies were circulated in Russia and two thousand were mailed to important people in Sweden and other neutral countries. Numerous newspapers in Russia, Ukraine, Sweden and the Baltic countries printed extracts from the memorandum and published original articles dealing with the international importance of settling the Irish question.[51] Significantly, they managed to convince the conference executive committee to include the Irish question in its programme for the future peace. By the time their stay in Stockholm came to an end, Gaffney could boast that the Swedish press gave considerable publicity to articles dealing with the Irish question and that numerous interviews were printed in the leading papers. They were in receipt of many manifestations of sympathy and support from unexpected quarters, while "very effective propaganda work was also done in Norway and Denmark".[52]

The sympathy from unexpected quarters was an allusion to Dr Troelstra, a member of the new executive committee composed of three Dutchmen. Gaffney had several interviews with Troelstra during which they discussed the Irish question. Troelstra was evidently in favour of Irish independence. He demonstrated "the greatest sympathy with the cause of Irish freedom and indignation at the misrule to which [Ireland] had been subjected by the English". Another sympathiser of the Irish demand for self-determination was the Russian, Nicolas Roussanof, member of the Committee of the Socialist Revolutionary Party and editor of the propaganda organ, *L'oeuvre du peuple*. According to Gaffney, Roussanof professed himself to be an advocate of Sinn Féin, closely following the movement since its inception and was a deep sympathiser with its programme. Before the outbreak of the war he had advocated a similar organisation for Russia in a series of articles in his paper, but some of these had been suppressed and others modified by the Russian censor almost beyond recognition. "I am a friend of Ireland and Sinn Féin and will gladly enlist the support of my colleagues in the interest of your native land" was his assurance to Gaffney.[53] Not everyone at the conference was friendly to the Irish deputation. As would prove to be the case at the Paris Peace Conference in 1919, the Irish representatives found themselves at the mercy of wider international forces beyond their control. The Belgian members of the Socialist International, for example, were transparently anti-German, and to an extent pro-British, which made the Irish guilty by association. Emile Vandervelde, the Belgian Chairman of the Socialist International Union, refused to meet with Gaffney and Chatterton-Hill when they sought him out for an interview. Gaffney explained this refusal to pro-British pressures on Vandervelde and his hostility to any associations with Germany:

> In certain circles, however, there is a tendency to designate every person who has any kind of relation to Germany as a German agent. As soon as an Irishman, Persian, Finn or Egyptian appears they say in the neutral circles of the socialistic committee he is a German agent.[54]

In the end, the Socialist Peace Conference did not take place. After various postponements from May until autumn it was ultimately abandoned due to the non-arrival of the British and French socialists. However, a series of preliminary negotiations had taken place among the various delegates at the conference which caused disappointment for the Irish and Indian delegates when it emerged the deliberations of the planners of the projected conference had failed to include the issue of subject nationalities. The German delegation did in fact include India, Ireland, Egypt, Korea, Tripoli and Morocco in their plan to promote self-determination, although not from the perspective of a principled anti-imperialist stance.[55]

This chapter has demonstrated the existence of an Indo-Irish nexus and explored its spatial dimensions. Irish and Indian nationalists moved within a transnational milieu which facilitated the integration of hitherto disparate independence movements and sparked British fears about a collective anti-imperialist politics which, as they perceived it, represented a threat to imperial stability. The shared anti-imperialist identity and fraternisation between Irish and Indian agitators served to reinforce the respective claims of both independence movements. Throughout the course of the war British intelligence closely monitored the activities of Indian radicals as the latter sought to maximise the opportunities afforded by the war to instigate anti-imperialist rebellion. The intrigues of the German-sponsored Berlin India Committee and the Ghadar Party in America endeavoured to smuggle weapons into India with the aim of creating a mass uprising that would capitalise upon Britain's difficulties. In America, Irish republicans provided logistical and financial support to these efforts. In Stockholm, Irish and Indian activists came into contact and fraternised, and conferred legitimacy upon the respective claims to independence that both nationalist movements aspired to achieve. The kinds of connections and interactions described in this chapter were not transient. Instead, they represented continuities from earlier periods and indeed they outlasted the war itself. Within the context of World War I and the particular anti-imperial moment of 1916–1917, they assumed a new dimension in which both Irish and Indian nationalists thought about each other's struggle in mutually supportive terms.

Notes

1 Keith Jeffery, *The British Army and the Crisis of Empire 1918–1922* (Manchester, 1984), 1. See also, Philip Orr, "200,000 Volunteer Soldiers," in John Horne, ed., *Our War: Ireland and The Great War* (Dublin, 2008), 63.
2 Keith Jeffery, *1916: A Global History* (London, 2015), 4.
3 Jeffery, *1916*, 3.
4 Christopher Andrew, *The Defence of the Realm: The Authorized History of MI5* (London, 2010), 86.
5 Matthew E. Plowman, "Irish Republicans and the Indo-German Conspiracy of World War I," *New Hibernia Review* 7.3 (2003), 88.
6 Plowman, "Irish Republicans," 4.
7 Matthew E. Plowman, "The British Intelligence Station in San Francisco during the First World War," *Journal of Intelligence History* 12.1 (2013), 8.
8 Plowman, "Irish Republicans," 90.
9 Reports on the Annie-Larsen-Maverick episode can be found in the wartime Foreign Office (hereafter FO) records. See "Maverick" FO 371/2786. See also, No. 392, Memorandum, FO 371/3065, National Archives United Kingdom (hereafter NAUK).
10 "Note on the German-Indian Plots for the supply of arms to Indian revolutionaries," FO 371/2786, NAUK.
11 "Documents Relative to the Sinn Féin Movement," FO 115/2673, NAUK.
12 Plowman, "The British Intelligence Station," 9.
13 Plowman, "Irish Republicans," 82.
14 "Documents Relative to the Sinn Féin Movement," FO 115/2673, NAUK, 9.
15 Ibid., 28.
16 Jérôme aan de Wiel, *The Irish Factor 1899–1919: Ireland's Strategic and Diplomatic Importance for Foreign Powers* (Dublin, 2008), 307.
17 Aan de Wiel, *The Irish Factor*, 307. See also Thomas St. John Gaffney, *Breaking the Silence: England, Ireland, Wilson and the War* (New York, 1930).
18 "Documents Relative to the Sinn Féin Movement", FO 115/2673, NAUK, 29. See also, J. Balfour, comment on a file containing a letter from Lord Kilmarnock, British chargé d'affaires in Berlin, to the Foreign Office, 4 March 1921, FO 371/5969, NAUK.
19 Nirode K. Barooah, *Chatto: The Life and Times of an Indian Anti-Imperialist in Europe* (Oxford, 2004), 101.
20 Home Department Political Proceedings, "B" Series, "Weekly Report of the Director of Criminal Intelligence," 21 July 1917, No. 429, British Library (BL), India Office Records (IOR) NEGATIVE (NEG) 10513. See also Home Department Political Proceedings, "B" Series, "Weekly Report of the Director of Criminal Intelligence," 25 January 1919, BL, IOR NEG 10515. The Department of Criminal Intelligence was the central domestic and foreign intelligence organisation in India under the British Raj established in 1904. The DCI served as a repository of information received from other intelligence agencies abroad that were not under its direct control.
21 Home Department Political Proceedings, "B" Series, "Weekly Report of the Director of Criminal Intelligence," 20 October 1917, No. 469, BL, IOR NEG 10514. See also Virendranath Chattopadhyaya Papers, National Archives of India (NAI), "My Dear Padman," 2 April 1955, 3.
22 Home Department Political Proceedings, "B" Series, "Weekly Report of the Director of Criminal Intelligence," 20 October 1917, No. 469, BL, IOR NEG 10514.
23 Home Department Political Proceedings, "B" Series, "Weekly Report of the Director of Criminal Intelligence," 20 October 1917, No. 469, BL, IOR NEG 10514.

24 No 8 Biographical Notes on Revolutionaries, 1907–1917, 442, P. C. Joshi Archives, Jawaharlal Nehru University (JNU), New Delhi.

25 No. 3 Terrorists Who's Who – Compiled in the Office of the Director, Criminal Intelligence, January 1914, Home Department, Government of India, 204–5, P.C. Joshi Archives, JNU.

26 No 8 Biographical Notes on Revolutionaries, 1907–1917, 442, P. C. Joshi Archives, JNU.

27 Noor-Aiman I. Khan, *Egyptian-Indian Nationalist Collaboration and the British Empire* (New York, 2011), 139. IPI was an independent intelligence organization formally established as a consequence of the development of Indian nationalist activities abroad at the turn of the nineteenth century. IPI's role was essentially a "catch-all" coordinator of information about anything relating to India and to Indians within the empire and it relied heavily on MI5 and Secret Intelligence Services (SIS) reports to supplement this.

28 "Profile on Chattopadhyaya, Virendranath," BL, IOR/L/P&J/12/667/13393. See also, No. 8 Biographical Notes on Revolutionaries, 1907–1917, 407, P. C. Joshi Archives, JNU.

29 Richard J. Popplewell, *Intelligence and Imperial Defence: British Intelligence and the Defence of the Indian Empire, 1904–1924* (London, 1995), 227–28.

30 W. Somerset Maugham, *Ashenden: Or The British Agent* (London, 1928).

31 For biographical information on Gifford see Gerald Hamilton, *As Young as Sophocles* (London, 1939), 166, Gaffney to Victor Collins, 12 and 13 June 1919, John Devoy papers, NLI, MS 18,001(15), Gavan Duffy to Dublin, 30 March 1920 and 15 August 1920, Gavan Duffy papers, National Archives of Ireland (NAI), 1125/1.

32 Gavan Duffy to Dublin, 1125/1, 15 August 1920, Gavan Duffy papers, NAI, cited in, cited in, Jennifer O'Brien, *Separatist Ireland and Germany, 1919–1923* (Unpublished PhD dissertation, Trinity College Dublin, 2011), 36.

33 Home Department Political Proceedings, "B" Series, "Weekly Report of the Director of Criminal Intelligence," 13 April 1918, No. 24, IOR NEG 10514, BL.

34 Home Department Political Proceedings, "B" Series, No. 397–400, February 1917, PC Joshi Archives, Jawaharlal Nehru University (JNU). See also, Home Department Political Proceedings, "B" Series, "Weekly Report of the Director of Criminal Intelligence," 13 January 1917, IOR NEG 10512, BL.

35 Home Department Political Proceedings, "B" Series, "Weekly Report of the Director of Criminal Intelligence," 21 April 1917, IOR NEG 10513, BL.

36 For "ideological promiscuity" see Eunan O'Halpin, *The Geopolitics of Republican Diplomacy in the Twentieth Century* (Dublin, 2001), 3. For message to ex-Khedive Abbas Hilmi see, Home Department Political Proceedings, "B" Series, "Weekly Report of the Director of Criminal Intelligence," 7 December 1918, IOR NEG 10515, BL.

37 Home Department Political Proceedings, "B" Series, "Weekly Report of the Director of Criminal Intelligence," 5 January 1918, IOR NEG 10514, BL.

38 Home Department Political Proceedings, "B" Series, "Weekly Report of the Director of Criminal Intelligence," 20 October 1917, No. 469, IOR NEG 10514, BL.

39 Home Department Political Proceedings, "B" Series, "Weekly Report of the Director of Criminal Intelligence," April 1919, Nos. 192–95, IOR NEG 10515, BL.

40 Home Department Political Proceedings, "B" Series, "Weekly Report of the Director of Criminal Intelligence," 28 September 1918, No. 469, IOR NEG 10515, BL.

41 Home Department Political Proceedings, "B" Series, "Weekly Report of the Director of Criminal Intelligence," 20 October 1917, No. 469, IOR NEG 10514, BL.

42 Nirode K. Barooah, *Chatto: The Life and Times of an Indian Anti-Imperialist in Europe* (Oxford, 2004), 118.

43 No. 12465, Sir Esme Howard to Hubert Montgomery, 17 January 1918, FO 395/190, NAUK.

44 No. 11625, Sir Esme Howard to Hubert Montgomery, 9 January 1918, FO 395/190, NAUK.

45 Stephen Hartley, *The Irish Question as a Problem in British Foreign Policy, 1914–18* (London, 1987), 99.

46 FO 395/190, NAUK. See also, Nirode K. Barooah, *Chatto: The Life and Times of an Indian Anti-Imperialist in Europe* (Oxford, 2004), 127.

47 No. 114239, "Translation of Letter by Mr. Chattopadhyaya in Aftontidning," 29 May 1918, FO 395/190, NAUK.

48 No. 114239, "Translation of Letter by Mr. Chattopadhyaya in Aftontidning," 29 May 1918, FO 395/190, NAUK.

49 Thomas St. John Gaffney, *Breaking the Silence: England, Ireland, Wilson and the War* (New York, 1930), 223.

50 Gaffney, *Breaking the Silence*, 209.

51 Ibid., 212, 221.

52 Ibid., 235.

53 Ibid., 219, 221.

54 Ibid., 224.

55 Fritz Fischer, *Germany's Aims in the First World War* (London, 1967), 389.

10 From Dublin to Turgai

Discourses on Small Nations and Violence in the Russian Muslim Press in 1916

Danielle Ross

In 1910, Alibi Jangil'din, an ethnic Kirghiz (Kazakh) and a former student of the Moscow Ecclesiastical Academy set out on foot to St. Petersburg with a pair of good hiking boots, a felt hat, a camera and twenty-five rubles. Once he reached the Russian capital, he decided to undertake a longer walking journey. He headed to Warsaw, Cracow, through the Carpathian Mountains, and eastward through Austria-Hungary to the Ottoman Empire. In the next two years, he travelled by train, steamship and on foot through Egypt, the Sudan, the Levant, India, China, and Japan. He supported himself by selling postcards, taking pictures, and delivering lectures on his experiences. In 1912, he finally returned to Russia via Siberia. However, his travels were not yet over. Taking a Pathéscope K.O.K cine projector, 40 short films and a bedsheet wound around a wooden pole (to be used as a screen), he and his childhood friend, Amangeldy Imanov, wandered among the towns and herding camps of their native Turgai Province in the Kirghiz Steppe, holding cinema screenings accompanied by explanations of filming technology and lectures on the exploitation of workers around the world. Jangil'din's career as an itinerant projectionist came to an abrupt end in 1913. At the Yasawi shrine in the town of Turkistan, a popular Muslim pilgrimage destination in what is now southern Kazakhstan, the police surrounded the building where Jangil'din was holding a public screening. To avoid arrest, Jangil'din abandoned his projector and dove out the window.[1] He fled to Crimea and remained there until summer of 1916, when violence broke out in the governor-generalship of Turkestan and the Kirghiz steppe in response to the emperor's mobilisation order. Jangil'din returned to Turgai province, where he and Imanov took the lead in organising local rebels into an army.

In rebel leader Jangil'din's story of the 1916 Turgai Uprising, he emerges as a committed socialist, a world traveller, and a technophile, in short, someone very much aware of the events and debates of his day. Such international aspects have played little part in analyses of Russian Central Asian uprisings of 1916. Despite their scale, the uprisings have received little attention in general studies of World War I. In western-language scholarship on the revolts themselves, the 1916 uprisings have been largely subsumed into the study of the Russian Empire and its colonial policy. Edward Dennis Sokol's *The Revolt of 1916 in Russian Central Asia* focuses on how declining economic fortunes and mismanagement by Russian officials fu- elled the rage among colonial subjects that eventually burst forth in 1916.[2] Daniel Brower opens his study of Russian Turkestan with an account of the uprisings. He positions them as the outcome of Russia's failed colonial project.[3] Jörn Happel's *Nomadische Lebenswelten und zarische Politk: Der Aufstand in Zentralasien 1916* focuses specifically on how the seizure of nomads' pastureland and the arrival of Russian settlers in the steppe contributed to the revolt.[4] Brower similarly highlights the ethnic and colo- nial economic factors (nomadic Kirghiz vs. sedentary Russian) motivating violence and retribution during the revolt.[5] Jonathan Smele argues for the uprising not only as the death knell for Russian colonialism, but for the empire as a whole. He proposes that the revolt was the first act in a Russian civil war that continued until the mid-1920s.[6]

All of the studies discussed above measure the 1916 uprisings' significance in terms of what they reveal about Russian governance, and, not surpris- ingly, all of them draw their data primarily from Russian-language sources. Studies by western and Japanese scholars that examine Turkic-language sources from 1916 to 1917 tend to focus on the activities of the liberal democratic faction of the Kirghiz intelligentsia, a group that spoke out in opposition to the uprisings.[7] Two exceptions are Martha Olcott's *The Ka- zakhs*, which notes the participation of a small number of intellectuals in the rebellion, and Tomohiko Uyama's "Two Attempts at Building a Qazaq State", which argues for Jangil'din and Imanov's organisation during the uprising as an effort on the part of its leaders to form a quasi-state.[8] In Soviet-era Russian and Kazakh-language scholarship, historians viewed the uprisings through the lenses of anti-colonial and class struggle. In the post- 1991 period, the uprising has been recast as a national liberation movement and a precursor to the modern Central Asian nation states.

The uprisings in the Kirghiz steppe included a variety of actors, from the Russian-educated, German and English-speaking Jangil'din to impover- ished Kirghiz herdsmen, who could neither speak nor read Russian.[9] While anger over old and new insults by the imperial government may have driven Kirghiz nomads to take up arms in 1916, it was the ability of educated leaders to organise and channel that anger that enabled the more successful rebel groups to persist as long as they did. However, a consideration of the frameworks and sensibilities that rebel leaders brought to the uprising is largely absent from the existing western scholarship. This article attempts a partial reconstruction of the intellectual world in which Olcott's "maverick Kazakh intellectuals", (Kirghiz rebel leaders who had received their educa- tion in traditional Muslim seminaries or Russian schools), took part on the eve of the uprisings. In particular, it examines coverage of Ireland's Easter Rising of April 1916 in the three Russian Turkic papers published in closest proximity to Turgai Province, where Jangil'din and Imanov's rebellion, one of the best-organised of the uprisings in Russian Central Asia, took place.

The Easter Rising presents an intriguing case for several reasons. First, historians of Russia's Muslims have emphasised the tendency of Turkic-speaking Muslims in Russia to take particular interest in the condition of Muslim and Turkish populations in other parts of the world.[10] The Easter Rising was neither Russian nor Turkic nor Muslim nor Asiatic, and yet it provoked responses in all three papers, and it suggests Russian Muslim intellectuals' sense of belonging to yet another international community, that of small nations. This sense of kinship among small nations was not confined to the Muslim newspapers' reactions to the Irish case, but also found expression in Muslim intellectuals' participation in conferences on small nations' issues during World War I.[11] Second, an examination of the presentation of the Easter Rising in various Muslim newspaper reveals the regional and political rifts among educated Russian Muslims concerning the questions of empire, nation, and the permissibility of using violence in the pursuit of national ends. This helps to situate Muslim rebel intellectuals within the broader milieu of their society and consider whether their views were as divergent as their exclusion from studies of the Muslim and Kirgiz intelligentsia would suggest. Third, while there is no evidence that rebel leaders in Turgai or elsewhere in Central Asia claim to have been directly inspired by events in Dublin, Muslim newspapers did draw explicit and implicit parallels between the Irish case and their own. When it came to the practical business of planning and organising an uprising, there are also interesting similarities between the two rebellions that suggests broader patterns in small nation politics and anti-imperial revolts during World War I.

The *Star* (*Ioldyz*) was founded in Kazan in 1906 and was published by Òmid Press. It appeared three times per week until its closure in June of 1918.[12] The paper identified itself as "a paper beholden to no political party". However, the *Star's* owner and head editor, Ahmad Hadi Maqsudi was the elder brother of State Duma member Sadreddin Maqsudi, a member and active promotor of Russia's Constitutional Democratic (Kadet) party.[13] Although leftist writers such as Gabdulla Tukai, Majit Gafuri and Galimjan Ibrahimov published in the *Star*, the paper's overall political profile was liberal democratic and Turko-Tatar nationalist.[14] The *Star* claimed to speak to and for all of the Muslims of the empire. However, much of its content focused on debates and events in Russia's Volga-Ural region.[15]

In 1906, the *Star* was one of three Turkic-language newspapers published in Kazan. However, the other two, the *Kazan Messenger* (*Qazan Mòkhbire*) and *The Foundation of Truth* (*Bayan ul-Haqq*), closed in 1910 and 1914 respectively, leaving the *Star* as the only Turkic-language newspaper in Kazan during World War I.[16]

The Easter Rising received front-page coverage in the *Star* for one day on 2 May (20 April), three days after rising had ended.[17] That coverage occupied less than three columns, each of them a length of less than half a page. The anonymous author characterised the participants in the uprising as "creators of disorder" (*fitnachelar*), who had seized control of several Dublin factories and a train station, forcing the British troops to fire upon them and arrest them.[18] In the midst of this outbreak, "base sorts of people who had come [to join] the movement robbed some of the city's [Dublin's] major stores".[19] While the author failed to offer any explanation of the participants' motivations, he devoted nearly half of his article to discussing the Germans' involvement in the affair, reconstructing in detail the sea route of the failed German arms delivery to the rebels.[20]

There was no follow-up to this article, either to expand on the information given or to provide resolution. The outbreak had occurred, it had been put down and it was finished, which was for the best, in the opinion of the article's author. As portrayed in the *Star*, the Rising was a story of unnamed and "base" subjects putting their empire in jeopardy by rioting, looting and colluding with the enemy in the middle of the War.

The apparent aversion of the *Star*'s writers to small nations taking up arms armed against their imperial government was not limited to the Irish case. It had found expression several years earlier, as the paper's writers had looked with dismay upon the growing aggression of the Balkans League. This dismay was inspired not only by the fact that the Balkans nations laid claim to Ottoman territory, but by their apparently insatiable appetite for territory and by the support that their territorial claims received from various European powers. To the *Star*'s writers, this situation created perpetual chaos (*fitna*) in southeastern Europe that had the potential to destabilise the broader international order.[21] As one of the *Star*'s writer had noted in 1913, in relation to growing European entanglement in the Balkans, "if a war starts in Europe, by the next day, trade and commerce would be ruined".[22]

Thus, while the editors and writers of the *Star* generally wrote strongly in favour of the development of national culture (*milli mădăniyyat*) and national literature (*milli ădăbiyyat; Tatar ădăbiyyaty*), they simultaneously remained acutely conscious of the ties the bound them both to the Russian Empire and to neighbouring Europe. Their outlook and circumstances were not such as to make armed rebellion seem appealing and they were quick to decry national groups who employed violence to achieve their ends.

The *Times* (*Vaqıt*) was founded in Orenburg in 1906 by Shakir and Zakir Ramiev, brothers who had made their fortune running a gold mine in the South Urals.[23] The *Times* began as a tri-weekly paper, but, by 1913, it had become a daily.[24] The paper's owners and editors defined it as "a national organ for all of the Muslims of eastern Russia, Central Asia and Siberia".[25] Although it had a print run of only 2,500 copies, it boasted subscribers and contributors from across the empire. Outside of Orenburg and Kazan, it proved particularly popular in Muslim communities in Siberia, the Kirghiz steppe, Turkestan and the Russia-Chinese borderlands, which lacked well-developed local publishing industries.[26] Also, while the *Star*'s international coverage often focused on the Ottoman Empire and Europe, the *Times* also gave attention to events on the southern and eastern frontiers of the Russian empire, including East (Chinese) Turkestan, the Ili

Valley, and the political situation in China after the overthrow of the Qing dynasty in 1911.[27]

In addition to Orenburg Tatar merchants, townsmen, and peasants, the *Times'* subscribers included educated members of nomadic Kirghiz and Bashkir society as well as Muslim merchants and political dissidents living in the Russian-Chinese trade towns of Kulja and Chawchak. The fact that the *Times* enjoyed a more diverse audience than the *Star* meant that, despite the fact that Alexandre Bennigsen and Chantal Lemercier-Quelquejay identify both publications as liberal and progressive, the two papers sometimes took quite different stances on the same issues.

The *Times* began its coverage of the Easter Rising on 28 April (15 April), a day before the surrender of the Rising's participants. Instead of starting with a description of the uprising, it began with a history of Ireland:

> Though Ireland is a part of Great Britain, there are many there who would demand to be out from under British rule. In its own history and in its present condition, Ireland has many reasons to be dissatisfied with England, and being dissatisfied, it has thought to try to break away [from Great Britain] in order to achieve its own desires.[28]

The article went on to explain English-Irish relations to its readers, beginning with the tenth century when it claimed that Ireland had been forced to recognise English rule and then jumping forward in time to Elizabeth I's attempts to enforce Anglicanism upon Ireland's Catholics, supposedly forcing "most" to flee to America. The paper related that those Irish Catholics who remained in their homeland were denied representation in Parliament and faced other oppression because of their faith. It then turned to a discussion of the arrival of the English lords, who "took" Irish land and subsequently enriched themselves by renting it to Irish farmers.[29] The second half of the article chronicled nineteenth-century British concessions to Irish demands for Home Rule and the various "Irish congresses", highlighting repeatedly the limits of the British government's willingness to relinquish control over Ireland. It ended with the split between those Irish who chose to support Britain in World War I and those who saw the war as an opportunity to attain independence. The last lines addressed Germany's agreement to arm the pro-independence faction. Here, unlike in the *Star*, German intervention was portrayed as a logical conclusion of Great Britain's history of mistreatment of its national-confessional minority.[30]

This first article set the tone for the rest of the *Times'* coverage of the uprising. That tone was extremely specific to the Orenburg region. The Irish were presented as a once-independent ethnic group conquered, oppressed on the basis of their religion and dispossessed of their land by their conquerors. Though their imperial masters had subsequently permitted them certain institutions and rights, those masters still stopped short of granting them their full equality and autonomy; they remained second-class citizens within a multi-ethnic empire. The *Times'* summary may not have been the most accurate portrayal of Irish history, but it would have been highly familiar to the *Times'* educated Kirgiz readers, for whom the questions of loss of political independence, seizure of grazing lands by the Russian state, lack of political representation and pressure to convert to Orthodox Christianity formed the core of their grievances toward the Russian government. The anonymous writer of the *Times'* article of 28 April (15 April) "In Relation to the Disorder in Ireland" both summarised the issues confronting Kirghiz subjects of the Russian empire and positioned the Irish rebels as primarily sympathetic actors by drawing implicit connections between their plight and that of a particular segment of the *Times'* readers.

On 30 April (17 April), the day after it had ended, the Easter Rising remained on the front page of the paper as part of an article relating all of the disasters that had recently befallen Britain: setbacks in the Middle East, the approach of the German Navy to England's west coast and, finally, the uprising (*ikhtilal*) in Ireland. As in the *Star*, the author writing for the *Times* labeled the uprising's participants as "rebels" (*ikhtilalchelar*). The German involvement in the uprising was also discussed. However, the ordering of events and the emphasis in the *Times'* presentation were significantly different. The German naval manoeuvres were presented ahead of the discussion of the uprising and not immediately connected to it. In fact, the author laid the blame for the breach of coastal security at the feet of the British Navy itself, noting that: "The English Navy *let the Germans get close and let them stay there* for about half an hour. The reasons for this remain unknown".[31] In the latter part of the article, after a description of conditions in Dublin, the author finally returned to the question of the boat loaded with weapons that had been intercepted and was traced back to a German cruiser, but he did not seem to blame either the Germans or the Irish rebels for the incident.[32] Whereas the *Star* had emphasised the illegitimate activities of the "rioters", the *Times* focused much more upon the Parliament, its reactions to the crisis, and the ramifications of the uprising for the British Isles as a whole. The activities of the rebels were barely discussed, save that they had "occupied several large buildings" and engaged in armed conflict with the British authorities.[33]

The *Times* continued its coverage of the Irish uprising on 3 May (20 April), though the subject was now relegated to the second page. It reported not only that the uprising had come to an end, but how it had ended: the British government had sent out a call, by way of the "police and clergymen", for participants to surrender and, in Dublin, 707 individuals had complied. The link between the German naval presence off Britain and German intentions to smuggle arms to the Irish rebels was now made explicit, though instead of ending on that note, the author used the German presence as a pretext to paraphrase a claim from the German press that the uprising had been supported not only by Sinn Féin, but by all of

Ireland and "not only poor people supported the Irish uprising; rich people backed it as well".[34]

The *Times'* turn to the German press for information marked a new phase in the newspaper's coverage of this event. The uprising was at an end, but the analysis had only just begun. The *Times* now gave a full account of the disorder (*tertipsezlek*), supposedly basing its narrative upon a combination of reports taken from Reuters and the German press. This lengthy article laid out the process of the Dublin uprising, including such details as the participants' targeting of police and army officers, their seizure of strategic buildings around the city, and the cutting all of the telegraph and telephone lines.[35] It provided equally vivid descriptions of the uprising's participants, including details such as wardrobe and gender:

> Beside each man walked a women dressed in military clothing. These women went along, carrying sacks of bullets in their hands and, during the battle, and they stood handing the men ammunition.[36]

The *Times'* portrayal of the Irish rebels was much more ambiguous than the depictions given in the *Star*. The author of the 3 May (20 April) article repeatedly emphasised the negative characteristics of the rebels' adversaries. He described how opponents of the Rising had gathered in the street outside of the General Post Office, but failed to act because "the rebels had scared them".[37] While he admitted that the rebels had committed violent acts such as "killing some dogs" and "wounding some soldiers and civilians" he drew repeated attention to the British soldiers' and police's use of excessive force (in the form of bombs and mortars) against rebel-occupied buildings. The looting of Dublin's stores, attributed in the *Star* to people who had come to take part in the Rising was attributed in the *Times* to the town's "dark masses" (*qara khalyq*), not associated with the Rising, who took advantage of the confusion caused by the fight to enrich themselves. Through these criticisms and revisions, the *Times'* portrayal of the Rising began to shift the responsibility for the destruction wrought in Dublin from the rebels to the British government and disorderly elements in the urban population.

That shift was continued in the 6 May (23 April) issue of the paper. It began with the trial of the Rising's leaders before a military court, but quickly shifted focus to discuss the rebels' goal of breaking away from the British Empire and the declaration of the provisional Irish Republic. For the information in the article, the author claimed to have relied on British newspapers, and, particularly, the *Daily Mail*. Again, as had been the case with the description of the attempted seizure of Dublin in the article from 3 May (20 April), the process of declaring a national republic, from "distributing flyers in all directions" to appointing a president to how exactly the promised German arms had failed to reach the rebels, was laid out in detail.[38] The article also included a statement from Easter Rising leader Patrick Pearse (taken from the British press and translated into Tatar) explaining that the Rising's participants had represented the independent republic of Ireland and that they had only surrendered because they had been hopelessly outmanned and outgunned by the British army.[39] The article ended by returning to the question of how widespread the support for the Rising had been, noting that "millions" of Irish men and women in the British Empire and America supported Irish independence and the main division had been between those who wanted to break away from the Empire during the war and those who saw wartime as an inopportune moment to pursue national independence. The former group had sent money to support their "holy warriors" (*mujahidlar*) as they set out to overthrow British rule.[40] As in the earlier articles, any time that the author strayed into potentially controversial territory, he credited the information to various European newspapers. For readers, this strategy may have added an air of legitimacy and objectivity to the information. It also enabled the author (or authors) to disavow responsibility in the face of wartime censorship; in effect, they were not expressing his own opinion, but merely repeating already-acknowledged "facts" reported in the European press. As can be seen in a comparison with the coverage in the *Star*, however, even if the authors were quoted and paraphrased from other newspapers, they also chose what to present and how to present it. These choices shaped the view of events that readers received.

The *Times'* coverage of the Easter Rising continued until 11 May (28 April) and ended with a summation of an official statement from the British government reporting that the Rising had been put down, communications with Dublin had been restored, and Pearse, leader of the revolt and a signatory of the Proclamation of the Irish Republic, had been executed. The other signatories had been arrested and awaited the same fate. The article ended with military governor General Sir John Maxwell's praise to the British soldiers for the bravery they had shown in putting down the uprising.[41]

The 11 May (28 April) report was situated among coverage of various fronts of the War. However, it also shared the page with an article entitled "Government, Religion, and Nation". This was the latest entry in Jamaladdin Validi's study of the origins and nature of nations and nationalism. It discussed the role of language and literature in creating coherent national identities in European empires such as Germany and Austria-Hungary.[42] The proximity of these issues – the progress of the war, small-nations uprisings, discussions of the roots of nationalisms in European empires suggests how interwoven they had become in the *Times* by 1916 and the World War I period.

The journal *Qazaq* was established in Orenburg in 1913. It began as a weekly paper, but became bi-weekly by 1915.[43] It editors, Mustafa Urazaev and Ahmad Baitursynov were ethnic Kirghiz, but, like many Kirghiz publications, the paper was printed by a Tatar press, the Karimov and Khussainov Printing House.[44] Its print run ranged between 3,000 at the time of its debut and 8,000 copies in its later year.[45] The journal remained in print until March of 1918. In contrast to the *Times*, which was marketed to a Muslim audience across Russia, *Qazaq* was targeted to an ethnic Kirghiz (Kazakh) audience and was written with orthography and lexical items that made its language more closely resemble the Kirghiz vernacular. *Qazaq's* main mission was the promotion of Kirghiz national culture and political literacy. To this end, it presented readers with a combination of news, political commentary, didactic and educational articles, and poetry. Popular topics in the pages of *Qazaq* included the seizure of nomadic grazing land by Slavic settlers and the Russian state, the need to improve native education, women's rights, and the problem of Kirghiz representation (or lack thereof) in the Russian State Duma.

Of the three newspapers examined, *Qazaq* covered the Easter Rising the latest and the least. The only mention of the Rising occurred on 7 May (24 April), well after it had ended. That coverage was slipped into two paragraphs at the end of a brief section entitled "The War", which provided information on events across the various fronts. It was placed at the end of a long list of recent misfortunes to befall Britain.

> The Germans have fired poison gas at England's troops and put them in difficulty. The Germans have also robbed the English of peace in their own land. In the daytime, they send zeppelins and drop bombs and these have caused great damage to the buildings. And they have not just sent the zeppelins, but warships and the Germans cause trouble, putting the English cities on the coast under fire and killing people. On top of this, Ireland, which is under English rule, staged an uprising (*bunt*).[46]

After this introduction, the final paragraph of the section briefly explained the context of the Irish uprising, informing the reader that "England, Ireland and Scotland were once three kingdoms each under its own rule". Then, England had brought the other two under its rule and the Irish, being dissatisfied with this, "fought many struggles to gain self-rule"[47] They had awaited England's granting of this self-rule before the War, but then the War began and the question was not resolved. Finally,

> As was sometimes Ireland's custom, it understood that England was in a difficult situation. Being armed for war, they said "In this difficult situation, England's neck will be broken. Let Ireland take what it needs."[48]

At first glance, *Qazaq's* coverage of the uprising seems to fall at a point somewhere between that of the *Star* and the *Times*. Like the *Times*, it placed the uprising within a historical context of lost independence and unfulfilled demands for self-rule. However, the emphasis on religious oppression, colonial relations and political disempowerment prominent in the *Times'* coverage was absent in *Qazaq*. So, too, was any mention of liberal democratic, parliamentary politics, or, for that matter, of the modern nation. In *Qazaq*, Ireland was introduced as a kingdom [*karol jurty*] engaged in ongoing hostility with another kingdom, England. With this description of British-Irish relations, *Qazaq* managed to exclude the historical details that had made the rebels sympathetic actors in the *Times'* coverage. Moreover, by placing the Rising beside German suffocation of English soldiers with gas and German bombing of civilian targets, *Qazaq's* coverage not only conditioned the reader to sympathise with the English, but implied that the uprising was an equally immoral and horrific act. This suggestion became explicit by the end of the article, when the author not only stated that the rebels had knowingly exploited their empire's weakness, but had "had words" with the Germans, (their empire's wartime enemies), before doing so. This gave the appearance that the rebels had set out to cripple their empire in the face of a direct enemy attack.

When this article appeared, a lively debate was already underway in the paper over whether Kirghiz men should be recruited to fight in World War I and, if so, under what conditions. (Until June 1916, the Kirghiz were exempted from the draft.) This debate intersected with questions about the relationship between the Russian government and its Kirghiz subjects and what concessions each side should or should not make to the other. With the larger issues looming behind the mobilisation question – the loss of pastureland to Russian settlers, exclusion from the State Duma since 1907, the division of the Kirghiz people over multiple administrative jurisdictions, and the inferior legal status of Islam in Russia – the compression of the Irish problem into a few sentences was not accidental. As the *Times* had drawn implicit parallels between Ireland and the steppe by highlighting certain Irish grievances, *Qazaq's* editors avoided the discussion by leaving them out and offering an unflattering portrayal of a people who committed violence against their imperial ruler. It also condemned, by extension, the numerous unsuccessful Kirghiz rebellions of the nineteenth century. This stance re-enforced the liberal editors' view that the Kirghiz would obtain political and cultural rights through education and democratic process rather than violence.

In June 1916, two months after the Easter Rising, the Russian government called for the mobilisation of male steppe Kirghiz and Turkestanis between the ages of 19 and 43. The new recruits were supposed to fill support positions at the rear, freeing up more reliable Russian troops to be sent to the front. However, poor organisation and lack of communication during the announcement of the draft gave rise to rumours that they would be sent to the trenches without weapons. By early July, recruitment lists in Turkestan were seized and destroyed. Young men went into hiding or fled into the steppe, and, in some districts, recruitment officials were attacked and killed.[49]

In July 1916, Jangil'din was still in Crimea. His friend, Imanov sent him a letter informing him of the mobilisation and the resulting protests and asking what should be done. Jangil'din instructed him to begin organising people in his province while he set out for Turgai, taking a film projector with him.[50] Upon arriving, he organised a war council with Imanov and the leaders of several thousand rebels from the Argyn and Kipchak tribes (*ru*), who had organised themselves into an army. Together they laid plans for how to capture the town of Turgai.[51] After a direct assault on the town failed, a smaller force entered the city in secret, with the goal of seizing control of the main post office, the other official buildings and the arsenal.[52] Despite occupying about a third of the town, most of Jangil'din's men were still poorly armed, and the Russian garrison defending the town forced the Kirghiz to withdraw. Though the rebels failed to take Turgai, Jangil'din viewed the effort to occupy the town as the true beginning of the uprising.[53]

Still lacking adequate weapons and supplies, Jangil'din and his men withdrew into the steppe to regroup. They formed a government consisting of a khan and twelve ministers. This new government set about recruiting blacksmiths and craftsmen to produce and repair weapons, securing horses and supplies, and sending out agitators with declarations in the Kirghiz language on the formation of the new, independent state. The rebels' ranks soon swelled to 20,000 men.[54]

Not everyone in Russia's Muslim communities reacted as enthusiastically to the uprising as Jangil'din did. In the Turkic-language press, the coverage of the Easter Rising proved a reliable indicator for how Muslim newspapers reacted to events in Central Asia. In Kazan, far from the Central Asian uprisings, the *Star* offered little coverage of the revolts and referred to the Kirghiz and Turkestani populations as *inorodtsy*, the term used by the Russian government to refer to many of its non-Russian subjects. The use of this term not only ignored the differences among the various peoples affected by the 1916 mobilisation, but reinforced the legal and cultural hierarchy between subjects of the empire who enjoyed greater legal and political rights, (a category in which the *Star's* Tatar editor and writers included themselves) and the colonial Central Asian Other.

The *Times* provided ongoing coverage of events in Turkestan and the steppe from August through the end of 1916. In addition, during the same period, they published a series of letters from writer Shakir Mukhamed'iarov, documenting his travels through Turkestan during the August 1916. Even when not focusing directly on the uprisings and their causes, the letters provided a humanising narrative; Turkestan was complex region populated by friendly and mostly reasonable people, not by savages and fanatics.[55] As it had in its coverage of the Easter Rising, the *Times* gave much more attention to local grievances and the specifics of regions and peoples. It referred to the participants in the uprising as Turkestanis and Kirghiz rather than *inorodtsy*. This interest in detail and, possibly, excessive sympathy for the uprising participants eventually put the *Times* into conflict with the wartime censorship regulation with the result of some articles having as much as half of their content cut before the final printing.[56] Despite their coverage of the uprisings, however, the *Times* did not go so far as to express support for open rebellion. On 21 July (8 July), the paper directly addressed the Kirghiz in Turgai Province, informing them that the Russian government had issued a declaration clarifying that Kirghiz recruits would not be sent into combat, but only assigned to work in the reserves and at the rear. The declaration pointed out that the other peoples of the Empire had sent their husbands, fathers and sons to defend the fatherland, and the Kirgiz needed to do their part as well. Their "ignorance of Russian language and European culture" was no excuse for exemption from their duty to their emperor.[57] Most of the article was a direct translation of the declaration from Russian into Turkic, but it posed a question than must have been on the minds of Orenburg's Muslims: The Tatars and Bashkirs of Orenburg Province had been sending their men into combat for two years. Why should the Kirghiz in neighbouring Turgai Province not do the same?

Qazaq had provided minimal and negative coverage of the Easter Rising. However, with the Kirghiz and Turkestani uprisings on their own doorstep, *Qazaq's* writers could not readily dismiss the complaints and demands made by their own readership, and the newspaper published letters and articles that highlighted abuses in the mobilisation process. At the same time, it tried to maintain an overall narrative of the steppe as part of the Russian Empire and the uprisings as part of a conflict that could be resolved through cooperation and mutual understanding between Russian officials and Kirghiz society. This rhetoric reached its apex in the announcement that General A.N. Kuropatkin would be arriving in Turkestan. With his previous employment under M. D. Skobelev in Central Asia and his service in the Russo-Japanese war, "soft" Kuropatkin, who "administered the country by means of cultured laws", was characterised as the perfect person to restore peace to the steppe.[58]

Land seizures, growing gaps between the wealthy and the poor, lack of political representations and corruption by local officials fed the anger and frustration that found expression in the Kirghiz and Turkestani uprisings of 1916. However, these uprisings also took place in the midst of a world war and against a background of international debates over the destiny of small nations and their relationship to great empires. An examination of the coverage of the Easter Rising in Russian Muslim newspapers demonstrates that lack of knowledge of Russian or western European languages was no barrier to following the small nations issue. With basic literacy in their native language or a literate friend or neighbour, Tatar, Bashkir and Kirghiz subjects of the empire could receive detailed news of events in Europe within a few days of those events' occurrence.

Within the newspapers themselves, writers not only reported international events such as the Easter Rising, but, rather, wove them into local discussions of nationhood and colonial relations, and, in the process drew explicit and implicit parallels between the plight of Russia's minorities and that of colonised and minority groups around the world. By the time the Central Asian uprisings began in summer of 1916, Muslim intellectuals had developed a sophisticated and multi-vocal discourse on nation, empire and how politics between imperial governments and their minorities were to be carried out. For those intellectuals who sought a peaceful resolution to Russia's fraught relationship with its Muslim minorities, this discourse served a bulwark against violence: the destructiveness, immorality, and ultimate futility of armed resistance was demonstrated through other nations' failed uprisings. For, others, such as Jangil'din, the discourse invested local conflicts with deeper significance: by taking up arms, seizing control of a town and forming their own government the Kirghiz rebels of Turgai joined the ranks of other oppressed and marginalised groups in opposing their colonial oppressors and asserting their right to national independence.

That is not to say that the Turgai Uprising was the "national liberation struggle" that modern Kazakh historians have characterised it as, but, rather, that Jangil'din and other literate men who joined the rebel forces possessed the intellectual frameworks and access to international news to interpret it as such. Nor do I wish to suggest that, as Jangil'din planned the attack on Turgai, he consciously recreated the events of the Easter Rising. Rather, the commonalities between the two movements suggest the existence of models, ideals and rituals in anti-imperialist revolt and state-founding that transcended national and imperial borders and that lent a consistency to many of the protests and uprisings of World War I.

Notes

1 Alibi Dzhangil'din, "Moi Put'," *Alibi Dzhangil'din: Dokumenty i materialy* (Almaty, 2009) 18–32.
2 Edward Dennis Sokol, *The Revolt of 1916 in Russian Central Asia*, 2nd ed. (Baltimore, MD, 2016).
3 Daniel Brower, *Turkestan and the Fate of the Russian Empire* (London and New York, 2003).
4 Jörn Happel, *Nomadische Lebenswelten und zarische Politk: Der Aufstand in Zentralasien 1916* (Stuttgart, 2010).
5 David Brower, "Kyrgyz Nomads and Russian Pioneers: Colonization and Ethnic Conflict in the Turkestan Revolt of 1916," *Jahrbücher für Geschichte Osteuropas* 44 (1996), 41–53.
6 Jonathan Smele, *The "Russian" Civil Wars, 1916–1926: Ten Years that Shook the World* (Oxford, 2016).
7 Tomohiko Uyama, "The Alash Orda's Relations with Siberia, the Urals, and Turkestan: The Kazakh National Movement and the Russian Imperial Legacy," in Tomohiko Uyama, ed., *Asiatic Russia: Imperial Power in Regional and International Contexts* (London and New York, 2012) 271–287; Pete Rottier, "Creating the Kazak Nation: The Intelligentsia's Quest for Acceptance in the Russian Empire, 1905–1920," PhD diss., University of Wisconsin-Madison, 2005; Ayse Deniz Balgamis, "The Origins and Development of Kazakh Intellectual Elites in the Pre-Revolutionary Period," PhD diss., University of Wisconsin-Madison, 2000.

8 Martha Brill Olcott, *The Kazakhs*, 2nd ed. (Stanford, 1995) 118–25; Tomohiko Uyama, "Two Attempts to Build a Qazaq State: The Revolt of 1916 and the Alash Movement," in Stéphane A. Dudoignon and Hisao Komatsu, eds., *Islam in Politics in Russia and Central Asia (Early Eighteenth to Late Twentieth Centuries)* (London, 2001), 77–98.

9 Dzhangil'din, "Moi Put'," 35, 42.

10 James Meyers, *Turks across Worlds: Marketing Muslim Identity in the Russian-Ottoman Borderlands, 1865–1914* (Oxford, 2014); Cemil Aydin, *The Politics of Anti-Westernism in Asia: Visions of a World Order in Pan-Islamic and Pan-Asian Thought* (New York, 2007).

11 Salavat Iskhakov, "Muslim Political Activity in Russian Turkestan, 1905–1916," in Uyama, ed., *Asiatic Russia*, 247.

12 Alexandre Bennigsen and Chantal Lemercier-Quelquejay, *La Presse et la Mouvement National chez les Musulmans de Russie avant 1920* (Paris, 1964), 67; Ismăgyil Rămi and Răis Dautov, *Ădăbi süzlek* (Kazan, 2001) 116.

13 Rămi and Dautov, *Ădăbi süzlek*, 157–58; Bennigsen and Lemercier-Quelquejay, *La Presse*, 67.

14 Rămi and Dautov, *Ădăbi süzlek*, 115–16; Bennigsen and Lemercier-Quelquejay, *La Presse*, 68.

15 See, for example, "Bez Tatar tugel!," *Ioldyz* 3 (1906), 1; Gainetdin Akhmerov, "Tatarcha – Türkchä – Musulmancha," *Ioldyz* 6 (1906), 1.

16 Rămi and Dautov, *Ădăbi süzlek*, 47, 119; Bennigsen and Lemercier-Quelquejay, *La Presse*, 67, 70–72.

17 All dates in the newspapers discussed here are from the Julian calendar, which was in use in Russia until 1918. All dates in this article will be given according to the Gregorian calendar first and then according to the Julian calendar (in parentheses).

18 "Irlandiyada," *Ioldyz*, 20 April 1916, 1.

19 Ibid.

20 Ibid.

21 "Nishliylăr?" *Ioldyz*, 3 January 1913, 1; H.M. "Ni bulachaq?," *Ioldyz*, 10 January 1913, 1.

22 "Sugysh vă aqcha," *Ioldyz*, 7 January 1912, 1.

23 Rămi and Dautov, *Ădăbi süzlek*, 60, 82; Bennigsen and Lemercier-Quelquejay, *La Presse*, 72.

24 Bennigsen and Lemercier-Quelquejay, *La Presse*, 72.

25 Ibid., 73.

26 Bennigsen and Lemercier-Quelquejay, *La Presse*, 73, 148; In the towns of the steppe and Turkestan, there were relatively few publishing houses. Those that existed were closely regulated by the imperial government. Many of the 900 Kirghiz-Qazaq titles that appeared in the early 1900s were sent for publication to printing houses in Kazan and Orenburg and the finished books were shipped to the steppe. Writers from the steppe and Turkestan also published letters and articles in Kazan and Orenburg's Turkic-language newspapers (Adeeb Khalid, *The Politics of Muslim Cultural Reform: Jadidism in Central Asia* (Berkeley, CA, 1998) 85–89; Zh. Shalgynbai, *Istoriia kazakhskoi knizhnoi kul'tury (XIX v.-1917 g. – 1991–2001 gg.)* (Almaty: "Baspalar uiy, 2009), 129–61). While copies of the *Times* have not survived well down to the twenty-first century, copies of the newspaper's literary-cultural supplement, *Shura*, can be found today in the book collections held at mosques and museums in steppe towns such as Semey (Semipalatinsk).

27 See, for example, "Qytai musulmannarynyng taliby," *Vaqyt*, 25 May 1912, 1; "Ili wilayaty waqigalary," *Vaqyt*, 19 April 1912, 3.

28 "Irlandiyadagy tertipsezlek mönasãbãtelã," *Vaqyt*, 15 April 1916, 1.
29 "Ibid.
30 Ibid.
31 "Ingletara vaqiygalary," *Vaqyt*, 17 April 1916, 1 [emphasis added by author].
32 Ibid.
33 "Irlandiya ikhtilaly," *Vaqyt*, 20 April 1916, 2.
34 Ibid.
35 "Irlandiyya tertipsezlekãre khaqynda tãfsyilat," *Vaqyt*, 22 April 1916, 2.
36 Ibid.
37 Ibid.
38 "Irlandiya Ikhtilaly," *Vaqyt*, 23 April 1916, 2.
39 Ibid.
40 Ibid.
41 "Irlandiyya ikhtilaly," *Vaqyt*, 28 April 1916, 2.
42 Jamal al-Din Validi, "Khokumat, din, va millat," *Vaqyt*, 28 April 1916, 2.
43 "Qazaq," *Alash Orda: Entsiklopediia* (Almaty, 2009) 206.
44 Bennigsen and Lemercier-Quelquejay, *La Presse*, 152.
45 Bennigsen and Lemercier-Quelquejay, *La Presse*, 152; "Qazaq," *Alash Orda*, 206.
46 "Sogys," *Qazaq* 178, 23 April 1916, 2.
47 Ibid
48 Ibid
49 Sokol, *The Revolt of 1916*, 80–83.
50 Jangil'din, "Moi Put'," 34–35.
51 Ibid., 36.
52 Ibid., 37.
53 Ibid., 38.
54 Ibid., 39–40.
55 Sh. Mukhammadyarov, "Turkestan maktuplare: Iuldan," *Vaqyt*, 24 August 1916, 2–3; Sh. Mukhammadyarov, "Turkestan maktuplare: Iuldan," *Vaqyt*, 30 August 1916, 3; Sh. Mukhammadyarov, "Turkestan maktuplare: Iuldan," *Vaqyt*, 2 September 1916, 3; Sh. Mukhammadyarov, "Turkestan maktuplare: Iuldan," *Vaqyt*, 13 September 1916, 2; Sh. Mukhammadyarov, "Turkestan maktuplare: Iuldan," *Vaqyt*, 16 September 1916, 3; Sh. Mukhammadyarov, "Turkestan maktuplare: Iuldan," *Vaqyt*, 24 September 1916, 2; Sh. Mukham-madyarov, "Turkestan maktuplare: Iuldan," *Vaqyt*, 11 October 1916, 3; For more on the biography and career of Mukhamed'iarov, see F. N. Bagautdinov, "Chelovek velikogo vremeni – Shakir Mukhamed'iarov," *Nauchnyi Tatarstan*, 2 (2009) 118–121, accessed 19 May 2014. www.antat.ru/cgi-bin/img.pl/files/NT%202%202009/Nt-2-2009-12.pdf.
56 See, for example "General Kuropatkinnyng noqtasy," *Vaqyt*, 4 September 1916, 1.
57 "Qirgizlarga Khitaby," *Vaqyt*, 8 July 1916, 1.
58 A.N. Kuropatkin, *Qazaq*, edited by Ü. Sūbkhanerina, S. Dәūitov, and Q. Sakhov (Almaty, 1998), 323.

11 "To be Avoided at all Hazards" – Rebel Irish and Syndicalists Coming into Office"

The Easter Rising, Climatic Conditions and the 1916 Australian Referendum on Conscription

Daniel Marc Segesser

In Volume 11 of *The Official History of Australia in the War of 1914–1918* published for the first time in 1936, Ernest Scott dealt at length with the issue of interconnections between the Easter Rising in Ireland in the European spring of 1916 and the opposition of considerable parts of the Irish Catholic population to the adoption of conscription for overseas military service in Australia in October of the same year. He claimed especially that Irish-born Archbishop Daniel Mannix of Melbourne was "an uncompromising opponent of conscription [and had] an influence among the Irish Catholic population of Australia, far exceeding the range of his ecclesiastical jurisdiction".[1] Ever since that time historians in Australia have discussed the contribution of the "Irish vote" to the No result on conscription.[2]

There was, however, another actor on stage, one whose role has been underestimated in the historiography for a long time. That is the natural environment, whose influence on human history can provide stimulation for the reinterpretation of older findings[3] and which "played an active role in moulding human actions".[4] 1916 was not only a year of large battles as in the case of Verdun, the Somme or the Brusilov Offensive, or a year of political turmoil, but it was also a year, in which global grain production was reduced to a considerable extent, especially in important producer countries such as the United States, Canada or Argentina.[5] This had a considerable influence on what has been called the "farmers' vote", which besides class, gender, birthplace or religion played an important role in the 1916 conscription referendum. As Joan Beaumont has recently written, "none of these variables were exclusive", as some voters defected from their class or normal political allegiances, but one thing, which was clear was that "each Australian cast his or her vote in a way that was personal and idiosyncratic".[6] As the referendum resulted in a No vote with a small margin of only 3.2 per cent of the valid votes cast,[7] every single factor which contributed to it must be considered. This is what this chapter proposes to do, talking about the role of the "Irish" and the "farmers'" vote in the conscription campaign of 1916 and the attempts to keep the Hughes government in power, to keep "rebel Irish and Syndicalists"[8] from coming into office. To do this the contribution will first look at reactions in Australia to the 1916 Easter Rising in Ireland, then move on to the role of Australia's agricultural production – and especially wheat – in 1916 before presenting some conclusions on the Australian conscription referendum in a global perspective.

As already indicated the reactions in Australia to the 1916 Easter Rising in Ireland have been a topic which has been debated in Australian historiography from as early as the interwar period. As Alan Gilbert, Stephanie James and Jeff Kildea have shown it would be simplistic to say that the Irish Catholics in Australia, who, according to the census of 1911, constituted about a quarter of the population of the country, generally opposed conscription and did so in most cases as a consequence of the British suppression on the 1916 Easter Rising. On the one hand, loyalty or disloyalty to the empire was a complex thing and needs to be understood along a continuum, which changed rapidly during the war in one or the other direction. On the other hand, the extent of Irish loyalty was again and again challenged by the dominant Anglo culture, in which anti-Irish prejudice resurfaced in times of crisis such as the conscription referendums of 1916 and 1917. In this context, the fact that Irish-Australian money was not only collected for the war effort, but also for Catholic schools as well as the fact that reports were published in Irish Catholic newspapers in Australia – but ignored in the mainstream press – about the discrimination against Irish regiments by the War Office sparked anger amongst dedicated war supporters in mainstream Australian society.[9]

At the time of the Easter Rising at the end of April 1916 most Irish Catholics in Australia trusted that Home Rule would be the right path for Ireland's future. Only a small minority joined the clandestine branches of the Irish Republican Brotherhood in Melbourne, Sydney or Brisbane. On 27 January 1916 the *Catholic Press*, a Sydney-based newspaper, stressed the fact that Ireland should not be depressed and that patience would now be required:

> it would be the sheerest folly and nonsense to suppose that all their sagacity and patriotism, all their gifts of leadership, and all their political instincts and talents, had [...] left [the leaders of the Irish Parliamentary Party] since August 1914.[10]

When the Rising took place in late April 1916 the first reactions even in the Irish Australian community were critical of the insurrectionists. While the mainstream press such as the Melbourne-based *Argus* spoke of "sanguinary riots" caused by "disaffected elements" or an "ill-conditioned minority", which no other section of the British people as much as the loyal Irish were "eager to see [...] punished",[11] the *Catholic Press* deplored that "unlike [...] other rebellions, [this one] had a sectional rather than a national character [.... ...] the only effect has been to lay many of the principal buildings in Dublin in ruins and to bring grief to thousands of homes".[12] Acting Prime Minister George Pearce, as well as the United League of Irishmen and many Catholic Church leaders, condemned the uprising. They made it clear that the Irish community in Australia repudiated the "criminality of the Dublin fanatics".[13] There were, however, already subtle differences between Catholic office holders and war-supporters in mainstream Australian society. While Archbishops Kelly and Mannix claimed that the British government bore some responsibility for the incidents in Dublin, because it had not punished Ulsterite offenders earlier on,[14] John A. Baker, the Grand Secretary of the Loyal Orange Institution, accused Mannix in particular of excusing traitors, who in reality were German tools and who had stabbed the Empire in the back. In his view Mannix therefore deserved to be interned like enemy citizens in Australia.[15]

The rift just described widened quickly as more details became known in Australia regarding the ways that the British troops had put down the uprising in Dublin and in regard to the punishment meted out to the leaders. While the United League of Irishmen advocated clemency[16] and others hoped that "enough sanctity and common sense [was] left to restrain the military",[17] the British authorities decided that only a quick and hard response would be adequate.[18] This came at a time when the topic of conscription was on the political agenda in Australia too. While the Universal Service League and the Australian Native Association launched a campaign for conscription at the end of April and the beginning of May 1916, the Political Labor Conference of Victoria and leading Labor politicians from Queensland came out against it, at almost the same time.[19] Prime Minister William Morris Hughes, then in Britain[20] and much to the dismay of his party, began to favour the introduction of conscription for overseas service, probably also because the home country had introduced conscription for single men in January 1916 and did so for married men in May.[21] Hughes' colleague and Acting Prime Minister George Foster Pearce, on the other hand, preferred to delay the issue at the end of April, mainly because he knew exactly how divisive the issue was within his own party.[22]

The issue was therefore only taken up after the return of Hughes to Australia in August 1916. At that time the prime minister was, however, convinced that his country needed to introduce conscription, in order to be able to replace the heavy losses that the Australian Imperial Force had already suffered at Fromelles and Pozières in the battle of the Somme.[23] Due to the split on the issue within his own party, Hughes was not able to achieve his aim by parliamentary means. He therefore decided to put the question to the people in a referendum, hoping that a mandate from the people would force the opposing senators to back down.[24] Like the whole country the Irish community was split on the issue, some opposing conscription from the beginning, while others supported it for some time. At the beginning, this was even the case of *The Catholic Press*, whose editor had written in

July 1915 that "in an hour of national danger it seems to us that those who do not realise their duty should not be allowed to evade it".[25] Later this paper was amongst the greatest critics of conscription.[26] While the country hotly debated this issue, Australian farmers still faced another challenge, which was to become relevant for the conscription referendum. They – and especially the government, which had become responsible for financing, marketing and shipping Australian wheat in 1915[27] – still had to sell the country's record wheat crop in the European spring of 1916.

At the beginning of the War as well as in 1915 Australian farmers did not have to worry about how to sell their produce. Most of the 1913/1914 wheat crop earmarked for export had already been shipped, when the war began and in 1914/1915 the wheat crop had been a failure owing to drought. In 1915 Australia even had to import wheat. This in turn led the government to call for an increase in the acreage to be put under wheat for the coming year.[28] Already by the middle of 1915, however, it became clear that the coming crop would probably be much larger than it had been before. Yet in the face of the existing shipping crisis due to a good harvest in the United States, Canada and Argentina the imperial authorities saw no way of purchasing large quantities of Australian wheat.[29] Early on the Australian government, which was paying for the troops of the Australian Imperial Force and therefore depended on earnings from the sale of primary commodities, indicated to its British counterpart that "war expenditure daily increasing Commonwealth largely depends upon satisfactory sale of this year's [i.e. 1915/1916s] wheat, wool and produce".[30] In early 1916 therefore Prime Minister Hughes not only travelled to Britain to discuss the future conduct of the war with members of the imperial government, as other Dominion prime ministers had done earlier on,[31] but also as the government's primary sales agent with regard to the country's vital export products. On this point his negotiations with British cabinet members between March and July 1916 proved difficult as he faced serious opposition from the Admiralty and the Shipping Control Committee. Although the Australian prime minister pointed to the fact that his government had to bear the cost of equipping, arming, feeding and sending Australian troops overseas while being unable to generate revenue from the sale of primary commodities, he was only able to gain concessions on wool, but not on wheat.[32]

It was only after Hughes returned to Australia that the wheat situation changed and the negotiations resumed.[33] The reason was that in July and August 1916 it became clear that the harvest of wheat in the United States and Canada would be considerably reduced. This was on the one hand due to the appearance of rust, but also a consequence of cold winter months. Both had a negative effect on winter grain, while above average rainfall in May and June as well as high temperatures in July and August in the grain-growing parts of the United States and heavy rainfalls in July 1916 in Saskatchewan negatively affected the maturation of the grain in spring and summer.[34] As wheat prices began to go up, farmers throughout Australia saw a chance that they might be able to sell more wheat at higher prices, not only for the 1916 crop, but also subsequently. Furthermore the bad prospects in Canada and the United States also seemed, at least temporarily, to ease the pressure on freight rates.[35] On the other hand farmers were well aware that the Admiralty still decided how many ships would be released to carry wheat from Australia to Europe and that the crop stored in Australia suffered from the effects of the weather, mice and weevils.[36] Hughes, however, was in no hurry and declined early offers and appeals from the Secretary of State for the Colonies to Empire solidarity.[37] His hand had been strengthened by a cablegram from High Commissioner Andrew Fisher which suggested that "it seems probable that owing to poor harvest in the U.S.A. and Canada, and bad outlook in Argentina, the British government will find it necessary to direct tonnage to Australia to secure supplies for themselves and the Allies".[38] While Hughes knew that he was in a strong bargaining position, he did not realise that the fact that no agreement had been reached in regard to the selling of the Australian wheat crop also raised the uncertainty amongst farmers, and this at a time when preparations for sowing were underway. Officially farmers' associations fully supported the government's effort to introduce conscription for overseas service,[39] but, as Jenny Tilby Stock and the following examples show, critical voices also existed. They related mainly to the fact that especially for small farmers it proved almost impossible to keep their business running. This was due, on the one hand, to a shortage of rural labour, as many experienced rural labourers as well as many farmers' sons had already volunteered. On the other hand, the government had called up eligible men already under the pre-existing Defence Act for Home Defence. Although it promised that none of these men would be sent overseas against their will, this caused distrust, as the intention to send them overseas, if the referendum was carried, seemed nevertheless obvious.[40] A further problem resulted from the fact that even for farmers not enough exemptions from the call to arms were granted.[41] Against this background promises to farmers that "men will be released from camp to harvest this season's crop and take off the wool"[42] or that "all eligible men will be exempted to take off the Harvest"[43] sounded hollow.[44] Hughes and his fellow campaigners also pointed to the fact that the Allies were buying Australian grain and farmers therefore had to honour Australia's promise. The prime minister issued a statement in which he pointed out to farmers that without the war effort of Australia and the Allies "not one bag of wheat could have been transported overseas".[45] For Hughes, Australian farmers were better off than their colleagues in Europe and the government would do all it could to help farmers with the harvest as well as making sure that the eligible men in the cities would be compelled to do their duty. Therefore, they should now agree to conscription.[46] Nevertheless at the same time Hughes still continued in his bargaining with the British government. He still objected to the terms offered by the Colonial Office, pointing to higher prices for wheat in America,[47] while at the same time reminding his farmers that without the Royal Navy such prices would mean nothing.[48] Although the majority of primary producers still accepted conscription, a substantial minority, especially in South Australia, could not be convinced and they accordingly voted against it.[49]

Only after the referendum had been lost did the Colonial Office and the Australian government finally reach an agreement. This was due also to a most secret and personal memorandum from Governor-General Sir Ronald Munro-Ferguson, in which he pointed to the fact that "Anti-British sentiment prevails [...] mainly Irish and Syndicalist".[50] Although many Irish-born Australians moved closer towards the disloyalty end of the spectrum after the Easter Rising and the conscription referendum of 1916, the major problem for Irish-born Australians was, however, elsewhere. Any engagement with or interest in Ireland became synonymous with disloyalty to Australia.[51] For the government that remained in place after the split of the governing Australian Labor Party, it was more important to retain the farmers' vote. Therefore Munro-Ferguson warned the Secretary of State for the Colonies, Andrew Bonar Law, that

> rebel Irish and Syndicalists would come into office [which would be] most disastrous to Imperial Unity and [had] to be avoided at all hazards. [...] Only hope of preventing Government of country falling into hands of extremists and rebels is to secure [the] farmer's and rural vote, but this we most assuredly shall lose if we sell wheat, wool, etc. at below market rate. [...] Imperial interests would receive vital injury, if Government passed from hands of loyalists, and money saved by cheap wheat would be dearly purchased by handing over Commonwealth into Anti-British hands.[52]

Bonar Law could not ignore such pressure, also because in November 1916 it became clear that Argentina, the last country after India and Australia that could provide the Allies with the necessary wheat after the crop failures in the United States, was also having large problems with a locust plague. After a final appeal to Australian loyalty to the Empire, Bonar Law had to give in and accept a price that was 20 per cent higher than that originally considered.[53] The British government had to give "cordial encouragement [to] Australian wheat growers"[54] and finally agreed to buy "the entire new crop [i.e. 1916–1917] less local requirements" at the same price.[55] The final agreement was made on 27 April 1917, the British government guaranteeing to the annual purchase of 3 million tons of wheat.[56]

In the meantime, Hughes lost control of his party and was forced into a coalition with his former political opponents in the Liberal Party, as they agreed that it was essential for Australia to remain in the War, even if soldiers could only be recruited on a voluntary basis. In order to keep up the numbers the new government favoured nationwide action and set up a new recruiting scheme.[57] The new Hughes government had to stay in power, meanwhile, if Munro-Ferguson's prediction of "rebel Irish and Syndicalists [...] in office"[58] was to be averted. Hughes and his fellow campaigners, who now operated as "nationalists" at first toyed with the idea of prolonging the term of parliament, but as this idea proved unpopular they finally decided to go to the polls before the end of the three-year term in May 1917. Promising that conscription would not be introduced unless the people accepted it in another referendum, Hughes and his nationalists won a landslide victory taking 53 of the 75 seats in the House of Representatives and all 18 seats up for election in the Senate, giving the new government a majority in the upper house as well. Many farmers, and others, who had voted against conscription had returned to their "normal" (Conservative) allegiance and voted to continue the war.[59] Munro-Ferguson had been right to say that the government needed to secure "farmers' and rural vote". The money spent "dearly" by buying up Australian wheat had avoided the "handing over [of the] Commonwealth into Anti-British hands".[60]

As indicated in the beginning, it is not possible to ascertain which part of the No vote in the 1916 conscription referendum tipped the balance. It was all a matter of loyalty, but of loyalty to different things. For those in favour of conscription it was the loyalty to Britain and the Empire, loyalty to their own soldiers that needed reinforcements and a willingness to share the military burden. Opponents of conscription were loyal to their class, to their religious denomination and demanded an equivalent sacrifice not only in terms of men, but also in terms of money.[61] In this context some arguments were even used for opposing ends. Trying to convince farmers to vote for conscription Hughes argued that "not one bag of wheat" would have been transported overseas without the Royal Navy,[62] At the same time he reminded the Secretary of State for the Colonies that Australia would also be able to sell wheat freely to Africa, the United States, Norway or South America should Britain not offer a better price.[63] Global climatic conditions and pests in countries as far away as Argentina, Canada or the United States and their effects on Hughes' bargaining position with the imperial government played as important a role in the No vote in the Australian conscription referendum of 1916 as had the Easter Rising. The 1916 conscription referendum in Australia was a national event with many global ramifications and a strong Irish imprint. Climatic conditions, farmers' concerns and the Easter Rising all contributed to the No result, which made Australia the only country with large numbers of soldiers in the First World War not to introduce conscription. It would nevertheless be wrong to say that it was the weather or a climate phenomenon alone which determined the outcome of the 1916 conscription referendum in Australia,[64] but nature was one of the important factors amongst others.

Notes

1 Ernest Scott, *The Official History of Australia in the War of 1914–1918*, vol. 11, *Australia during the War* (St. Lucia, 1989), 346.
2 Examples are Alan D. Gilbert, "The Conscription Referenda, 1916–17: The Impact of the Irish Crisis," *Historical Studies* 14 (1969): 54–72; Stephanie James, "Loyalty Becoming Disloyalty? The War and Irish Australians Before and After Easter 1916," in Michael J. K. Walsh and Andrekos Varnava, eds., *Australia and the Great War: Identity, Memory and Mythology* (Melbourne, 2016), 110–27; Jeff Kildea, "Australian Catholics and Conscription in the Great War," *Journal of Religious History* 26 (2002), 298–313.
3 John M. Mackenzie, *Empires of Nature and the Nature of Empires: Imperialism, Scotland and the Environment* (East Linton, 1997), xi–xv.
4 Dipesh Chakrabarty, "The Climate of History: Four Theses," *Critical Inquiry* 35 (2009), 205.
5 Marco Alexander Jeker, *Klimaimpacts auf die Landwirtschaft Europas und wichtiger Exportländer während des Ersten Weltkrieges* (Unpublished Lizentiats-Thesis, University of Bern 2007); Daniel Marc Segesser, "Zwischen Weiji und dem Tod von Marie Ankenhafen: Globale Herausforderungen und Krisen in der Ressourcenmobilisierung," in Daniel Krämer, Christian Pfister, und Daniel Marc Segesser, eds., *"Woche für Woche neue Preisaufschläge": Nahrungsmittel-, Energie- und Ressourcenkonflikte in der Schweiz des Ersten Weltkrieges* (Basel, 2016), 29–55.
6 Joan Beaumont: Conscription (Australia), in: 1914–1918-online. International Encyclopedia of the First World War, ed. by Ute Daniel, Peter Gatrell, Oliver Janz, Heather Jones, Jennifer Keene, Alan Kramer, and Bill Nasson, issued by Freie Universität Berlin, Berlin 2015-02-16. doi:10.15463/ie1418.10554 (April 7, 2017).
7 Beaumont: Conscription (Australia).
8 This is a quotation from a most secret and personal memorandum cabled to Secretary of State for the Colonies by Governor-General Ronald Munro-Ferguson, dated 13 November 1916. National Archives of Australia, Canberra, NAA (ACT): CP 78/31/3.
9 Gilbert, "Conscription Referenda," 54–56; James, "Loyalty," 110–13; Kildea, "Australian Catholics," 305–6.
10 *The Catholic Press*, 27 January 1916, 8.
11 *The Argus*, 28 April 1916, 6.
12 *The Catholic Press*, 4 May 1916, 19.
13 Message of Acting Prime Minister George Foster Pearce via the Governor-General to the Secretary of State fort he Colonies, printed in the *Geelong Advertiser*, 1 May 1916, 3 and *The Advocate*, 6 May 1916, 18, but not in mainstream papers like *The Age* or *The Argus*. For the protest of the United League of Irishmen in Melbourne cf. *The Age*, 29 April 1916, 4 or *The Adelaide Chronicle*, 29 April 1916, 35.
14 *The Catholic Press*, 4 May 1916, 21, 24.
15 *The Argus*, 5 May 1916, 7.
16 Ibid., 9 May 1916, 7.
17 *The Catholic Press*, 18 May 1916, 19.
18 See Gilbert, "Conscription Referenda," 61–63.

19 See *The Age*, 29 April 1916, 11; *The Adelaide Chronicle*, 29 April 1916, 13; or *The Catholic Press*, 11 May 1915, 22.

20 See below.

21 See Beaumont: Conscription (Australia); Joan Beaumont, "Australia's War," in Joan Beaumont, ed., *Australia's War 1914–1918* (St. Leonards, 1995), 19–20. To what extent Hughes was also influenced by the fact that New Zealand also introduced conscription for non-Maori males is not clear.

22 Beaumont: Conscription (Australia); John Connor, *Anzac and Empire: George Foster Pearce and the Foundations of Australian Defence* (Cambridge, 2011), 87. News of the Easter Rising seems not to have played a role in Pearce's decision.

23 For a detailed account of the battles of Fromelles and Pozières, see Charles E. W. Bean, *The AIF in France 1916*, vol. 3 of *The Official History of Australia in the War of 1914–1918* (St. Lucia, 1982), 328–861. See also Beaumont, "Australia's War," 14–19.

24 Beaumont: Conscription (Australia); Jeff Kildea, "Paranoia and Prejudice: Billy Hughes and the Irish Question 1916–1922," in Jeff Brownrigg, Cheryl Morgan, and Richard Reid, eds., *Echoes of Irish Australia: Rebellion to Republic* (Galong, NSW, 2007), 157.

25 *The Catholic Press*, 15 July 1915, 26. See Gilbert, "Conscription Referenda," 67–68.

26 Gilbert, "Conscription Referenda," 69–70; Kildea, "Australian Catholics," 301.

27 Scott, *Australia during the War*, 584–88.

28 Daniel Marc Segesser, "Saving the Australian War Effort in 1916? Global Climatic Conditions, Pests and William Morris Hughes's Negotiations with the British Government," in Michael J. K. Walsh and Andrekos Varnava, eds., *Australia and the Great War: Identity, Memory and Mythology* (Melbourne, 2016), 100.

29 NAA (ACT), A2939/SC41, Cablegram received in Australia from the Secretary of State for the Colonies, 6 September 1915.

30 NAA (ACT), A2939/SC41, Letter of Malcolm Lindsay Shepherd, Official Secretary to Prime Minister Andrew Fisher to the Official Secretary of Governor-General, Sir Ronald Munro-Ferguson, 13 July 1915, inviting him to send a cablegram to the British Secretary of State for the Colonies with the respective content. In a cablegram dated 22 November 1916 the new Prime Minister, William Morris Hughes, showed that he was very much aware how vitally important it was for his country to sell its wheat at as high a price as possible.

31 Daniel Marc Segesser, *Empire und Totaler Krieg: Australien 1905–1918* (Paderborn, 2002), 142–45, 227–35.

32 NAA (ACT), CP 359/2/2, Memorandum on Australian Wheat position sent to the First Lord of the Admiralty on 4 May 1916. On the wheat negotiations, see Segesser, "Saving the Australian War Effort," 101–2, and, on wool, see Kosmas Tsokhas, *Markets, Money & Empire: The Political Economy of the Australian Wool Industry* (Melbourne, 1990), 24–30.

33 Segesser, "Saving the Australian War Effort," 102–3.

34 Jeker, *Klimaimpacts*, 105–18.

35 *The Advertiser*, 7 August 1916, 8.

36 Ibid., 4 August 1916, 6.

37 NAA (ACT), A2939/SC41, Decypher of cablegrams from the Secretary of State for the Colonies dated London 26 September as well as 3 and 16 October 1916 and letters of the Official Secretary of the Prime Minister, Malcolm Lindsay Shepherd, to the Official Secretary to the Governor-General of 29 September as well as 10 and 19 October 1916 inviting him to send a

cablegram to the British Secretary of State for the Colonies with the respective content.

38 NAA (ACT), A2939/SC41, Cablegram received from High Commissioner Andrew Fisher 9 October 1916.

39 *The Advertiser*, 11 October 1916, 9.

40 NAA (ACT), A 11803 1914/89/385, Statement made by Prime Minister on 30 August 1916 in regard to conscription, 3–4.

41 *The Advertiser*, 2 October 1916, 9; *Daily Herald*, 18 October 1916, 6; *West Coast Sentinel*, 14 October 1916, 2. Jenny Tilby Stock, "Farmers and the Rural Vote in South Australia in World War I: The 1916 Conscription Referendum," *Historical Studies* 21 (1985), 398–99.

42 *West Coast Sentinel*, 21 October 1916, 2.

43 Ibid., 28 October 1916, 2.

44 General promises for exemptions were made in regard to Catholic brothers and seminarians in the second referendum campaign in 1917, but they could not convince many Catholics, not least because a similar promise had been broken in New Zealand and because no specific exceptions were set down in law. (See Kildea, "Australian Catholics," 306–11.) There is a good chance that in 1916 farmers did not trust Hughes and his government for similar reasons.

45 *The Advertiser*, 25 October 1916, 7.

46 *The Advertiser*, 7–8.

47 NAA (ACT), A2939/SC41, Letter of the Official Secretary to the Prime Minister, Malcolm Lindsay Shepherd, to the Official Secretary to the Governor-General 13 November 1916, inviting the latter to send a cablegram to the British Secretary of State for the Colonies with the respective content.

48 *The Advertiser*, 25 October 1916, 7.

49 Tilby Stock, "Farmers and the Rural Vote," 392. For the general tendency of primary producers to vote for conscription, see Glenn Withers, "The 1916–1917 Conscription Referenda: A Cliometric Re-Appraisal," *Historical Studies* 20 (1982), 42.

50 NAA (ACT), CP 78/31/3, Most secret and personal memorandum cabled to Secretary of State for the Colonies by Governor-General Ronald Munro-Ferguson, dated 13 November 1916.

51 James, "Loyalty," 123.

52 NAA (ACT), CP 78/31/3, Most secret and personal memorandum cabled to Secretary of State for the Colonies by Governor-General Ronald Munro-Ferguson, dated 13 November 1916.

53 Segesser, "Saving the Australian War Effort," 104.

54 NAA (ACT), A2939/SC41, Decypher of cablegram from the Secretary of State for the Colonies dated, London 24 November 1916.

55 NAA (ACT), A2939/SC41, Decypher of cablegram from the Secretary of State for the Colonies dated, London 27 November 1916.

56 See Command Papers Cmd. 1544, Royal Commission on Wheat Supplies, *First Report of the Royal Commission on Wheat Supplies*, (London, 1921), 30.

57 Leslie Lloyd Robson, *The First A.I.F.: A Study of Its Recruitment 1914–1918* (Melbourne, 1982), 123–41.

58 NAA (ACT), CP 78/31/3, Most secret and personal memorandum cabled to Secretary of State for the Colonies by Governor-General Ronald Munro-Ferguson, dated 13 November 1916.

59 Russel Ward, *A Nation for a Continent: The History of Australia 1901–1975* (Richmond, VIC, 1988), 117.

60 NAA (ACT), CP 78/31/3, Most secret and personal memorandum cabled to Secretary of State for the Colonies by Governor-General Ronald Munro-Ferguson, dated 13 November 1916.

61 Beaumont: Conscription (Australia). Another argument was that some anti-conscriptionists feared for White Australia, once the country had been depleted of its fighting men.
62 *The Advertiser*, 25 October 1917, 7.
63 NAA (ACT), A2939/SC41, Letter by the Official Secretary to the Prime Minister, Malcolm Lindsay Shepherd, to the Official Secretary to the Governor-General 3 November 1916, inviting the latter to send a cablegram to the British Secretary of State for the Colonies with the respective content.
64 On the dangers of a climate (or weather) determinism, see Heinz Wanner, *Klima und Mensch: Eine 12.000-jährige Geschichte* (Bern, 2016), 181–88.

Section IV

European Responses and Parallels

12 British Labour and Irish Rebels

"Try and Understand"

Geoffrey Bell

In a plea written in response to the Easter Rising the English socialist intellectual Harold Laski, asked, "Surely, for the first time England can try and understand".[1] This chapter explores the extent to which Laski's words were heeded in his own British labour movement. It examines the reactions to and explanations of the Rising and its immediate aftermath offered by the Labour Party and other left-wing parties in Britain. These include the Independent Labour Party (ILP), the Fabians, the British Socialist Party (BSP) and the Socialist Labour Party (SLP), of which James Connolly had been the first national secretary. These reactions will be located in the context of the British labour movement's ideological traditions with respect to Ireland, contemporary British politics, the British socialist world, the Irish in Britain and the wider world of international socialism.

A useful event with which to commence, as with other narratives of the 1916 Easter Rising, is the Dublin Lockout of 1913; that "desperate, anguished and brutal affair", as the eloquent George Dangerfield described it.[2] The Lockout was preceded by a transport-workers' strike against the Dublin Tramway Company, owned by William Martin Murphy, Dublin's leading capitalist who was also owner of the *Irish Independent* daily newspaper. The strike was organised by the Irish Transport and General Workers Union (ITGWU), led by James Larkin and James Connolly. A week after it began, in August 1913, Murphy organised Dublin employers to exclude the ITGWU and its members from their work places across the city. The "Lockout" lasted until February 1914 and ended in defeat for the union. That defeat had been signalled on 9 December 1913 when the British Trades Union Congress (TUC) withdrew its support for the Irish workers. Many of the leaders of the TUC had never forgiven Larkin and Connolly for breaking away from the British-based union movement. This in itself has an important relevance, indicating, among other things that the British labour movement had something of a proprietorial attitude towards their Irish counterparts. Similarly, the political organisations of the British working class, notably the Social Democratic Federation (SDF) and the ILP, had, during the closing decades of the nineteenth century, opposed the Irish forming parties separate from them.[3]

Different attitudes were suggested at a rally in support of the Dublin Lockout workers, held on 1 November 1913 in London's Albert Hall. Four of 13 speakers at the rally have significance. The first was Connolly himself. "You cannot build a free nation built on slavery", he was reported as saying. He went on to declare he was "against the domination of nation over nation, of class over class and of sex over sex". He insisted, "You cannot have freedom or self-respect whilst you have starvation, whether it is the green flag or the Union Jack that is flying over our head".[4] The speech, said the British labour movement's newspaper, the *Daily Herald* was, "A masterpiece... Here was a man with more statesmanship in his little finger than in the whole Cabinet heaped together".

Following Connolly, the *Daily's Herald*'s George Lansbury spoke. In his autobiography Lansbury was to remember how as a child in East London he had joined his London-Irish school friends in singing "God Save Ireland" in the playground, defying teachers who had dared to criticise the Fenians.[5] He showed similar belligerence decades later when he told the Albert Hall, "We are out for a fight. In Dublin as in London, property must take second place".

Even more militant was George Bernard Shaw, the Dublin-born playwright and member of the socialist inclined Fabian Society, which in the opening decades of the twentieth century played a significant role in shaping the ideology of the Labour Party. On this occasion, Shaw was some distance from the usual Fabian moderation. His speech was a call to arms, literally. Criticising the role of the Dublin police in the Lockout, he observed,

> It has been the practice, ever since the modern police were established, in difficulties with the working class, to let loose the police and tell them to do their worst with the people. Now if you put the policeman on the footing of a mad dog it can only end in one way – that all respectable men will have to arm themselves. I suggest you arm yourselves with some something that would put a decisive stop to the police.

This indeed was fighting talk: the headline in *The Times* was, "Mr Shaw on Arming Against the Police".[6] Interestingly, it was just two weeks later that James Connolly played a leading role in forming the Irish Citizen Army. No biographer of either Connolly or Shaw has argued this was all Shaw's big idea, but perhaps, it can be suggested, he did give it a nod of encouragement.

The other dramatic intervention came from Sylvia Pankhurst, the daughter of Emmeline and sister of Christabel. Sylvia had always been on the socialist wing of the suffragette movement. As she told the Albert Hall rally she had already been arrested five times and expected to be so again that evening. She declared, "Women had no votes ... the only thing they could do was fight". Sylvia soon had a different sort of fight on her hands when she was thrown out of the Women's Social and Political Union (WSPU) by her mother and sister because of her appearance at the Albert Hall rally; this they argued had compromised the independence of the WSPU.[7] Pankhurst, Lansbury and Shaw were to have significant and important reactions to the Easter Rising, but, before we come to these, a more general context about the 1916 British labour movement, including its policies on Ireland, can be noted.

That movement was headed by the Labour Party which had been founded in 1906, evolving from the Labour Representation Committee (LRC) founded in 1900. The early motivation of the LRC was to increase the number of working class individuals in the House of Commons, to which the Labour Party added the reversal of anti-union legislation. Many of the early protagonists of the party came from trade unions. Others had served their political apprenticeships in the Liberal Party, which had encouraged working class representation in parliament and in pursuit of this, had formed an early pact with Labour. Consequently, Labour won 42 seats in the 1910 general election. The party had no individual membership until 1918; the 2,220,000 membership in 1916 were all affiliates from the unions or political organisations. In 1916 there were 4,644,000 trade unionists in Britain, of whom just over three million were affiliated to the TUC. Of the political organisations affiliated to the Labour Party, the most prominent was the ILP, founded in 1891, which had also played a role in forming the Labour Party but whose membership was much more overtly political. In 1914 the ILP had between 20,000 and 30,000 members. To the left of the ILP was the BSP, established in 1912. It had evolved from the Marxist-oriented SDF. In 1914 the BSP had a membership of just fewer than 14,000. Definitely non-Marxist was the Fabian Society, founded in 1884, which, in today's language, was a think-tank, whose influence over the Labour Party was greater than suggested by its total membership, which never exceeded several thousand. To the left of these was the SLP, which was largely confined to Scotland, and the Workers (previously Women's) Suffrage (later Socialist) Federation (WSF) led by Sylvia Pankhurst and based in East London. Neither the WSF nor the SLP ever had a membership which reached four figures, but again they had an influence beyond their numbers.

For the purpose of this essay, an ideological audit of the British Labour movement is also required specifically in respect to Ireland and to the Great War which had commenced in 1914. Neither the TUC, which had been established in 1868, nor the LRC, nor the Labour Party, nor the ILP, nor the BSP had ever discussed Ireland at their conferences, despite the significant part Ireland played in British politics in the latter half of the nineteenth century and, more specifically the "Ulster Crisis", of 1912–1914, which brought Ireland and Britain to the verge of civil war, prevented, at least in part, by British participation in the Great War. This was supported by the Labour Party and the TUC. It was opposed by the ILP, the WSF and the SLP; but much of this opposition was on pacifist grounds, especially in respect of the ILP. The BSP also supported the British war effort until its conference held, coincidently, in Easter 1916. The Fabians had no official position on the conflict, although a majority of its membership approved of British participation. Ramsay MacDonald who resigned as Labour Party leader because of his opposition to the war, summed all this up by saying, "When the war broke out organised Labour in this country lost the initiative. It became a mere echo of the old governing classes' opinion".[8]

In assessing whether the British working-class movement echoed its rulers on the Easter Rising, or whether the spirit of the Albert Hall in 1913 prevailed, three features of its 1916 politics briefly just described had pessimistic implications for the Irish rebels: the lack of discussion of Ireland, the support for the war, or, if not, pacifism. These were also likely to prove barriers to sympathy.

So it certainly seemed in the House of Commons on May 1916 when Will Thorne rose to ask a question of Prime Minister Asquith. Thorne was in many ways an embodiment of British Labour. He was born into a working-class family in Birmingham in 1857, moved to London where he became a member of the SDF, and was an active trade unionist who in 1889 helped to form the National Union of Gasworkers and General Labourers, one of the first unions in Britain for unskilled workers. He was elected to the leadership body (Parliamentary Committee) of the TUC, was a Labour local councillor and became a Labour MP for West Ham in 1906. On the outbreak of the Great War he signed up and became a lieutenant colonel in the Essex Regiment. He was the first Labour MP to raise the issue of the Easter Rising in the House of Commons. The day he did so saw the first three executions of the leaders of the Rising. Thorne asked, "Can the Prime Minister state when the man Sir Roger Casement is going to be tried. He was the forerunner of this movement?"[9] During the following three days nine more of the Rising's leaders were executed. Two days later Thorne asked, this time the Attorney General, when Casement's trial would proceed.[10] By this time Casement had been in prison for a mere two weeks, so Thorne's concern was not a liberal one that Casement had been held without trial; to put it bluntly, Thorne was out for blood.

Three days later the House of Commons had a limited debate on the Rising. No Labour MP spoke, but the same month J.H. Thomas did make a speech in which he referred to the Rising. Thomas was a prominent Labour MP, a railway workers' union leader, and was on the leadership bodies of both the Labour Party and the TUC. On 14 May at a meeting in Ashford, Kent, he said "Labour leaders deplore Irish Rebellion".[11] No such leaders have been recorded as contradicting this in the weeks that followed.

By the time the House of Commons started a full debate on Ireland in October 1916, the occasional Labour MP was becoming more understanding. In particular, James O'Grady, MP told the Commons that "I know some of the men who were unfortunately executed... They were absolutely sincere". O'Grady, who was second-generation Irish, even complained, "Englishmen never can and never will understand Ireland". However, he ended his speech promising, "We will not do anything to embarrass the Government in carrying out the war".[12] The war not only came first, apparently it overrode all other considerations.

There was a flaw in this logic, certainly if it meant abhorring the Easter Rising. That was spotted by one of those who had spoken so militantly at the Albert Hall in November 1913. George Bernard Shaw, writing in the *Daily News*, maintained, "those executed for their part in the Rising were prisoners of war and therefore it was entirely incorrect to shoot them". Moreover, "An Irishman resorting to arms to free his country is only doing what an Englishman would do if it be their misfortune to be invaded and conquered by the Germans in the course of the present war".[13] Shaw elaborated on this in an article in the *New Statesman*, the house journal of the Fabians. In this, he described himself as a "pro-British Pacificeist" (sic), which was hardly the image he projected at the Albert Hall. But in a sense, that makes what he wrote now on the Easter Rising all the more significant:

> He who fights for the independence of his country may be an ignorant and disastrous fool; but he is not a traitor and will not be regarded as one by his fellow countrymen. All the slain men and women of the Sinn Fein Volunteers fought and died for their country as sincerely as any soldier in Flanders who fought and died for his.[14]

We will return to the *New Statesman* and its more general views on the Rising later, but for the moment, what of the others on the 1913 Albert Hall platform? Did they stay true to that appearance, or were they part of the chorus of condemnation noted by Thomas?

The immediate comment of Sylvia Pankhurst in her newspaper, *Woman's Dreadnought*, began, "Justice can make but one reply to the Irish Rebellion and that is the demand that Ireland should be allowed to govern itself". She continued, "The Irish Rebels find today almost every man's hand against them, yet reckless though they may have been, their desperate venture was undoubtedly animated by high ideals". She gave as an example of those ideals the Rising's promise of universal male and female suffrage. She concluded, "We understand why rebellion breaks out in Ireland and we share the sorrow of those who are weeping today for the Rebels whom the Government has shot".[15]

The following issue of *Woman's Dreadnought* contained an eye-witness account of the aftermath of the Rising written by Patricia Lynch, later to become, arguably, Ireland's greatest writer of children's fiction but then living in London and a comrade of Sylvia. Her article "Scenes From the Irish Rebellion" was a moving and fascinating mix of factual reporting and revolutionary journalism. Exceptionally, most of those interviewed by Lynch were women. The reporter also had her own observations:

I have seen the military search suspected houses. I have seen gangs of prisoners – mostly boys and grey-bearded men – marched into Dublin Castle, wet, weary haggard, but their eyes shining and their heads erect.... I have listened to many reasons why the rebellion should have taken place at all... Poets and dreamers alone cannot make a rebellion. There must be popular unrest behind even the smallest revolt. In Dublin it is impossible for men and women of the working class to live like human beings; out of every six children born one dies. Can we wonder that high spirited men and women, seeing their wrongs so ignored have allied their discontent to that of political reformers?[16]

Woman's Dreadnought continued in this vein. A front-page lead story in August 1916 was a poem saluting the memory of Easter's 1916 pacifist martyr Francis Sheehy Skeffington.[17] Two weeks later there was something of a scoop, an article by Sir Francis Vane, a Dubliner and British army commander against the Rising, who testified, "after poor Skeffington had been shot by an officer under my command... I ventured to call on his widow" to express "personal horror at the deed".[18]

Afterwards, writing in 1932 in her book, *Home Front*, Pankhurst put the Rising both in a personal and a broader context. She mourned James Connolly as

one who had lived laborious days in the service of human welfare; a man of pity and tenderness, driven to violent means, from a belief that they alone would serve to win through to a better life for the people.

More generally, she insisted, "All that had happened in Ireland was but the logical conclusion of the great war-time propaganda that the small nations should take up the sword against their oppressors".[19]

The other member of the 1913 Albert Hall platform of militancy did not see things this way at all. George Lansbury was now editing the *Herald* (the now-weekly version of the *Daily Herald*) and, while the Great War had been the priority for the Labour Party, for Lansbury and his newspaper it was his pacifism and, to a lesser extent, British Empire unionism which were the yardsticks:

No lover of peace can do anything but deplore the outbreak in Dublin. Over and above the horrors of war, as such, with all its train of disasters – death, mutilation, madness, heartbreak, and despair – there has throughout history been, and necessarily must be, a special sense of horror attaching to anything in the nature of warfare within the bounds of a single nation... Fighting between men of the same nation is – again apart from the question of whether any particular rebellion is justifiable – in a special and terrible sense a war of brothers.... The whole case of ... the moderate and constitutional [Irish] Nationalists who wish to remain within the Empire, is founded on the contention that Ireland is a real and indissoluble part of Great Britain. The extreme Nationalists, it is true, have always claimed separation; but that, we repeat, cannot any of us from deploring that they should sought to have gain separation by bloodshed.[20]

There is a suggestion of inconsistency in George Lansbury, who as a child sang *God Save Ireland*, now deciding that Ireland was something of an abstract concept, but personality aside, and pacifism aside, there is something significant here. What was involved was not simply an argument about means, but about ends: an opposition both to the use of physical force and Irish separation.

This attitude is also reflected in a further response, two weeks later, from the *Herald*. In a personalised editorial Lansbury reported that he had received a message from Tom Johnson of the Irish Trades Union Congress and Labour Party that said that "most of the Trade Union leaders in Dublin have been put in prison; that the authorities have taken it for granted that men who were Larkinites or Irish Volunteers have been put in prison". Accordingly, Johnson and Lansbury were proposing that the British trade union movement send in reinforcements. They centred on Robert Williams, a left-wing British union leader who, incidentally, was also present at the Albert Hall 1913 rally. However, what is telling is the role Lansbury wanted to assign to Williams. He wrote:

> I believe that this would assist in quieting things down and would show the Irish working people that their comrades in Britain were willing and anxious to assist in the work of restoring order... It is not the object of the Government to crush the Constitutional Labour Movement, and Robert Williams would certainly conduct the movement on constitutional lines.[21]

What the Irish needed, apparently, was a good dose of British moderation, and in this sense Lansbury's suggestion smacks more of British missionaries sorting out the culturally deviant Irish natives than working-class solidarity. And what of James Connolly, whom, remember, the *Daily Herald* had praised for his "statesmanship" in November 1913? In the same edition of the *Herald* as the above, Lansbury just said of Connolly, "We hope the executions will have been stayed before his turn comes".[22]

The *Herald/Daily Herald* was, it should be underlined, generally on the left of the British labour movement. So too was the ILP and its publications – *Labour Leader*, *Forward* in Scotland and *Socialist Review*. They also shared the *Herald*'s pacifism. *Socialist Review* did publish an article in its August/September 1916 edition by Eva Gore-Booth, the sister of Countess Markievicz, which argued that "desperation" had "found an outlet in rebellion". However, the same issue of the journal declared, "In no degree do we approve of the Sinn Fein rebellion. We do not approve of armed rebellion at all, any more than any form of militarism or war. Nor do we plead the rebels' cause". Here again then is criticism both of means and ends. In *Labour Leader*, it was the pacifist objection which was most prominently aired, saying in its first issue after the Rising, "We are opposed to armed force, whether it be under the control of a Government or a Labour organisation".[23] More generally, the following issue said, "We condemn as strongly as anyone those who were responsible for the revolt".[24]

That condemnation would have come as no surprise to James Connolly, who was executed on 12 May, eight days after these words appeared, and who just before his execution had asked his daughter Nora what the socialist press were saying about the Rising. He predicted, "They will never understand why I am here. They will all forget I am an Irishman".[25] The accuracy of that forecast was already apparent before he died, in the words quoted above, but most of all in the ILP dominated *Forward*, for which Connolly himself had written. No punches were pulled in a long front page of 6 May. This sought to condemn Connolly by his own political assumptions:

> To the Socialist – on this side of the Irish Channel, at any rate – the mysterious and astounding part of the insensate rebellion past week was the fact that James Connolly was not only implicated in it, but seems to have been one of its organisers. All Connolly's past history, his quite unassuming manner, his public writings, his wise historical knowledge, marked him out as the last man who would encourage, much less mix himself up with an obvious futile insurrection were hundreds of lives would be lost to no end or purpose.... A hundred times. a thousand times has Connolly by eloquent words and pen proved to the people of Ireland that Home Rule in itself matters nothing, and that as long as they supported or acquiesced in a system of private ownership and capital there would be misery and degradation.

The article went on to say that "no mere change in the form of the name of the "Executive Government" would challenge "landlordism and capitalism"; that Connolly "had frequently disavowed any desire for a resort to physical force to secure political ends"; and that accordingly his "appearance in the Dublin outbreak is to Socialists on this side wholly inexplicable".[26]

This article was written by Tom Johnston, the editor of *Forward* (not to be confused with Tom Johnson of the Irish Trade Union Congress and Labour Party (ITUCLP)), and perhaps more than anything illustrates the recklessness of rushing to judgement. Even more so the following week:

Even at this short distance of time it is possible to be sure of one count of the verdict which will stand – the absolute folly of the attempt, folly military, political and moral ... [the] leaders now pay a heavy price and have done nothing but harm to their unfortunate country.[27]

Of course, it is easy with hindsight to titter at this dismissal of the event which more than any other in the twentieth century was to prove to have a seminal impact on the course of Irish history, but Johnston's attack on Connolly on socialist grounds is not so easy to disparage; indeed, Connolly's remark to Nora suggested he expected as much.

Yet even at the time it was surprising that Johnston appeared to think Connolly would be involved in an endeavour seeking what he characterised as "Home Rule". Indeed in the first article quoted above he admitted that "recently in his writings" Connolly "has been more syndicalist and Sinn Fein Nationalist in character". Moreover, it certainly was not the case that Connolly's writing had rejected the use of physical force, as Johnston also said. As early as 1899, Connolly summed up his position, on " the use of physical force in a popular movement", saying "we neither exalt it or repudiate it as something not to be thought of ... the use or non-use of force ... has always been determined by the attitude, not of the party of progress, but of the government class".[28] While a full explanation of the motivation of Connolly's participation in the Rising is beyond the scope of this chapter, it is clear from his other writings, particularly on partition and the Great War that it was the "attitudes" of the "governing class" that persuaded him of the necessity of the use of force in 1916.[29]

Forward was not alone in scratching its theoretical head. The *Socialist*, the newspaper of the SLP, of which, it bears repeating, Connolly had been the first national secretary, made no comment whatsoever on the Rising or on Connolly's participation in it, and it was three years before it printed his obituary. The most likely explanation of this is that the SLP, as with *Forward*, did not understand "Why I am here".[30] On the other hand, another "hard left" newspaper, the BSP's *Call*, while labelling the Rising "foolish", also said, "We [...] can understand this effort of the Irish people to throw off the alien yoke".[31]

Other socialists outside of Ireland were not so sympathetic. Among the critics were John Leslie, the Scottish socialist, who in many ways had been Connolly's mentor, the leading US socialist Victor Berger, the Socialist Labor Party in the United States, of which Connolly had been a member and the Russian Marxist Plekhanov, who said the Rising was an attempt at a "putsch", which in Marxist terminology meant a group of individuals substituting themselves for a mass movement. Leon Trotsky condemned Plekhanov, but while saluting the heroism of the 1916 insurgents also drew the lesson that, "the experience of the national revolution is over".[32] Lenin attacked all those on the left who criticised 1916, for apparently not being socialist enough, summing up his scorn in the phrase "whoever expects to see a 'pure' revolution will never live to see it".[33]

The French trade unionist and socialist Léon Jouhaux (who himself supported the French war effort as a defensive war against invasion and German imperialism) also came to the defence of the Irish insurgents. The *Herald* reported,

> He notes that the Irish question is a longstanding one, which the Irish people have time and again given proof of their national faith and passion for freedom... And he stresses that the general war of today is declared on all hands to be on behalf of nationalities. He urges that French and English workers, in the name and cause of solidarity, should speak out against repression in Ireland ... on behalf of clemency, justice, humanity, and ideal of the rights of peoples.[34]

It is worthwhile to observe that the discussion of Connolly's role in the Rising continued among Marxists long after his death. Tom Bell, one of England's foremost left activists of the first half of the twentieth century, wrote in 1941 that, "If the Easter Rising did not realise Connolly's highest expectations, he at least fulfilled his international duty as a socialist and revolutionary leader".[35] Eric Hobsbawn, on the other hand, echoed Plekhanov in describing the Rising as "a small putsch".[36]

Leaving aside such controversies, possibly the most thoughtful and sustained explanation of 1916 in its immediate aftermath in the British socialist press came from the *New Statesman*. A week after Easter it wryly observed,

> The Sinn Feiner would probably say that the original cause of the outbreak was the landings of Strongbow in Ireland in the reign of Henry II, and the secondary cause was the destruction of Gratten's [sic] Parliament at the end of the eighteenth century.

A more contemporary context was then outlined: "The chain of events goes back to the revival a few years ago of the physical force idea in Irish politics. That as everyone knows began in Ulster". Perhaps more interestingly, there was also criticism of John Redmond, that, "he has seen Home Rule as a question to be debated in parliament, rather than a faith to be guarded in Ireland". And

> Then came the hanging-up of the Home Rule Bill, and week by week score of eager young Nationalists abandoned Mr. Redmond's body the National Volunteers, for the more extreme body [the Irish Volunteers] and they found effective allies in the underpaid workers of Dublin, who had banded themselves together first under Mr. Larkin and later under Mr. Connolly.[37]

Other newspapers on the British left were to join the *New Statesman*, in blaming Sir Edward Carson. The *Herald* printed a disparaging front page cartoon of him and said that he and the Ulster Volunteers of 1912–1914 "set an example which they can blame others from following",[38] an observation also made *by Labour Leader*[39] and *Forward*.[40] There was a superficiality about such indictments. Truth to tell, neither the Irish Republican Brotherhood nor Connolly needed Carson's example to point out that violence in Ireland could have an effect when more peaceful means did not. However, by also putting Redmond and Redmondism in the frame, the *New Statesman* was more perceptive. The editor of the *New Statesman* at this time and throughout the period of the Irish revolution was Clifford Sharp. Sharp had a strong interest in Ireland and ensured that from 1916 to 1921 his journal offered full and often shrewdly analytical coverage.[41] His and Shaw's commentary on 1916 in the same journal, together with Patricia Lynch's report in *Woman's Dreadnought*, showed that it was possible, even in the immediate aftermath of the emotional storm which 1916 let loose, to detect the historical, contemporary, political and material influences which produced the Rising and the participation of socialists in it; something *Forward*, ILP, the SLP, the Labour Party and the *Herald* seemed unable to do. Of course, the majority of the British left were by no means alone in reacting as critically. For example, in Britain the Liberal-supporting *Manchester Guardian* described Sir Roger Casement as a "half-mad traitor" and lumping together the Irish and French commented that, "not all are revolutionaries, but both countries in the past have taken these bloody and muddy short-cuts to what they want, which Englishmen instinctively shun". Accordingly, "The issue is not one between England and Ireland ... but simply between opposing political ideas, one of ordered progress and the other of violent revolution".[42]

Also significant was that sections of the Irish in Britain reacted with alarm and condemnation to the Easter Rising. The *Catholic Herald*, which had an Irish editor, Charles Diamond, and a large Irish readership spoke of the "treachery to Ireland and her cause",[43] and of "the inconceivably wild, irresponsible, pathetic outburst ... it is difficult to speak with restraint of the mad folly of it all".[44] The same newspaper also reported condemnations from Irish organisations in Britain. These included branches of the United Irish League, Irish Societies and the Ancient Order of Hibernians in Birmingham, Manchester, Leeds, Sheffield, Salford, Cardiff, South Shields and Newcastle, Bradford, Teesside, Hartlepool and Wigan. To take just one example, Aberdeen AOH, "view[ed] with horror and intense indignation the rebellion".[45]

All of this was to change in the months and years which were to follow. The *Catholic Herald* was to later criticise the Labour Party for not doing enough on Ireland, while the founding and growth of the Irish Self-Determination League from 1919 onwards replaced the traditional and more conservative organisations, and became the voice of Irish militancy in England. It is also the case that changes of attitude were also seen in the British working-class movement, especially once the War of Independence was underway. All the British left were critical of the Government's policy in pursuit of this. Yet the Labour Party remained opposed to complete Irish separation, the "soft left" showed similar inclinations and the "hard left", Pankhurst and a couple of others excepted, still found it difficult to embrace the cause of Irish self-determination with enthusiasm or relate this to revolutionary socialism.[46]

It was not lack of knowledge which was at play. George Lansbury had grown up with the London Irish and played an important part in organising support for the Dublin workers victimised by the 1913 Lockout; Tom Johnston of *Forward* knew Connolly and the politics of Ireland well, Will Thorne related in his autobiography how he had often visited Ireland and, on one occasion had suffered police harassment there.[47] But being aware of the politics of Ireland and being sympathetic to the political direction the Irish were travelling in the opening decades of the twentieth century were two different things. In a 1907 pamphlet, written for the Labour Party, Ramsay MacDonald insisted that the British Empire "must exist, not merely for safety or order, or peace but for richness of life".[48] It can be suggested he spoke for many of his comrades here. Accordingly, the aspiration of Irish separation from the Empire was something the British labour movement had difficulty seeing as a cause to endorse. Yes, they could rally round the victims of the Lockout, a demonstrably workers' struggle, and in so doing show that Connolly's much-quoted words, "the cause of Labour is the cause of Ireland" had a relevance to them. What they did not so easily comprehend was the other part of Connolly's phraseology, "The cause of Ireland is the cause of Labour". Hence the ILP and the TUC opposed the Irish forming their own labour movement organisations. Hence the reluctance of all wings of the Labour movement to discuss the Irish issue in conference. Hence, the rush to judgement and the superficiality of many of the reactions to the Rising. Hence George Lansbury, writing in the *Herald* a week after the Rising ended, stated

> I do not believe in the narrow patriotism which would keep any nation, however large or small separate from its neighbours.... 'Ireland a nation' is a great and lofty ideal. She could be all this as a partner of Britain and her Dominions.[49]

This resembled a plea to the Irish to be reasonable, as, in British eyes, the men and women of Easter 1916 were clearly not. All of this represented an ideological gulf between the British and Irish comrades. Accordingly, for many in the British working-class movement, the Easter Rising was, at the very least, an unwelcome intrusion into the politics of what mattered to them at the time: the war or the struggle of trade unionists versus employers. This is why a columnist in the *Herald* warned a month after the Rising, "Generally speaking, the average Britain is heartedly sick of the Irish problem".[50] Unfortunately, the malady was about to become a lot worse.

Notes

1 *Herald*, 27 June 1913.
2 George Dangerfield, *The Damnable Question* (London, 1979), 3.
3 Geoffrey Bell, *Hesitant Comrades: The Irish Revolution and the British Labour Movement* (London, 2016), 159.
4 For this and subsequent excerpts from speeches at the rally, *Daily Herald*, 3 November 1913.
5 George Lansbury, *My Life* (London, 1926), 27–28.
6 *The Times*, 3 November 1913.
7 On Pankhurst and Ireland see Geoffrey Bell, "Sylvia Pankhurst and the Irish Revolution," *History Ireland*, 24 (2016), www.historyireland.com/volume-24/sylvia-pankhurst-irish-revolution/.
8 Quoted in Ralph Miliband, *Parliamentary Socialism* (London, 1972), 59.
9 House of Commons Debates, 3 May 1916.
10 Ibid., 8 May 1916.
11 *Morning Post*, 15 May 1916.
12 House of Commons Debates, 18 October 1916.
13 Quoted in Geoffrey Bell, *Troublesome Business: The Labour Party and the Irish Question*, (Basingstoke, 1982), 34.
14 *New Statesman*, 6 May 1916.
15 *Woman's Dreadnought*, 6 May 1916.
16 Ibid., 13 May 1916.
17 Ibid., 5 August 1916.
18 Ibid., 19 August 1916.
19 Sylvia Pankhurst, *Home Front* (London, 1987, first pub. 1932), 321–22.
20 *Herald*, 29 April 1916.
21 Ibid., 13 May 1916.
22 Ibid.
23 *Labour Leader*, 27 April 1916.
24 Ibid., 4 May 1916.
25 Samuel Levenson, *James Connolly* (London, 1973), 324.
26 *Forward*, 6 May 1916.
27 Ibid., 13 May 1916.
28 *Workers Republic*, 22 July 1899.
29 Connolly's participation in the Rising has attracted much controversy. For contrasting views, see Desmond Greaves, *The Life and Times of James Connolly* (London, 1973), David Howell, *A Lost Left: Three Studies in Socialism and Nationalism* (Manchester, 1986) and Austen Morgan, *James Connolly* (Manchester, 1988).
30 Bell, *Hesitant Comrades*, 19–21.
31 *Call*, 18 May 1916.
32 *Nashe Slovo*, 4 July 1916.
33 For more on this see Peter Beresford Ellis, *James Connolly, Selected Writings* (London, 1973), 35–36.
34 *Herald*, 20 May 1916; On Jouhaux and the French context, see John Horne, *Labour at War: France and Britain, 1914–1918* (Oxford, 1991), 45.
35 Thomas Bell, *Pioneering Days* (London, 1941), 50.
36 Eric Hobsbawn, *The Age of Empire*, 2nd ed. (London, 1989), 287.
37 *New Statesman*, 6 May 1916.
38 *Herald*, 29 April 1916.
39 *Labour Leader*, 27 April 1916.
40 *Forward*, 20 May 1916.

41 Bell, *Hesitant Comrades*, 120–24.
42 *Manchester Guardian*, 2 May 1916.
43 *Catholic Herald*, 6 May 1916.
44 Ibid., 13 May 1916.
45 Ibid., 6 May 1916.
46 For detailed coverage of this, see Bell, *Hesitant Comrades*.
47 Will Thorne, *My Life Battles* (London, 1998, orig. 1925), 120–21.
48 James Ramsay MacDonald, *Labour and Empire* (London, 1907), 49.
49 *Herald*, 4 May 1916.
50 Ibid., 27 May 1916.

13 The Execution of Cesare Battisti

Loyalty, Citizenship, and Empire in the Trentino in World War I

Vanda Wilcox

A sprawling edifice dating back to 1300, the Castello del Buonconsiglio was for centuries the seat of Trento's prince-bishops; by the early twentieth century it was best known for its extraordinary medieval frescoes and fine Gothic architecture. On 12 July 1916, it would gain a new, darker fame when in a dank corner of the castle's rear courtyard the Habsburg Empire executed a former member of the Austrian *Reichsrat* for treason. Cesare Battisti (1875–1916), an Italian-speaking socialist elected in 1911 for the Tyrol constituency, was hanged just two hours after his conviction by a court martial after Austrian forces had captured him fighting for Italy. The case acquired instant notoriety, in large part due to the circulation of a series of images of the event. Remarkably, the capture and transport of Battisti, and his fellow Italian irredentist Fabio Filzi (1884–1916), were recorded by Austrian photographers: the two men are shown together at the front, their wrists in chains, while later images show Battisti en route to the place of execution.[1] He was driven through the crowded streets of his hometown to the castle in a tumbril. Other photographs show the preparation of the gallows in the courtyard, with Battisti surrounded by a large crowd of officers and men; in the background civilians clamber onto piles of rubble to get a better view while many of the watching officers are keenly photographing the entire event. Finally, the most famous photograph shows Battisti's corpse displayed on a board by the grinning hangman, Josef Lang (1885–1925), who had travelled specially from Vienna for the occasion.[2] Lang and Battisti are surrounded by both uniformed officers and civilians, posing for the camera as if proud of the day's work. This was death-as-spectacle with a vengeance; rumours even circulated that some officers took their wives along to watch.

In recent years the dissemination of graphic images of executed enemies, such as those produced by ISIS, has highlighted the immense political power of such photographs, particularly with reference to punishing betrayal. As Michel Foucault argued, public spectacle has historically been an essential part of the punishment of treason.[3] In the modern era, the trial itself generally serves as a "theatre for a public power struggle", in Mark Cornwall's words.[4] Battisti's abbreviated military trial, however, could not serve this purpose, and perhaps this drove the production and dissemination of the images of his death.[5] The long tradition of the public display of executed corpses was always particularly associated with cases of treason; while Battisti's body was buried immediately, the photographs served the same purpose as the public gibbet on an eighteenth-century highway.[6] As well as enhancing the effect of the moral example, public display heaped further shame and dishonour upon the convicted criminals, and emphasised their expulsion from the community: denying the customary dignities to the deceased body was another way to indicate the guilty party's outcast status.[7]

These images shocked and enraged the public when they reached Italian publications from April 1917 onwards: the photograph of Battisti's corpse provoked particular outrage.[8] Perhaps its most celebrated denunciation, though, was from Austrian playwright Karl Kraus, who selected it as a frontispiece for his extraordinary masterwork, *The Last Days of Mankind*. Battisti's execution "epitomizes the sadistic attitude towards persecuted minorities" and was the target of a prolonged critique, voiced by Kraus' *raisonneur*, the Grumbler.[9] For Kraus, while the hangings were cruel in themselves, it was the circulation of images of the corpse which was the true disgrace.

THE GRUMBLER: The Viennese hangman, on a picture postcard of the dead Battisti, holding his paws over the head of the man he has just executed, standing there like a stuffed dummy in smug triumph and "just look at us" geniality. Grinning faces, both civilians and officers proud of their honour, crowding around the corpse to make sure they all get their picture on the postcard.

THE OPTIMIST: What? Is there really such a picture postcard?

THE GRUMBLER: It was produced on official instructions, circulated at the scene of the crime [...] and now it's on display in the shop windows of all enemy cities as a group portrait of Austro-Hungarian humanity.

[...]

THE OPTIMIST: The English also executed their traitors. Think of Casement.

THE GRUMBLER: I possess no picture postcard about that case. Apart from the fact that Casement was condemned to death by a court of law and then executed, while not much time was wasted on Battisti, who was captured and simply strung up, though the death sentence was indeed aggravated by making him first stand and listen to the Habsburg national anthem – it is unlikely that official photographs were taken of Casement's execution, which England did not celebrate as if it were some country fair.

(Act IV, Scene 29)

The comparison with the execution of Sir Roger Casement is instructive. For the Grumbler, despite the similarity of the cases, there were essential differences in both legal and moral terms: he objected not to the conviction for treason, or even the execution, but to its degrading and improper circumstances, which were a throwback to a less civilised culture of execution as spectacle. The Grumbler's outrage continues for another 30 lines, part of a prolonged critique of Austrian journalism about the war, which he sees as publicising Austrian barbarism and brutality. Kraus also linked Battisti's death to the brutal Austrian suppression of the 1848 uprisings, with mass executions in Mantova and elsewhere.[10] In his analysis, Italians under Austrian rule had no reason to trust the Empire, and could scarcely be considered as treacherous, when it was Austria which had proven itself barbarous and cruel.

Of course, Kraus' views were hardly typical of Austro-Hungarian opinion. For the Dual Monarchy, the entire Italian state was guilty of betrayal, after its abandonment of the thirty-year-old Triple Alliance. Although Italy justified its choice for neutrality in 1914 by correctly pointing out that the *casus foederis* had not been fulfilled, to Austria this position was unconvincing. If the failure to join the war in August 1914 was treacherous, the sense of betrayal when war was declared in May 1915 was enormous. The operation in which Battisti was taken prisoner was known as the *Strafexpedition* or "punitive expedition", to punish Italian treachery. By this reckoning, Battisti and Filzi were guilty twice over: *all* Italians were treacherous, Austrian Italians even more so. This view was manifested in some of the pettier humiliations heaped on the two men, such as the tumbril ride through the city. Likewise, Battisti was hanged rather than shot because the Austrian authorities refused to recognise his military status and executed him as a civilian, not a soldier. Captured on the battlefield, he was of course wearing Italian army uniform; prior to the hanging, he was stripped and dressed in a hastily gathered selection of rather tattered civilian clothes, not his own. All aspects of the execution were designed to carry a considerable symbolic weight.

Battisti was not the only irredentist volunteer to fall into Austrian hands: both Filzi and Damiano Chiesa, (1894–1916) executed in May of that year, were born in Rovereto, close to Trento. Nazario Sauro (1880–1916), born in the Slovenian port Koper, (or Capodistria), volunteered for the Italian Navy and was hanged in Pola after his submarine sank in the Adriatic. Yet Battisti has been the most prominent both during and after the war, serving as the archetypal Italian martyr and symbol of the Trentino. A closer examination of his pre-war career will partially explain his unique prominence in Italian patriotic culture.

Born in Trento into a comfortable middle-class family, Battisti's political instincts were clear even in high school: finding his history classes – which ended with the Napoleonic wars – to be outdated, he attempted to organise a student protest calling for an updated and Italianised curriculum. At university in Florence he met his future wife, the writer Ernesta Bittanti, one of the first women in Italy to earn a degree. She worked closely with Battisti throughout the marriage and edited his works for publication after his death (as well as adopting a determined stance against fascism). As a student, Battisti was attracted to socialism and to a romantic vision of Mazzinian nationalism which soon centred on the Trentino region. He wrote several important works on the history, geography, economy and culture of the Trentino, focusing on its scope for future development within the Italian state; journalism – including his role as editor of the local socialist newspaper for the Trentino, *Il Popolo* – and political activism soon became his chief interests.[11]

Battisti's first political success was in organising workers' protests in Trento, successfully involving peasant groups in the wider socialist movement. However, unlike the Italian Socialist Party, he saw the national question as an essential one, incorporating Mazzinian elements into his rhetoric and focusing on the crucial role the proletariat should play in achieving national liberation. The Habsburg ruling classes, he considered, must be forced to grant autonomy to the Trentino by a popular movement; he saw no contradiction between nationalism and the international solidarity of the working class. This redemptive nationalism was to be promoted through the rediscovery of local history and culture, with the foundation of an Italian-language university in Austria-Hungary high on his list of priorities. At Innsbruck, there were moves to develop two parallel university structures in German and Italian, allowing Austro-Hungarian citizens to choose their language of study, but the idea was controversial and attracted a series of protests. When in 1904 the imperial government approved the creation of an Italian faculty of jurisprudence, German-speaking opponents rioted at its inauguration, leading to one death and the arrest of 138 Italians, including Battisti. The new faculty was immediately shelved, but the debate rumbled on for the next decade.

Elected to the Vienna parliament and the Tyrol Diet in 1911 representing the socialist party, Battisti continued to promote Italian universities and language rights within the Empire and protested over police mistreatment of the Italian minority. His address to the Vienna parliament in October 1911 compared Austria unfavourably to colonial regimes, noting that even "colonizing states [...] in their own interests end up by erecting schools and building works of civic improvement" in their conquered territories, whereas Austria treated "Italian lands of high and ancient civilisation as if they were lands of conquest".[12] Other speeches highlighted the economic exploitation of the region, linked to a culpable failure to promote modernisation or industrial and technological development. He also repeatedly described the Austrian army's presence in the region and their programme of road and fortress-building in the Trentino as a form of oppressive military dictatorship.[13]

After the assassination of Franz Ferdinand in 1914, Battisti initially hoped that war could be avoided; the failure of Austrian socialism to mobilise effectively against the war was a great disappointment to him, but once it became clear that conflict was imminent he turned his thoughts to how the Trentino might benefit. On 8 August 1914, he composed an appeal to the King of Italy, urging him to intervene in the war against Austria, and on 12 August he fled to Milan where he joined the liberal-democratic wing of the interventionist movement. During the period of Italian neutrality, from August 1914 until May 1915, Battisti emerged as one of the country's leading irredentist voices, writing for *Il Secolo* newspaper and publishing an appeal for intervention, *Ora o mai*, which proved very influential in student circles.[14] He travelled around the country addressing public meetings with his distinctive brand of democratic, secular, Risorgimento-inspired rhetoric. Battisti's nationalism had for years coexisted with reformist democratic socialism, and he used his previous campaigning experience to develop a highly effective mobilisation campaign, reaching communities across northern and central Italy who had ignored the pro-war appeals of conservative militarists and nationalists.[15] He formed a vital link between democratic interventionists and nationalist irredentists, while his experience of activism among peasants and workers allowed him to influence both the moderate left and groups closer to revolutionary syndicalism.[16]

Once war was declared Battisti immediately volunteered for Italy's elite mountain unit, the *Alpini*, and with them was deployed in the fierce fighting on the Asiago plateau during the 1916 Austrian *Strafexpedition*. As lieutenant, he and his unit were attempting to recapture Monte Corno when he was captured on 10 July. Although certain dynamics of Battisti's capture remain unclear, Austrian troops learned of his presence in the sector – most likely thanks to deserters from his own unit who perceived him as a fanatic – and set out very deliberately to seize him.

News of Battisti's death reached Italy very rapidly, where he was well known to the public thanks to his interventionist activism, and was unanimously condemned by the media. Celebrated illustrator Achille Beltrami, who for over forty years produced the front covers for *La Domenica del Corriere*, chose to depict Battisti as he was prepared for his execution on the 30 July cover.[17] In Beltrami's drawing, Battisti stands proudly while several brutish individuals in civilian dress hold him fast and the executioner slips the noose over his neck. The rope is clearly visible, but the executioner – who took centre stage in the notorious Austrian photograph – is completely obscured by his assistants. Where the Austrian image highlighted the contrast between the erect, grinning, living figure of Josef Lang and the limp corpse below him, for Beltrami the hangman was completely unworthy of any attention. Nothing should detract from the dignity and determination of Italy's newest martyr.

Formal commemoration soon followed: on 20 September 1916 (the anniversary of the capture of Rome in 1870) a plaque was unveiled in Piazza Venezia in the centre of Rome, directly opposite the Vittoriano monumental complex which honours Italian Unification and Italy's first king. The inscription on the new monument both exalted Battisti's sacrifice and denounced Austrian barbarism:

Wretched Austrian savagery
sought to punish and humiliate
in CESARE BATTISTI
ancestry and faith
love for the fatherland and freedom
and through the blind barbarism of torture
condemned itself to the world's opprobrium
while raising him to the admiration of the centuries to come.

Battisti's death was absorbed into more informal elements of patriotic wartime culture too, with many songs written in his honour. The "Hymn to Battisti" was perhaps the best known:

> Hangman, your victory / is vain [in the face of] the immortal, / the flame of [our] ideal /will burn more brightly. / Prodigy! To the new martyr / a tricolour will be raised, / a blast of trumpets played, / "Italia" will resound.
>   [Chorus:] Freed on the wings of the wind / an eagle of Trento / went to the Campidoglio... / went to the Campidoglio. / Glimpsed by the Italian ranks / a wave of flags / saluted Battisti.... / saluted Battisti.[18]

Battisti and the other wartime irredentist "martyrs" were quickly incorporated into long-standing nationalist narratives of redemptive sacrifice, using rhetoric which had evolved about the very first of their number, the Trieste-born Guglielmo Oberdan (1858–1882). As a young man, he embraced Mazzinian ideals of independence for all the subject nationalities of the Habsburg empire; in 1878, he deserted the army rather than take part in the occupation of Bosnia-Herzegovina. In 1882, after several years in Rome, he decided that only violent insurrection could liberate his hometown and embarked on a poorly conceived and unsuccessful plot to assassinate the emperor. He was hanged on 20 December 1882, despite many pleas for clemency; almost immediately he underwent a kind of secular beatification, with the poet Giosuè Carducci (later winner of the Nobel Prize for literature) leading the literary tributes. Carducci's epigraph was a model for the later memorial to Battisti: "Guglielmo Oberdan, Died Devoutly for Italy. Terror, Punishment, Reproof to Tyrants from Abroad and Cowards at Home".[19] If the Habsburgs were tyrants, then resistance was noble, even saintly. The cult of Oberdan's martyrdom was a key element in the clandestine irredentist schools which operated in the Trentino before the First World War – one of which was run by Cesare Battisti – and greatly escalated upon the outbreak of the war.[20] A film was made of his life in 1915, and his image and name were used in patriotic publications and songs such as the "Hymn to Oberdan", with an aggressively anti-Austrian refrain ("Death to the Emperor, Long live Oberdan").[21] The song "Col capestro d'Oberdan", another early celebration of his martyrdom, became a particular wartime favourite: "With Oberdan's noose, / we will strangle the emperor! / Trieste of my heart, / we will come to liberate you!"[22] The two were often rhetorically linked during the war: on a poster urging the liberation of Trieste and Trentino, Oberdan and Battisti were placed alongside Mazzini, Garibaldi, Cavour and the king as heroes of Italian unification. The texts of the "Hymns" to Oberdan and to Battisti were also included on the image.[23] Likewise, both men were added to the "Busti del Pincio" memorial garden within the park of Villa Borghese in Rome, an important collection of patriotic sculptures dating back to the 1849 Roman Republic. Alongside a collection of Italy's greatest artists, philosophers, writers and political figures, busts of Battisti and Nazario Sauro were erected in 1917 and joined by Oberdan in February 1918.[24] Such initiatives firmly embedded Battisti and his fellow irredentists as Italians (despite their Austrian citizenship) and as national heroes over whom no shadow of betrayal or disloyalty fell.

If for Italians, Battisti was a hero, there was no doubt in Austria-Hungary as to how he should be seen. From a legal standpoint, it was clear that he had indeed committed one of the most serious forms of treason imaginable: liable to conscription into the *k.u.k* army, he instead took up arms against the land of his birth. As the prosecutor in the trial of Sir Roger Casement stated in his opening remarks, just a fortnight before Battisti's capture and trial, "The charge [...] is a grave one. The law knows none graver".[25] Battisti and his fellow irredentist volunteers knew the risk they were running, and whatever the moral or political status they claimed, the legal consequences of their actions were clear. Admittedly the later years of the Habsburg Empire were marked by acute concern, even paranoia, over treason and disloyalty which was reflected in a very high number of political trials immediately before the war.[26] Socialists and irredentists were considered suspect in their allegiance even in peacetime, making Battisti politically unreliable twice over. As soon as the war broke out, large swathes of the empire – the war zones close to the front– were handed over to the army authorities who pursued treason trials in the military courts with enormous vigour and enthusiasm. There was a sharp rise in cases, especially against civilians from the empire's minority nationalities, Czechs and Bosnian Serbs in particular. It has been estimated that around 88 individuals were executed for treason and a further 351 for less defined disloyalty to the "war power of the state".[27] Summary execution in treason trials was also a widespread phenomenon.[28] Yet while the judicial process in many of these instances was flawed, and however many examples may be found of jumped-up charges, show trials and open political persecution at work within the Habsburg state, the case again Battisti was legally straightforward. Far from a unique example of Austrian savagery, as the Italian cult of remembrance would have it, the verdict was unsurprising and Battisti's actions would have been popularly considered treasonous in any First World War combatant nation (including Italy). They were certainly well within the scope of Habsburg law, which set out the crime of *Hochverrat* in article §58 of the 1852 Austrian penal code.[29] Under section §58c, threatening state's external security or working to detach sections of the imperial territory were clearly defined as treason; taking up arms in irredentist groups was precisely the crime which §58c was designed to punish. For comparison, the Italian Penal Code of the day included not one but a whole series of "treason type" crimes, specifically including crimes against the territorial integrity of the state, under which Battisti's actions would certainly have come.[30] Furthermore the Military Penal Code clearly stated that in wartime, all crimes of treason and espionage came under the jurisdiction of the military authorities, so that even civilians charged with this crime would have been liable to court martial and execution in Italy just as they were in Austria-Hungary.[31] The Italian justification of Battisti's military service was predicated upon not a legal but a political case; as his birthplace, Trento, was rightfully Italian, his actions could not be seen as traitorous.

As Mark Cornwall has noted, the Battisti case presented the Habsburg authorities with a dilemma: how to effectively punish the individual traitor in an exemplary fashion, actively discouraging imitators, rather than creating a martyr? How would his death be perceived by fellow Italian citizens of the empire, or in other areas prone to irredentism and minority nationalism – not to mention within Italy?[32] Despite Austria-Hungary's strong legal case, a number of missteps were made from a public relations perspective: the great rapidity of both the trial and the execution – though not unusual – implied an act of vengeance rather than of justice. Worse still were the undignified circumstances of the hanging and the lack of respect shown to Battisti's corpse.[33] Not all deserters were treated alike: other Italians from the Trentino were arrested and after trial (some even in the Castello del Buonconsiglio of Trento) were given prison sentences or hard labour, while in cases of recidivism execution was by firing squad.[34] Battisti, however, was a high-profile figure whose betrayal could not be ignored; as a member of the parliament, he had also sworn a direct personal oath of loyalty to the Crown upon first taking his seat. The propaganda value at home and abroad of the execution was extremely unclear, and the way in which the case was handled meant that public reactions even at home were at best mixed. For Italy, by contrast, Austrian disrespect and inhumanity towards Battisti was all grist to the moral mill, a helpful justification of the national cause given the less than convincing process by which Italy had committed to war against its former ally.

In Italian mythology, a tradition persists of blaming a Trentino-born Italian serving in the Austro-Hungarian army, Bruno Franceschini (1894–1970), for the capture of Battisti and Filzi. After the war, Franceschini moved to Vienna, unable to return to his hometown lest the fascist regime arrested him. Articles in the Italian press in 1916 and 1917 denounced him as a coward and a traitor to his own land and people.[35] Within Italy it seemed unthinkable to consider that he was merely doing his duty as a citizen and soldier of the Habsburg Empire. Even at the time it was not clear whether he really was responsible for Battisti's capture, but this is in many ways unimportant; the Italian desire to attribute blame and moreover, to identify an act of betrayal, is extremely revealing. By law, the only treason was Battisti's, as an elected official of Austria-Hungary who had sworn a personal oath of loyalty to its emperor. The desire of Italian patriots to decry Franceschini's treachery displays not only the rejection of the legitimacy of Austrian rule and a recognition of a "natural" law by which the Trentino and its citizens must be Italian; it also speaks to a certain anxiety about this very issue. By creating and propagating a narrative whereby Battisti was betrayed, rather than the betrayer, the martyr's heroism could be shored up against the ugly sound of the word "traitor".

Ironically, Battisti was not the only Trentino deputy in the Reichsrat who would go on to become a political symbol in Italy. His colleague and opponent, Alcide De Gasperi (1881–1954), founder of the Italian Christian Democrat party, prime minister in eight successive governments from 1945 to 1953 and founding father of the Italian Republic, offered an alternate model of wartime conduct for Austrian Italians. Until 1918 De Gasperi was a member of the Austrian Partito Popolare, which, like similar Catholic, conservative parties belonging to other minority nationalities of the Empire, strongly supported the rights of national groups and promoted their equal status with German citizens but also continually reasserted loyalty to emperor and empire alike, denying any irredentist sentiment. Like Battisti, De Gasperi was both a member of the Reichsrat and of the Innsbruck Diet; like his political opponent he was also the editor of a local newspaper, *Il Trentino* (formerly *La Voce Cattolica*). From their respective press platforms, the two men conducted a long-running, vigorous and occasionally petty debate, disagreeing on nearly all local and national issues. Their sense of what it meant to be an Italian-speaking citizen of the Trentino differed considerably. Both shared a commitment to defending the language and culture of the region; De Gasperi strongly supported the university campaign, and as a young law student was even involved in the disorder at Innsbruck in 1904, where both future deputies were among the group of Italians arrested. But their differences were far more substantial than their points of agreement. In foreign policy, De Gasperi supported the Triple Alliance, which Battisti decried as an alliance of "governments not people", and hoped to maintain peace with Italy; he was much concerned by the death of Foreign Minister Alois Lexa von Aehrentahl in 1912, which he feared would lead to a decline in relations. He was very critical of the anti-clericalism of the Italian state (it was no coincidence that anti-clericalism formed an important strand of irredentist thought in the Trentino). He strongly denied the existence of widespread irredentism among his constituents, but embraced what he called "trentinismo" instead, the promotion and defence of the interests and traditions of the Trentino, which he hoped to achieve within the structures of the Austro-Hungarian state. The two men's reactions to the outbreak of the First World War were typically opposed. While in 1914 and 1915 Battisti was touring Italy giving impassioned public speeches in favour of intervention, Alcide De Gasperi travelled privately to Rome on three occasions in pursuit of a peaceful resolution to be negotiated behind the scenes. In autumn 1914, he met with both the Austrian ambassador to Italy and Pope Benedict XV; in March 1915 he held talks with Italian foreign minister Sidney Sonnino (1847–1922), who by that point was already privately determined on war. As well as supporting Italian neutrality, De Gasperi took a strongly Germanophile line in his newspaper, defending Germany after the sinking of the Lusitania and denouncing the Dardanelles campaign.

Once the war broke out, De Gasperi remained loyally in Vienna. The parliament was closed for much of the war, but when it reopened in 1917 after the death of Franz Josef, he resumed his seat. Clearly, he was perceived as politically reliable – some fellow Italians in the Reichsrat, Enrico Conci (1866–1960) and Guido de Gentili (1870–1945), were sent into exile, whereas De Gasperi retained his status, and indeed was even invited to observe the old emperor's funeral procession from the Imperial Reggia in November 1916. De Gasperi was appointed to the parliamentary commission for the treatment of refugees and internally exiled people, which gave him the opportunity to witness first-hand the attitudes of military authorities towards his fellow Italians, many of whom were interned in the notorious concentration camp of Katzenau. By 1917 he was angrily denouncing the mistreatment of exiled Italians from the Trentino, and by the war's end he was outspoken (like many of his parliamentary colleagues) in his criticisms of the state's treatment of minorities; it was the state's wartime policies which finally destroyed his faith that the Trentino's legitimate national aspirations could be met within the structures of the Habsburg empire.[36] When the war ended and Trento became Italian, he accepted Italian citizenship and transferred his political activities to Rome.

If De Gasperi was not necessarily typical of the Trentino's response to the war neither was Battisti: for the majority of the local peasantry Austrian rule might be unpopular but it was legitimate, though military service was never popular among the minority nationalities. Battisti himself, addressing the Vienna parliament in June 1914, stated:

> in Austria the army lacks one fundamental quality [...] Elsewhere the army is the genuine, characteristic expression of the fatherland. But in Austria the fatherland does not exist. Austria is an infernal cauldron in which fatherlands pile up one over the other, the stronger fight for territory against the weaker, and not only for land but for freedom, which is the air which peoples must breathe. So in Austria the living spirit of an army is lacking; it is not a centre from which affections and sympathies may radiate and towards which they converge. No. Here everyone

fears finding themselves within an army which may tomorrow be called upon to fight against their own mother country.[37]

For most men of the Trentino the war was simply a burden to be endured, much as it was for peasants from other parts of Italy (or, indeed, of Austria).[38] Battisti was one of Italy's relatively small band of volunteers – fewer than 10,000, perhaps one-fifth of whom were citizens of Austria-Hungary like him.[39] Overall some 40,000 Habsburg subjects were resident in Italy on the eve of the war, rising rapidly to 86,000 when war was declared; only a few thousand were irredentists of military age, yet their political activism in this period belied their small number.[40] As Marco Mondini has observed, the subsequent hagiographical treatment of the roughly 700 Trentini and 1,700 Triestini who volunteered for Italy has been allowed to obscure the fact that at least 100,000 Italians fought for the Dual Monarchy, including at least 55,000 from the Trentino (of whom around 10,500 died).[41] To be an Italian-speaking subject of Franz Josef was by no means synonymous with treachery to the Habsburg cause, and the vast majority did not share Battisti's position – only around 1per cent of Trentino men of military age volunteered for Italy, and these were mainly educated urban elites; workers and peasants overwhelmingly remained loyal (or at least obedient) to the state of their birth.[42] On the contrary, there was a widespread popular sense within the Trentino that Battisti had betrayed the region by helping to bring about the war. For years, when Battisti spoke of "mio paese" he meant the Trentino,[43] and for many of his fellow Trentini, this – not Austria or Italy – was his true homeland, the place to which loyalty was owed. For locals, his chief duty was to protect the interests of the region and not sacrifice its people for the Italian cause. Conservative tradition in the area blamed him for the war and the consequent sufferings it brought; this enduring local memory has been entirely ignored by the Italian nationalist myth which saw Battisti as representing the deep-seated aspirations of all Trentini.[44] News of Battisti's capture and death divided the Trentino and its political representatives. The local pro-imperial newspaper, *Il Risveglio Trentino*, proclaimed that a "sense of satisfaction pervaded the entire population" and launched a "patriotic subscription" for local soldiers in the Habsburg forces, in celebration of the event. Two Trentino members of De Gasperi's Popular Party – though not De Gasperi himself – subscribed to the fund. Other local people, regardless of party affiliation were shocked and dismayed; in death, as in life, Battisti provoked disagreement and highlighted contrasting and contradictory identities.[45]

One way in which Trentino, Italian and Austrian identities could co-exist was thanks to a careful separation of nationality and citizenship. A crucial insight into De Gasperi's complex view on this relationship can be found during the debates over the Italian intervention in Libya in 1911, which was much criticised in the German-language Austrian press. Angrily reminding his fellow Austrians of Vienna's long anti-Turkish history and invoking the defence of the city in 1683, he refuted allegations of Italian brutality and defended Italy's actions against the "rebellion" of the native population in Libya. On 8 November 1911, the anti-Italian *Reichspost* had described the Trentino fundraising in support of the Italian war dead as "an act of high treason". In response, De Gasperi wrote: "Reasonably, one's feeling of belonging to one's own nation should not be placed against one's political community".[46] This remarkable phrase suggests that he saw no contradiction, then, between his political community (Austria) and his nation (Italy) existing as two wholly separate entities. He also ironically noted that when it came to treachery,

> Perhaps the Tyrolese are lacking historic background in establishing the subjectivity of opinions on these conflicts, when they can read about their great national hero [Andreas Hofer] not only condemned in all the histories as a traitor but also commonly judged by European public opinion of the Napoleonic era as a common brigand?[47]

Treason and loyalty, he presciently observed, were always a matter of perspective.

For De Gasperi, then, citizenship and nationality were not the same. The relationship between the two is complex and in the Italian constitutional and juridical framework perhaps particularly so. The 1913 *Enciclopedia giuridica italiana* (Milan) revealed considerable confusion, defining citizenship through both horizontal links (in terms of shared membership of a collective body) and a vertical relationship (between individual and state).[48] For De Gasperi, these were two separate phenomena, but during the Risorgimento, Pasquale Stanislao Mancini and others evolved a juridical definition of nationality which became synonymous, in Italian legal thought, with citizenship: nationality was the feature which connected an individual to the state, the means for determining and identifying the citizens of each state and the basis for acknowledging the rights and responsibilities of each individual. This was an inherently political model specifically designed to support the process of Italian unification. If citizenship was derived entirely from nationality (rather than from membership in a political community), what then was the root of nationality? For Mancini, it was a "psychological element", in other words national consciousness, an inherently subjective and intangible phenomenon.[49] Under this definition, the irredentists of the Trentino or Trieste (or, earlier, the populations of Lombardy and Venetia) were Italian simply by virtue of believing themselves to be so; the right to citizenship of the Italian state followed logically and inescapably from this condition. This idea, which formed the basis of the Italian understanding of citizenship, was fundamentally incompatible with the structures and systems of the Austrian Empire, or indeed with De Gasperi's careful formula which enabled separate loyalties to coexist.

Perhaps inevitably, contrasting interpretations of Battisti's status – heroic martyr or treacherous betrayer – can still be found. Elected representatives of the Trentino Tyrolean Autonomist Party (PATT) have caused local uproar in recent years by describing Battisti explicitly as a deserter, and praising the loyalty of Franceschini, the man responsible for his capture.[50] In his history of betrayal, Marcello Flores notes that it "is the rupture of a bond of trust, faithfulness and loyalty which belongs to an aspect of our being, our identity", and that in order for it to take place "one must *belong* to the group which is betrayed".[51] Perhaps the key to Battisti's act, or at least the Italian interpretation of it, lies here: if he never identified as Austrian, never belonged to that group, could he really betray them? Flores also identifies the end of the nineteenth century as a watershed moment which completed an essential transition in the conception of treason: where once loyalty to the sovereign was the highest form of duty, and concurrently treason against the king the worst of all offences, now the highest form of loyalty was that owed to the national community. The only "true" treason, by 1915, was against the nation.[52] Weighed in this balance, Battisti's act is a symbol of modernity: eschewing the loyalty to the sovereign to whom he had sworn his oath as an older, dynastic form of obligation, Battisti perceived his overriding and transcendent duty to be owed to his nation, Italy. The nature of the complex and evolving relationship between citizenship and nationality lay at the heart of his choice to serve Italy and of his death; the fury with which Austria-Hungary punished him reveals the deep fears which this thorny question evoked within the Dual Monarchy.

Notes

1 The images are reproduced in Diego Leoni, ed., *Come si porta un uomo alla morte: la fotografia della cattura e dell'esecuzione di Cesare Battisti* (Trento, 2008).

2 In a bizarre irony, in 1900 Battisti witnessed Lang perform a hanging in Trento, an event loosely foreshadowing his own death. Leoni, *Come si porta un uomo alla morte*, 15–17.

3 Michel Foucault, *Discipline and Punish: The Birth of the Prison*, (New York, 1995).

4 Mark Cornwall, "Traitors and the Meaning of Treason in Austria-Hungary's Great War," *Transactions of the Royal Historical Society (Sixth Series)* 25 (2015), 115.

5 Postcards circulated within the Austrian army and were shown to Italian prisoners of war. Leoni, *Come si porta un uomo alla morte*, 224.

6 The three men hanged by Austria-Hungary in February 1915 for assassinating Archduke Franz Ferdinand were also photographed on the gallows, see http://gams.uni-graz.at/o:vase.2452.

7 Richard Ward, *A Global History of Execution and the Criminal Corpse* (Berlin, 2015), Introduction.

8 Postcards captioned in French and English also circulated among the Allied armies. Leoni, *Come si porta un uomo alla morte*, 228–29.

9 Karl Kraus, *The Last Days of Mankind: The Complete Text*, trans. Frederick George Thomas Bridgham and Edward Timms (New Haven, CT, 2015), xvi, xviii.

10 Kraus, *The Last Days of Mankind*, 385–86.

11 Gaetano Arfè, 'Cesare Battisti,' *Dizionario Biografico degli Italiani* (Milan, 1970).

12 "La Questione Universitaria," in Cesare Battisti, ed., *Al Parlamento Austriaco e al Popolo Italiano* (Treves, 1915), 4.

13 "La Questione Universitaria," 35–42, 52–55, 74–76.

14 Marco Mondini, *La Guerra Italiana: Partire, Raccontare, Tornare: 1914–18* (Bologna, 2014), 38–39.

15 Mondini, *La Guerra Italiana*, 53–55.

16 Leo Valiani, *Il Partito socialista italiano nel periodo della neutralità* (Milan, 1963), 51–52.

17 *La Domenica del Corriere*, 30 July 1916.

18 Virgilio Savona and Michele Straniero, eds., *Canti della Grande Guerra* (Milan, 1981), 188.

19 Eva Cecchinato and Daniele Ceschin, "Guglielmo Oberdan," in *Dizionario Biografico Degli Italiani* (Milan, 2013).

20 Quinto Antonelli, "Vita scolastica e formazione nazionale degli italiani d'Austria," in Fabrizio Rasera and Camillo Zadra, ed., *Volontari italiani nella Grande Guerra* (Rovereto, 2008), 124–25.

21 Savona and Straniero, eds, *Canti*, 200–2.

22 Savona and Straniero, eds, *Canti*, 70.

23 www.14-18.it/stampa/RML0194467_01.

24 Alessandro Cremona, Sabina Gnisci, and Alessandra Ponente, *Il giardino della memoria* (Roma, 1999).

25 Cited in Owen Dudley Edwards, "Divided Treasons and Divided Loyalties: Roger Casement and Others," *Transactions of the Royal Historical Society (Fifth Series)* 32 (1982), 157.

26 T. Mills Kelly, "Traitors Everywhere! Political Trials in the Late Habsburg Monarchy," *Nationalities Papers* 27.2 (1999), 175–89.

27 Cornwall, "Traitors and the Meaning of Treason," 120.

28 By contrast the notoriously repressive Italian military justice system executed only 28 men for treason during the war. Giorgio Mortara, *Statistica dello sforzo militare italiano nella Guerra mondiale. Dati sulla giustizia e disciplina militare* (Rome, 1927), 14–20.

29 Cornwall, "Traitors and the Meaning of Treason," 117–18, 121.

30 On the Penal Code see Andrea Bianchi, "Appunti sul diritto penale militare italiano in vigore durante la Grande Guerra," in Luciano Viazzi, ed., *Fucilazioni di Guerra: Testimonianze ed episodi di giustizia militare del fronte italo-austriaco 1915–1918* (Chiari, 1999).

31 Carlotta Latini, "Une justice 'd'exception'. La jurisdiction militaire et son extension au cours de la Première Guerre mondiale en Italie," in Jean-Marc Berlière et al., eds., *Justices Militaires et Guerres Mondiales (Europe 1914–1950) /Military Justices and World Wars (Europe 1914–1950)* (Louvain-la-Neuve, 2014), 141–56; See also Marco Pluviano and Irene Guerrini, *Le fucilazioni sommarie nella prima guerra mondiale* (Udine, 2004).

32 Cornwall, "Traitors and the Meaning of Treason," 121–22.

33 Leoni, *Come si porta un uomo alla morte*.

34 Quinto Antonelli, *I dimenticati della grande guerra: la memoria dei combattenti trentini, 1914–1920*, (Trento, 2014), 107–10.

35 Austria: Tribunale dell'I. e R. comando militare di stazione, in Archivio di Stato di Trento and Società di studi per la Venezia Tridentina Tridentina, ed., *Atti dei processi Battisti, Filzi, Chiesa/a cura dell'Archivio di Stato di Trento e della Società di studi per la Venezia Tridentina* (Trento, 1934).

36 Maurizio Cau and Marco Mondini, *De Gasperi e la Prima guerra mondiale* (Trento, 2015).

37 Battisti, *Al parlamento austriaco e al popolo italiano*, 78.

38 Antonelli, *I dimenticati della grande guerra*; Laurence Cole, *Military Culture and Popular Patriotism in Late Imperial Austria* (Oxford, 2014), chap. 4.

39 Rasera and Zadra, eds., *Volontari italiani nella Grande Guerra*.

40 Camillo Zadra and Fabrizio Rasera, "Patrie Lontane. La conscienza nazionale negli scritti di soldati trentini 1914–1918," *Passato e Presente* 14–15 (1987).

41 Mondini, *La Guerra Italiana*, 85; Antonelli, *I dimenticati della grande guerra*, 22–23.

42 Fabio Todero, "I volontari del litorale austriaco," in Rasera and Zadra, eds., *Volontari italiani nella Grande Guerra*, 185–86.

43 See his speeches in the Austrian parliament, in Battisti, *Al parlamento austriaco e al popolo italiano*.

44 Diego Leoni and Camillo Zadra, "Classi popolari e questione nazionale al tempo della prima guerra mondiale: spunti di ricerca nell'area trentino," *Materiali di Lavoro* 1 (1983), 24–25.

45 See diary extracts in Leoni, *Come si porta un uomo alla morte*.

46 Alcide De Gasperi, *Scritti e discorsi politici*, edited by Elena Tonezzer et al. (Bologna, 2006), 1871.

47 *Il Trentino*, 1 December 1911. De Gasperi, *Scritti e discorsi politici*, 1340–41.

48 Enrico Grosso, "La cittadinanza: appartenenza, identità e partecipazione dallo Stato liberale alla democrazia contemporanea," in Luciano Violante, ed., *Legge Diritto Giustizia*, vol. 14, *Storia d'Italia* (Turin: Giulio Einaudi, 1998), 108–9.

49 Grosso, "La cittadinanza," 111–12.

50 "'Battisti Era Un Disertore' Battaglia Su Facebook," *Trentino Corriere Alpi*, 11 July 2014.

51 Marcello Flores, *Traditori: una storia politica e culturale* (Bologna, 2015), 9.

52 Flores, *Traditori*, 401–2.

14 "The Same Thing Could Happen in Finland"

The Anti-Imperial Moment in Ireland and Finland, 1916–1917

Andrew G. Newby

As "small nations" forming components of globally significant empires, both Finland and Ireland were profoundly affected by the global "wave of challenges to imperialism" during the Great War.[1] A microcosm of the "anti-imperial moment" occurred during the Easter Rising, when Captain Liam Tannam, Captain of E Company, 3rd Battalion Dublin Brigade, was presented with two foreign volunteers in the GPO. Tannam described the scene:

> I asked him why a Swede and a Finn would want to fight against the British. I asked him how he had arrived. He said he had come in on a ship, they were part of a crew, that his friend, the Finn, had no English and that he would explain. So I said: "Tell me why you want to come in here and fight against England". He said: "Finland, a small country, Russia eat her up". Then he said: "Sweden, another small country, Russia eat her up. Russia with the British, therefore, we against".[2]

This story has been a recurrent *curio* during the centenary writing on 1916 and has been used to "prove", amongst other things, the international element of the Rising, and the relevance of Roman Catholicism to the rebels (the Finn, although he spoke no English, was said to have emerged from his experiences able to recite the Rosary *as Gaeilge*).[3] Volunteer Charles Donnelly provided further details of this encounter:

> On one of the barricades I saw a Finn and a Swede – two seamen. One had a shotgun and the other had a gun that was either a Martini or a shotgun. I was amazed and asked them what they were doing there. They told me they wanted to fight for small nationalities. One of them let off a shot accidentally and wounded a Volunteer in the foot. When James Connolly heard the shot, he came over and said: "The man who fires a shot like that will himself be shot".[4]

Whether James Connolly had time to pause and find out more about these reinforcements is not known, though it seems unlikely. It is interesting to note, however, that the billposters for Connolly's *Workers' Republic* that were pasted around Dublin during Easter Week proclaimed boldly: "WHY FINLAND WILL NOT FIGHT".[5] The article, in what turned out to be the final issue of *Workers' Republic*, described the tsar's decision to impose conscription on Finland, and the Finns' refusal to fight either for or against Russia or Germany: "The Finns are for Finland first, last, and all the time".[6] It is possible, of course, that such thoroughgoing anti-imperialism might have helped to persuade GPO guards that a Finn could be a valuable ally in the struggle.

While Finland had become one of several "Irelands of Russia" in the early twentieth century, comparisons between the two countries tended to be used as rhetorical devices, and direct contact between revolutionary na-tionalists on both sides was very limited, despite the concerns of Russian and British officials.[7] The sense of political flux that was created by the Great War, however, was recognised by nationalists in both Ireland and Finland. The war, and subsequently the Easter Rising, encouraged greater mutual interest and strengthened international parallels between the two nations, particularly regarding German intervention in both. This article investigates the ways in which the Finnish and Irish cases contribute to the more general sense that 1916 constituted an "anti-imperial moment".

Formerly a part of the Swedish kingdom, Finland was annexed to the Russian Empire in 1809, and was able subsequently to develop a largely autonomous political and economic administration.[8] As the century pro-gressed, a "top-down" nation-building project was developed by a group of academics and statesmen known collectively as Fennomans.[9] The Fen-nomans' programme encompassed various elements, including the distinc-tive Finnish language, the folklore of the Karelia region, and supposed Lutheran values (including self-sufficiency and forbearance) inherited from Swedish times.[10] Although its "home rule" senate in Helsinki prompted some interest from Ireland, the Finns' compliant approach to relations with Russia – their nation-building seemed to rely on the benign neglect of the Tsars – means that potential comparisons with Ireland cannot be based on the notion of anti-imperialism. Nonetheless, the *Nation* newspaper, which had emerged from the Young Ireland movement, argued in 1854 that "many a curious parallel and pregnant lesson" could be found for Ireland in the "condition and history" of Finland.[11] These lessons, it continued, were to be found especially in the Finns' development of their own language in an imperial context.[12] Finland also emerged as a potential model – among many others – for Ireland during the Home Rule debates of the 1880s. In general, though, Gladstonians and Parnellites used Finland to highlight the idea that national self-government, and a generally permissive approach on the part of the imperial power, could promote loyalty to the empire and dampen political separatism.[13]

The conditions under which Finland's autonomy had flourished came un-der pressure after the assassination of Alexander II in 1881. The developing imperial policy of Russification in the 1890s – overseen first by Alexander III and then by his successor Nicholas II, and which saw arch-Russifier Nikolai Bobrikov appointed as Finland's Governor General in 1898 – culminated in the 1899 February Manifesto, a decree which suspended many of Finland's privileges and commenced what became known as the "First Period of Oppression".[14] The February Manifesto prompted a wave of international sympathy for the Finns, and accelerated a move among Finnish nationalists away from compliance and accommodation with the Tsarist authorities, towards varying forms of passive and active resistance.[15] The Russo-Japanese War (1904–1905) persuaded some Finnish nationalists that, to paraphrase generations of Irish rebels, Russia's difficulty could be Finland's opportunity. A new radical organisation, the Finnish Active Resistance Party, sought alliances with Russian socialists.[16] Explicit anti-imperialism could also be seen in tentative collaboration with Japanese agents, whose failed gun-running through Finland in 1905 prefigured Roger Casement's activities a decade later.[17] These crisis years witnessed various acts of political violence, including the assassination of Bobrikov (an incident which reverberated around Europe in a way reminiscent of the Phoenix Park Murders of 1882), and the emergence of a secretive group called the *Verikoirat*, who conducted sporadic terrorist attacks and plotted (in vain) to assassinate Nicholas II.[18] Michael Davitt, the prominent Irish nationalist, visited Helsinki in 1904 and 1905, and observed that Russification was a self-defeating policy that had fomented anti-imperialism in Finland, which had been, hitherto, "the most loyal part of the Tsar's vast empire".[19]

The Finnish nationalists, through the underground Kagal movement, became adept at placing pro-Finnish news stories in the international press. The British, motivated by longstanding Russophobia as much as any concern for Finland, were particularly keen to highlight Tsarist oppression. This widespread outcry over Russia's treatment of Finland irritated many Irish nationalists, who, while generally sympathising with the Finnish case, accused the British of rank hypocrisy in championing the rights of a small nation against its imperial overlord.[20] Patrick Pearse's exasperation is illustrative. After an incident in which a Connemara child was caned by school inspectors for using the Irish language, Pearse bemoaned the fact that:

> If these things had happened in Poland or in Finland or in Alsace-Lorraine these islands would ring with denunciations ... but when Connacht is the theatre of tyranny the outside world hears nothing, for England controls the press agencies.[21]

Russia's military defeat against Japan in 1905 had widespread domestic consequences, one of which was the creation in 1906 of a new legislative assembly, the *Eduskunta*, in Helsinki. Ironically, the same forces that presented Finland with its own parliament, also created the State *Duma* in St. Petersburg, a body which fused autocracy with "a resurgent, crude

Russian nationalism" and which prompted a "Second Period of Oppression" in Finland.[22] In late 1909, the liberal St. Petersburg paper *Birzhevye Vedomosti* had expressed the fear that Finland was becoming "Russia's Ireland", and a year later the nationalist MP for South Down, Jeremiah McVeagh, claimed during a visit to Helsinki (accompanied by the Armagh-born Quaker socialist, Samuel Hobson) that the Finns now considered the Irish to be "brothers in misfortune".[23]

As a renewed effort was made to solve the "Irish Problem" in 1912, Samuel Hobson used his recent experience of Finland to paint a positive image of the potential benefits of Home Rule:

> What Ireland demands is independence of the British parliament combined with loyalty to the empire of which she is a part. Her case is analogous to that of Finland. Finland acknowledges the Tsar as her Grand Duke, but her diet claims to make laws independent of the Duma...[24]

Far from suggesting the arrival of an anti-imperial crisis, and ignoring the continued threat of Russification, this argument followed the old Gladstonian line that imperial coherence could be guaranteed by allowing self-determination to component nations. This type of rhetoric also persisted in the Irish Parliamentary Party as Herbert Henry Asquith's new Home Rule Bill started its tortuous progress through parliament. By May 1914, having passed three successful votes in the Commons, the bill was sent for royal assent. This seemed to be an outcome that persuaded Finnish nationalists of the righteousness of the Irish cause: a legal reform of the constitution that afforded autonomy to Ireland and, in all likelihood, would strengthen the union. It did not, however, imply any strong sense of shared anti-imperialism on the eve of the Great War.[25]

True anti-imperial sentiment – opposition to the principle of imperialism rather than a pragmatic nationalist reaction against the nation's own imperial power – tended to come from the Socialists. James Connolly argued that imperial powers were wont to highlight the excesses of their rivals, whilst suppressing the "small nationalities" under their own regime. Thus, he argued that the Tsar was just as guilty of hypocrisy as the British:

> The Russian Socialists have issued a strong manifesto denouncing the war, and pouring contempt upon the professions of the Czar in favour of oppressed races, pointing out his suppression of the liberties of Finland, his continued martyrdom of Poland, his atrocious tortures and massacres in the Baltic provinces, and his withdrawal of the recently granted parliamentary liberties of Russia.[26]

While the Irish rhetoric of "oppressed races" often included Finland, the Finns still tended to focus more specifically on fellow members of the Russian Empire.[27]

The outbreak of war in 1914 had a relatively small sociopolitical impact on Finland. As in Ireland, there was no conscription to a native army, but some Finns served as volunteers at all levels in the imperial forces.[28] Economically, the consequences were more noticeable. Finland's foreign trade was distorted, but problems were offset by demands of maintaining Russia's huge military effort. Politically, many Finns believed that a Russian victory over Germany would see Russia restore its full autonomy, comparable with the Redmondite faith in the inevitability of Home Rule in Ireland. In the first two years of the war, therefore, the economic dividend militated against popular disenchantment, and reduced the chance of Finns taking advantage of the chaotic international situation by instigating a genuine uprising. The length of the war meant that shortages were common by 1916, and general discontent increased.[29]

Nationalists in Helsinki, however, saw potential in strategic collaboration with the Germans, their mindset like those Irish nationalists who believed that Britain's difficulty was Ireland's opportunity. Although the Germans recognised the possible benefits of fomenting agitation in Finland, they had little faith in the Finns' readiness to commit. A German officer in Stockholm reported in August 1914 that Finland lacked the "guns, education, leaders and decisiveness" needed for an anti-Russian uprising.[30] The veteran Finnish nationalist Jonas Castrén was called to Germany at the beginning of the war to discuss matters that affected Finland. He suggested the creation of an independent buffer state between Russia and the Central Powers. There was some interest in this plan, but the German Department of Foreign Affairs considered that it would be sufficient simply to prepare Finnish and German public opinion to support Finnish separation from Russia.[31]

News emerged in September 1914 that a new wartime Russification scheme was planned, including the possible annexation of some Finnish border parishes to Russia proper.[32] Activity increased among those who hoped to take advantage of the international situation, and profit from German assistance, guns and pressure.[33] Secret negotiations took place between Finnish nationalists and representatives of the German government, and attempts to form a broader front against Russia saw the Åland Islands being offered up to Sweden in return for their military support.[34] Most significantly, a recruitment drive for the German army was launched, and from early 1915 some 2,000 Finns headed surreptitiously (in the guise of scouts) to Lockstedt Camp near Hamburg for military training, eventually forming the 27th Prussian Jaeger Brigade.[35] The establishment in Stockholm of a "Finnish Active Independence Bureau" supplemented the Jaeger project, and sought to educate and, following the Kagal's model, influence foreign public opinion.[36] While there is no strong evidence of direct contact between Irish and Finnish agitators, therefore, the parallels between the two cases, with Germany as a common denominator, were strong.[37] James K. Maguire's *What Could Germany Do For Ireland?* made an explicit comparison:

We turn now to Finland, where, like Ireland, the embers of revolution are smouldering. Finland is in the extreme of Russia, separated from Sweden by the Gulf of Bothnia… Finland was an independent kingdom for eight centuries, was conquered by Sweden in the twelfth century, and taken away from Sweden by Russia in 1809. Sweden has been the friendliest to Germany of all the neutral countries since the war, and undoubtedly is fostering the Finnish revolution.[38]

It was the potential for alliance with the imperial powers' enemies as a means of national liberation that prompted the regular comparisons between Finland and Ireland at this time. International commentary increasingly saw potential for Finland to be "Russia's Ireland", although the analogy was used in a very general and flexible way.[39]

As the Finns opened secret channels with Germany, Roger Casement's cooperation with the Germans began in August 1914, initially based on gunrunning but subsequently with the idea of training Irish prisoners of war in Germany for an Irish Brigade. Casement argued that this brigade would return and fight for Irish independence, aiding the Germans to defeat the British in the process. While the Germans were sceptical of any military benefits, they did acknowledge a propaganda use that might hinder British recruitment in Ireland.[40] Casement's earlier humanitarian and diplomatic work in Congo and South America had been noted in the Finnish press, so it was with some puzzlement that, in December 1914, their newspapers started to report Casement's attempts to agitate "on behalf of the Irish Party" in Germany.[41] It is quite clear that Finnish agents were aware of Casement's efforts to raise an Irish Brigade, and it is likely that the Irish agitators were aware of the Jaeger training. Rumours that Irishmen might have been approached to join the Jaegers are unsubstantiated, but there is some evidence of Finnish and Irish agents crossing paths at this time.[42]

With due regard to the reliability of the source material, Casement's diary for December 1914 demonstrates considerable frustration with the German authorities' ambivalence towards Ireland. After a speech by Bernhard Dernburg in New York, which proposed the idea of "small nationalities" such as "Finland, Poland and the Boers" being offered sovereignty in a post-war settlement if they had supported Germany, Casement was exasperated that Ireland had been "omitted from the list":

> I pointed out [to the German Foreign Office] that the Irish people had already given a much warmer and fuller support to the German cause than either Poles or Finns – that both Poles and Finns, no less than Irish, were in armies now attacking Germany and that if it came to public evidences of goodwill and "value received" Ireland had done much more than either "Poland" or Finland for Germany.[43]

Estonian historian Mart Kuldkepp has highlighted the potential that smaller national movements identified in the global uncertainty of 1914–1917:

the same mutual opportunism found, for instance, in the German General Staff's relations with Indian and Irish nationalists, brought together by common anti-British interests, was characteristic of the relationship between Swedish, Finnish and Estonian nationalists inside the larger activist movement.[44]

It is possible that negotiations with Casement were used to put moral pressure on Germany to support the Finnish Active Independence movement, and it has been noted that the "Germans rated the Finnish independence movement as equally worthy of support as the Irish", before a combined meeting of the German Foreign Ministry, Ministry of War, and General Staff confirmed their commitment to the Jaeger programme in January 1915.[45]

Harald Hornborg, who later published the story of his time as a Jaeger, claimed that one means of boosting recruitment for the force in September 1915 was "to follow the example of Sir Roger Casement and go carefully through the prison camps to find our countrymen as recruits for the battalion".[46] Although Hornborg claimed that the Jaeger programme was "without parallel in world history", he noted that the only similar movement had been Casement's attempt to develop an Irish battalion.[47]

The first reports of Roger Casement's gunrunning only appeared in Finland after the *Aud* had been captured off the Kerry coast: "The boat was sunk and many prisoners were taken, including sir Roger Kesmer [sic] who from the outset of the war has promoted an anti-English agitation in Germany and tried to convince Irish Prisoners Of War to turn traitor".[48] This commenced a fortnight of great confusion in the Finnish press, as it attempted to make sense of the apparent German intervention in Ireland.[49] Wartime censorship not only affected the news coming out of Dublin and London, it dictated what would then be reported in Russia and Finland.[50] Therefore, Finns were presented with rather garbled accounts of the Easter Rising, based on wire services and the major British, Swedish and Russian newspapers, amidst stories from the main theatres of war. Unlike, for example, its Norwegian and Danish counterparts, the Finnish press did not feature any reports from its own correspondents, or analysis from informed local experts.[51] The Finnish newspapers tended to stress that the Rising was carried out by a small group of extremists, that anti-imperial sentiment in Ireland was minimal, and that Redmond's Home Rule party was the true representative of the Irish people.[52] The Finnish papers proposed a variety of potential reasons for the German conspiracy: first, the Rising could have been part of a multi-pronged offensive against Britain; second, it could have been an attempt to damage Britain from within, particularly as the issue of military conscription had been causing problems for the government; and, third, it might have been a diversionary tactic to draw attention from other plans.[53]

Helsinki's influential Swedish-language daily, *Hufvudstadsbladet*, quoted the St. Petersburg *Novoye Vremja*, which called the rebellion "a new German farce", before recounting the history of the Irish parliamentary party and emphasising its broad popular support. According to *Novoye Vremja*, there was no realistic chance of a rebellion. "BUT IN THAT EVENT", demanded *Hufvustadsbladet* in upper-case exasperation, "WHAT IS THE CAUSE OF THE UPRISING THAT HAS ERUPTED IN DUBLIN?"[54] *Hufvudstadsbladet* argued that the only certainty was that the Rising did not reflect "the mood of the masses", nor that the Irish people had "any wish to take Home Rule or land reform from the hands of Germany".[55]

The Social Democrat newspaper *Työmies* demonstrated the clearest manifestation of Finnish anti-imperialism in its reporting of the Easter Rising, noting that the insurrection was an exceptional demonstration of popular unrest "almost at the heart of the kingdom".[56] As a labour advocate, *Työmies* downplayed reports seen in most of the other Finnish titles that the Irish labour movement had led a futile rebellion, and it mocked the German machinations: "the whole attempted coup has fizzled out without any military benefits for Germany. It has not tied up sufficient British resources in the home country to in any way weaken the British front in France".[57] Nevertheless, *Työmies* condemned the suppression of the Rising and attendant executions as a "tragedy".[58] After the dust had settled, *Työmies* and its political ally *Sosialisti* suggested that the Germans had used the naïve Irish nationalists to do their bidding, before betraying them and leaving them to be executed or detained in Prisoner of War Camps.[59]

No Finnish paper noted that one of the detained rebels, noted in some of the prisoner lists in the British press, was a sailor with a distinctly non-Irish name. The surname of "Makapaltis", a garbled or mis-transcribed version of "Mäkipaltio", would not have prompted any great suspicion that the imprisoned seaman was in fact a Finn, and indeed this connection was not made until eye-witness accounts were published in the 1920s.[60] Perhaps the most important conclusion to be drawn from this lack of interest is that, despite the well-grounded fear of German interference in both Finland and Ireland, there appears to have been no suspicion that the foreign national found in the GPO was anything other than an accidental rebel who had taken the opportunity for adventure. The tales of his general incompetence inside the post office, and his apparently unmistakable appearance as a merchant sailor, ruled out any possible suggestion that the Finn could be a stray Jaeger from Lockstedt, sent by the Germans to help destabilise the British. He was released after a short stint in Knutsford prison, and repatriated with his comrades to Dublin, from where he crossed the Atlantic and settled in the United States.[61]

If an isolated mercenary did not cause consternation, the Allied Powers were nonetheless well aware of the different national agitations in Europe, and their potential to draw power from each other. Indeed, this caused sporadic diplomatic problems. For the British, of course, the Irish Question made it hard to pontificate to the Russians about Poland or Finland, although when action on behalf of Finland was suggested in April 1916, Lord Crewe, the Liberal leader of the House of Lords, quipped that at least "we might get in return some good advice how to deal with Sein Fein [sic]".[62] The British Ambassador in Sweden, Sir Esme Howard, seemed to think a Finnish equivalent of the Easter Rising was inevitable. He claimed that, having failed in Dublin, and with the Verdun offensive having stalled, the Germans would be seeking new opportunities to create chaos: "something else has to be thought of. Undoubtedly the turn has now come to Finland and Sweden".[63]

Russian newspapers used the Easter Rising to highlight the dangers of a discontented portion of the empire being given special privileges, particularly when it was so close to the imperial core. These editorials were reported back to the Finnish people:

> When one takes into consideration the events in Ireland, it can't go un-
> noticed, that the same thing could happen in Finland once the Germans
> have arrived in the country. If we notice this, and believe it even partly
> to be true, then measures must be taken to render Finland harmless ...
> the Finns are given the example of Ireland, where the rebellion caused
> the government a great deal of trouble... It is difficult to believe, that in
> Russia at such a crucial time, there are "nationalists" who apparently
> help our enemy.[64]

Although this type of report carried a threatening tone, its description of the Easter Rising seemed as likely to increase anti-imperial contagion in Finland as to quell it. Shortly afterwards, Finnish newspapers reprinted further Russian reports of German agitation in Finland. The Russian government would not allow a local version of the Easter Rising, and threatened exile to anyone suspected of sedition.[65] The ominous tone of the Russian press continued:

> *Novoje Wremja* writes again in its editorial: a few days ago we high-
> lighted Finland's curious position. In the great fight against the German
> offensive, all countries that are politically or morally bound to Russia,
> France and England are participating. There is only one country left
> standing apart – the Grand Duchy of Finland... The false friends of
> Finland have taken a different tack. They say: there is no military con-
> scription law. Therefore no-one has the right to demand anything from
> us. Sit yourselves down, good friends, at home ... let the people of other
> states protect Russia, while you preserve your neutrality; hold tightly
> on to this right, and there is nothing wrong with your young men get-
> ting paid a good wage by the Germans, for you are a non-aligned state.
> You talk of the example of the Irish people, who struggle for the right of

national existence, as a common fight for freedom. But what have you to do with the Irish?[66]

As the Finns seemed to be moving ever closer to armed rebellion – either against the Russian Empire or in the form of a civil war – the relevance of the Irish "battle for freedom" began to receive widespread acknowledgement, and even occasional approval, in the Finnish press.

In the military environment of Lockstedt Camp, Ireland provided a useful case study. In September 1916, Major Maximilian Bayer, the Jaegers' Battalion commander, addressed his men with aggressive sarcasm:

> Is it really the case that every Finn is so stupid, that he thinks he can only fight for Finland on Finnish land?... When the Russian army is defeated, then Finland will be free. A local victory at the gates of Helsinki is no use whatsoever. If this is not understood, then ask, what benefit did the Irish get from their rebellion? The question of Irish freedom would not be resolved in Ireland, only on the fields of the Somme or in Egypt.[67]

In mid-December 1916 news emerged that the Russians were planning to conscript Finns to the imperial army, a measure that was sure to provoke widespread protest.[68] As an inducement, it was suggested that full autonomy would be returned to Finland, because the Irish had supposedly remained loyal to Britain after being promised Home Rule.[69] A further comparison with Ireland might have been equally relevant. After their training in Germany, the Jaegers had been returning to Finland and proving troublesome to the imperial Russian authorities. In some parts of Finland, as a result, the relationship between the Jaegers and the local police force – their compatriots – was comparable with that between the Royal Irish Constabulary and the IRA. Political violence and local score-settling seemed to be growing in Finland by December 1916, but the developing anti-imperial atmosphere convinced the Jaegers that such assassinations would unnecessarily alienate public opinion.[70]

Finland's potential metamorphosis from contented Home Rule society into a troublesome "Ireland of Russia" was acknowledged internationally by 1917.[71] As in the previous decades, friendly British commentators largely downplayed the strength of Finnish anti-imperialism. Rosalind Travers Hyndman, who in addition to her socialist connections had helped to found the Anglo-Finnish Society in 1911, recycled the old Fennoman trope of victory through patience:

> It seems pretty clear that there were several German agencies in more than one part of Finland trying to stir the people up to an armed revolt. Some say, humorously, that the failure of the Sinn Fein rising in Ireland last year was a warning to the Finns; but, in reality, such warning was

not needed, for they are the very last people in Europe to undertake so hazardous a business. They have practised passive resistance during the first period of oppression, and now, as then, the keystone of the country's policy is to be absolutely blameless towards Russia.[72]

Writing only a few months before "absolute independence" was realised, Hyndman was far from the only observer to present a moderate prognosis of the political situation. Given that Hyndman's article appeared in the same week that Joseph McGuinness won the South Longford by-election for Sinn Féin, its coda might also be read as a metaphorical, paternalistic warning against Irish anti-imperialism:

> Nor has the fiercest advocate of Finnish freedom ever contemplated absolute independence. The position of the country and its very small population wholly forbids it.[73]

Hyndman was writing in the aftermath of the February Revolution in Russia, which forced the abdication of Tsar Nicholas II and his replacement by a provisional government. The optimism represented by Hyndman was based on the new Russian administration's offer to revoke the restrictions that had been placed on Finland's autonomy since 1899.[74] The final Russian assault on the Germans had just commenced and they hoped that conciliation with Finland might persuade Finns to support the military offensive, and that any discussions of Finnish independence could wait until after victory was achieved. Irish polemicists and politicians had been eager to explore the lessons that could be learned for their own case, and expose any British diplomatic inconsistencies.[75] Laurence Ginnell, the vociferous Independent Nationalist MP for Westmeath North, asked Foreign Secretary Arthur Balfour in April 1917 whether the British Government would "follow, with regard to Ireland, the example of the Russian government?"[76] In fact, Home Rule remained in the background, and although Asquith and Lloyd George were reluctant, there was an increasing pressure from the British military in 1917 to extend conscription to Ireland.[77]

While the Easter Rising might have given a "warning to the Finns", there does seem to have been indirect communications between Finnish and Irish nationalists in Germany, Sweden and America. The Friends of Irish Freedom had been established in New York in February 1916 to advocate Irish independence, and had a significant *Clan na Gael* presence. The European branch was established at an office in Artillerigatan in Stockholm, which was shared with the "Indiska Central Committee" (described by the British as a "seditious Indian organisation").[78] Sinn Féin's accredited agents in Europe, Thomas St. John Gaffney and Georges Chatterton-Hill, worked energetically between Stockholm and Berlin to promote the cause of an independent Irish Republic.[79] With the Finnish National Committee also operating out of Stockholm and Berlin, there were good opportunities for sharing tactics.[80] Chatterton-Hill edited *Irische Blätter*, which promoted the Sinn Féin programme in Germany and the neutral European states. He wrote regular propaganda pieces in German, which were translated and reprinted in Finnish and Swedish newspapers. These articles generally sought to correct the prevailing British narrative and highlight Ireland's economic and political potential as an independent state.[81] Such despatches bolstered the London *Spectator*'s suspicions that pro-German agitation underpinned discontent in both Finland and Ireland:

> Now it is well-known that Finland, the Ireland of Russia, is in a state of intense disaffection. The Finns have never forgotten their grievances against Russia of the old regime. Germany – there is already evidence of this – is trying to bring the revolt to a head in Finland, just as she has tried, and perhaps is still trying, to engineer insurrection in Ireland.[82]

Finland held parliamentary elections in October 1917, at which the Social Democrats, despite remaining as the largest party, lost their overall majority. The Agrarian Party gained some strength, and with the Social Democrats divided internally, the political situation was highly combustible. The disturbed state of Ireland was perhaps more intelligible to Finns than during the settled years of the *Pax Russica*, and the socialist monthly *Säkeniä* reported in October 1917 that Ireland was "on the verge of revolution". Reprinting an article from the short-lived Russian Menshevik newspaper *Novaya Zhizn*, it described the work of the Irish Convention, and argued now that the "failed rebellion of 1916 was a turning point in Irish history". The Rising, it continued, had inspired a huge increase in "Sinn Féin clubs", and the idea of independence, a commensurate decline in support for Redmond, and Ireland now had "the old white-green-orange flag of the Irish Republic ... flying on streets around the country."[83] On the eve of the October Revolution, this report also noted with approval that the language being used by Sinn Féin against the partition of Ulster brought to mind the fiery rhetoric of street battles of Dublin during "Red Easter" 1916.[84]

The situation in Ireland seemed to excite the Finnish socialists in particular, albeit without drawing explicit comparisons. As the Social Democrats "had been Finnish democrats and Finnish nationalists, and had (in 1907) achieved access to power by constitutional means", they seemed to approve of the Sinn Féin policy in Ireland.[85] The Social Democratic *Kansan Lehti*, reported on the rise of Sinn Féin, borrowing stories from Swedish and Russian sources, concluding that

> It is much more likely that there will be a renewed armed insurrection. The Sinn Fein movement reflects the mood of contemporary Ireland. No plans to organise the condition of Ireland can now be implemented without considering the desires of the Sinn Feiners.[86]

In the same week, Lenin's Bolsheviks overthrew the provisional government of Russia, an event that gave increased urgency to the national question in Finland. The Social Democrats hoped to negotiate a settlement with Lenin, but the bourgeois parties would not countenance remaining part of a Russia ruled by revolutionary socialists. By the end of November, Per Evind Svinhufvud was chosen to lead a provisional Senate in Helsinki, and on 4 December, this Senate published a declaration of Finnish independence.

Some of the rhetorical similarities between the Finnish document and the 1916 Proclamation of the Irish Republic have been recognised. Alan Titley, for example, writing in the *Irish Times* in advance of the Easter Rising centenary, noted the "strong echoes" between the Finnish and Irish proclamations, but added that this represented "the international language of freedom" rather than Finns borrowing ideas from Ireland.[87] There is no strong evidence to suggest that any of the Finnish leaders would have been aware of Pearse's precise text, nor that the Irish proclamation influenced Finland in the same way that it later inspired Indian nationalists.[88] In fact, the Finnish demand for independence built on the same sort of legalistic argument that had been used since 1899: that Finland's fate was based on its "centuries-old cultural development"; that a "century-old desire for freedom awaits fulfilment", and, notably, that "the people of Finland feel deeply that they cannot fulfil their national duty and their universal human obligations without a complete sovereignty". Compared with the Easter 1916 text, the Finnish proclamation lacked references to a tradition of military resistance, and to aspirations for a future society. They believed that civil society was already well established and the main requirement was that the "people of Finland have to step forward as an independent nation among the other nations in the world".

Two days after the presentation of the Finnish declaration of independence, 6 December 1917, the Finnish parliament approved the measure and started to seek international recognition for its independence. Once the Russians had been convinced, other nations – with the exception of the United States and Great Britain – acknowledged Finland as an independent state.[89] Finland's case was again used to bolster arguments for Irish freedom, for example by Éamon De Valera in *Ireland's Case Against Conscription*,[90] by Arthur Griffith in a revised edition of *The Resurrection of Hungary*,[91] and by George Bernard Shaw, who claimed that "we have politicians here more unscrupulous than Bobrikoff..."[92]

The Jaegers, in fact, had been deployed on the German Eastern Front rather than being used for a German invasion of Finland, but they returned to Finland after the outbreak of Civil War in January 1918.[93] Finland might finally have been free from Russia, but the political divisions that had grown in the preceding years were now exposed. The Bolshevik takeover in Russia inspired the Finnish Social Democrats to seek a revolutionary takeover of the Finnish government, prompting a short but brutal Civil War. As Bill Kissane has noted, a key comparison between Finland and Ireland during the early twentieth century was that "the very moment Finland and Ireland asserted their claims to independence statehood revealed the depths of their internal divisions".[94] On 15 May 1918, the Whites completed a military victory. Approximately 39,000 people perished during Finland's Civil War, including 36,000 Finns, more than 1 per cent of the newly independent state's population. Finland looked set to become an independent monarchy, but the defeat of Germany in November 1918 made it impossible for the planned German monarch to assume office. An independent Republic of Finland emerged from the elections of March 1919. As polling day had approached, Ireland featured regularly in political columns. Sinn Féin's election victory of December 1918, and subsequent reassertion of independence, had created a stir internationally. In the years leading to the creation of the Irish Free State in 1922, and during the subsequent civil war in Ireland, there was general mutual (and international) recognition of parallels between Finland and Ireland.[95]

It is remarkable, however, how durable was the Finns' attachment to supposed forbearance and "vindication through legal right". Even during the "Continuation War" (1941–1944), which saw Finland and Germany battle the Soviet Union, the Finnish author and journalist Olof Enckell claimed that:

> ...the most valuable asset in our modern history, is that Finnish action was carried out with the assertion of the right as an unwavering beacon, even during a long succession of seemingly hopeless years. This strict, at times fanatical, adherence to the principle of law prevented us from lapsing into a series of chaotic or undisciplined acts of violence and desperate enterprises of the type that until recently made Ireland's fight for freedom so depressing.[96]

Reminiscent of the early Fennoman writing of the 1860s, Enckell's idealised image of Finnish "adherence to the principle of law" glosses over the political assassinations of the early twentieth century, the courting of Germany in both world wars, and a civil war that cost ten times more lives than its bloody Irish equivalent.

There were certainly parallels between the Irish and Finnish experiences during 1916–1917, some of which were encapsulated by "the Finn in the GPO" in his claim that he understood imperial tyranny and wished to take a stand against it. Both countries sought versions of Home Rule, and both had broad nationalist movements which contained great divergences in their approach to achieving this aim. As outlined above, despite Finland being a regular point of reference for Irish nationalists after the 1880s, it was rarely a point of direct contact until the early 1900s. Ireland's position in Finnish nationalist discourse shifted, gradually, towards a situation where the Finns recognised certain parallels, particularly the acceptance of Asquith's Home Rule Bill as a satisfactory conclusion to an age-old problem. As war erupted in 1914, however, the strength of "anti-imperialism" in both countries can be questioned. Many nationalists in Finland followed what might be called the "Redmondite" approach of supporting the empire's general war aims in the hope of being treated sympathetically when hostilities were over. As in many other cases, the "anti-imperialism" on show was often pragmatic or opportunistic. It was aimed specifically against the imperial ruler (Russia or Britain), and other than among Socialists/Social Democrats there was limited evidence of philosophical antagonism towards all forms of imperialism.

Thus, both the Irish and the Finns were happy to engage with the Germans if it meant achieving political independence, despite the Germans' own record regarding small nationalities. In this respect, both countries conform to a more general sense that 1916 was an "anti-imperial moment", forming part of a tapestry of causally (if sometimes loosely) connected reactions against imperialism, drawing on long-term resentment, the particular sociopolitical flux caused by war, and the interference and encouragement of the imperial powers' enemy.

Acknowledgements

The research for this article was funded by the Academy of Finland (grants #1264940 and #1257696).

Notes

1 Liam Ó Ruairc, "Easter Rising (1916)," in Immanuel Ness and Zak Cope, eds., *The Palgrave Encyclopedia of Imperialism & Anti-Imperialism: Volume 1* (Basingstoke, 2016), 622.
2 Witness Statement WS242 (Liam Tannam). Bureau of Military History, Dublin. For more on "Antti the Finn" (Antti Mäkipaltio), including a summary of contemporary and more recent references, and the difficulties inherent in confirming his identity, see A. G. Newby, *Éire na Rúise: An Fhionlainn agus Éire ar thóir na saoirse ["The Ireland of Russia": Ireland and Finland in search of freedom]* (Dublin, 2016), 76–90.
3 Greg Daly, *1916: The Church and the Rising* (Dublin, 2016). Quoted in Breda O'Brien, "We Must Not Play Down the Faith of the 1916 Leaders," *Irish Times*, 26 March 2016; Pól Ó Muirí, "Creideamh agus Cogadh," *Irish Times*, 25 April 2016.
4 Witness Statement WS824 (Charles Donnelly). Bureau of Military History, Dublin. The wounded volunteer seems to have been James Kenny. Witness Statement WS141 (James Kenny). Bureau of Military History, Dublin.
5 National Library of Ireland, EPH F242 [Broadside advertisement poster for display on sandwich board], *Workers' Republic*, 22 April 1916.
6 *Workers' Republic*, 22 April 1916; Newby, *Éire na Rúise*, 81.
7 Alexander S. Kaun, "The Slavic Enigma," *The New Republic* 5.62 (1916), 250–51.
8 Newby, *Éire na Rúise*, 12–64; Andrew G. Newby, "'Black Spots on the Map of Europe': Ireland and Finland as Oppressed Nationalities, 1854–1910," *Irish Historical Studies* 41 (2017, forthcoming), xx.

9 Johanna Rainio-Niemi, "A Nordic Paradox of Openness and Consensus? The Case of Finland," in Norbert Götz and Carl Marklund, eds., *The Paradox of Openness: Transparency and Participation in Nordic Cultures of Consensus* (Leiden, 2015), 35.

10 Henrik Stenius, "Paradoxes of Finnish Political Culture," in Jóhan Pál Árnason and Björn Wittrock, eds., *Nordic Paths to Modernity* (New York, 2012), 207–28.

11 *Nation*, 22 July 1854.

12 Kati Nurmi, "Imagining the Nation in Irish and Finnish Popular Culture in the Nineteenth and Early Twentieth Centuries," in Brian Heffernan, ed., *Life on the Fringe? Ireland and Europe 1800–1922* (Dublin, 2012), 39–61; Michael Coleman, "'You Might All Be Speaking Swedish Today!': Language Change in 19th-Century Finland and Ireland," *Scandinavian Journal of History* 35.1 (2010), 44–64. Bill Kissane has distinguished between Finland's largely "civic" nationalism and Ireland's "ethnic" nationalism in the nineteenth century. Bill Kissane, "Nineteenth-Century Nationalism in Finland and Ireland: A Comparative Analysis," *Nationalism and Ethnic Politics* 6.2 (2000), 25–42.

13 Newby, "'Black Spots on the Map of Europe'", xx.

14 Tuomo Polvinen, *Imperial Borderland: Bobrikov and the Attempted Russification of Finland 1898–1904* (London, 1995), 76–102.

15 Steven D. Huxley, *Constitutionalist Insurgency in Finland: Finnish "Passive Resistance" Against Russification as a Case of Nonmilitary Struggle in the European Resistance Tradition* (Helsinki, 1990), 51.

16 David G. Kirby, *Finland and Russia 1808–1920: From Autonomy to Independence* (London, 1975), 99–100.

17 George Maude, "Finland in Anglo-Russian Relations, 1899–1910," *Slavonic and East European Review* 48 (1970), 566. Antti Kujala, "The Russian Revolutionary Movement and the Finnish Opposition, 1905," *Scandinavian Journal of History* 5 (1980), 257–75.

18 "Verikoirat" translates loosely as "Killer Dogs". One of the group's leading members, Karl Emil Primus Nyman, later became a Finnish newspaper correspondent in London, and was briefly married to a Cork woman, Emily Graves Moynihan.

19 Andrew G. Newby, "'The Cold Northern Land of Suomi': Michael Davitt and Finnish Nationalism," *Journal of Irish and Scottish Studies* 6.1 (2012), 87, See also Patrick Salmon, *Scandinavia and the Great Powers 1890–1940* (Cambridge, 1997), 102.

20 Eino Lyytinen, *Finland in British Politics in the First World War* (Helsinki, 1980), 39; Maude, "Finland in Anglo-Russian Relations," 560–65; Newby, *Éire na Rúise*, 26–27.

21 P.H. Pearse, "'Education' in the West of Ireland," *Guth na Bliadhna* [Voice of the Year] 2 (1905), 379.

22 Kirby, *Finland and Russia*, 123–39.

23 McVeagh was in Finland in 1910 as part of a British press deputation arranged between Julio Reuter and Samuel Hobson. Hobson, *Pilgrim to the Left*, 162; *Veckans Krönika*, 1 October 1910; Lyytinen, *Finland in British Politics*, 48. For more on Finnish nationalists and their diverse Irish correspondents, see Newby, *Éire na Rúise*, 52–69.

24 Samuel G. Hobson, *Irish Home Rule* (London, 1912), 211.

25 Rudolf Holsti, "Irlannin Kysymys," *Historiallinen Aikakauskirja* xii (1914), 48. The article is a review of L. Maisonnier and G. Lecarpentier, *L'Irlande et le Home Rule* (Paris, 1912).

26 James Connolly, "The Friends of Small Nationalities," *Irish Worker*, 12 September 1914.

27 Seikko Eskola, *Suomen Kysymys ja Ruotsin Mielipide* (Helsinki, 1965), 37–38, 41.

28 Juhani Paasivirta, *Finland and Europe: The Period of Autonomy & The International Crises 1808–1914* (London, 1981), 214.

29 Jason Lavery, *The History of Finland* (Westport, CT, 2006), 84–86; Anatole G. Mazour, *Finland: Between East and West* (Princeton, NJ, 1956), 35–36; Henrik Meinander, *A History of Finland* (London, 2011), 121; George Maude, *Aspects of Governing the Finns* (New York, 2010), 10.

30 Aaro Pakaslahti, *Suomen politiikkaa maailmansodassa*, 2 vols. (Helsinki, 1933–1934), i, 13; Osmo Apunen, *Suomi keisarillisen Saksan politiikkassa 1914–1915* (Helsinki, 1968), 65.

31 Eskola, *Suomen Kysymys*, 41.

32 Edward Thaden, "The Russian Government," in Edward Thaden, ed., *Russification in the Baltic Provinces and Finland, 1855–1914* (Princeton, NJ, 1981), 87. Research suggests that the Finn in the GPO, Antti Mäkipaltio, was from Kivennapa, a parish approximately 60 km from St. Petersburg and one of the areas threatened with annexation. The extent to which this might have been a basis for his anti-imperial rhetoric, however, can only remain speculation. Newby, *Éire na Rúise*, 85–86.

33 Thaden, "The Russian Government," 87.

34 B.J. C. McKercher, *Esme Howard: A Diplomatic Biography* (Cambridge, 1989), 151, 187.

35 Mazour, *Finland: Between East and West*, 35–36.

36 This bureau was known as (Swedish) *Utlandsdelegationen för Finlands Frigörelse*, and (Finnish) *Suomen itsenäisyysliikkeen Ulkomaanvaltuuskunta*. Eskola, *Suomen Kysymys*, 201. Matti Lackman, *Suomen vai Saksan puolesta? Jääkäreiden tuntematon historia* (Helsinki, 2000), 141–43.

37 Harold Nicolson, a clerk at the British War Department, quoted in private correspondence (January 1916) a member of the Russian Embassy in London, who argued that "Finland was to the Russian government what Ireland was to the British government, only supposing that Ireland was in Essex." Quoted in Lyytinen, *Finland in British Politics*, 68.

38 James K. Maguire, *What Could Germany Do For Ireland?* (New York, 1916), 69. The *Freeman's Journal* review of this book implied that Maguire was turning a blind eye to German imperialism, particularly its treatment of the Polish. Róisín Healy, *Poland in the Irish Nationalist Imagination 1772–1922: Anti-Colonialism within Europe* (London, 2017), 245–46; *Freeman's Journal*, 9 February 1916.

39 John Foster Fraser, *Russia of To-day* (New York, 1915), 125.

40 Filip Nerad, "The Gallant Allies? German-Irish Military Cooperation Before and During World War I," *Prague Papers on the History of International Relations* (Prague, 2008), 223.

41 *Helsingin Sanomat*, 1 December 1914.

42 This does not imply that they were seeking cooperation. Indeed, the Finns passed intelligence about Casement to the British. Samuel Hoare, Conservative MP for Chelsea, claimed in 1921 that "I remember the year 1916, when I was in charge of our military intelligence in Russia, that I met a Finnish agent who came to give me news of Casement's doings in Germany." *Hansard*, HC Deb 14 December 1921, vol. 149 c. 8.

43 National Library of Ireland MS1690 (Roger Casement's 1914–1916, *German Diaries*), http://studylib.net/doc/8471283/roger-casement-s-1914 [20 February 2017]. Reproduced in *The Nation* (New York), 4 January 1922.

44 Mart Kuldkepp, "Hegemony and Liberation in World War I: The Plans for the New *Mare Nostrum Balticum*," *Ajalooline Ajakiri* 153 (2015), 252. See also Mikko Uola, *Jääkärikenraalin vuosisata: Väinö Valve 1895–1995* (Helsinki, 2001), 82.
45 Matti Lauerma, "Poliittisen luotettavuuden ongelma Jääkäripataljoona 27:ssä," *Historiallinen Aikakauskirja* 58 (1960), 117.
46 Harald Hornborg, *He Löysivät Tiensä: Pfadfindereiden Tarina* (Porvoo, 1965), 103.
47 Hornborg, *He Löysivät Tiensä*, 39.
48 *Aamulehti*, 26 April 1916.
49 The "plausible" possibility of an uprising in Finland was used as a cover story as Casement's gun-running mission passed through Danish waters. Shaw Desmond, *The Drama of Sinn Fein* (London, 1923), 156. Tony Griffiths, moreover, speculated that the *Aud*'s stash of weapons were "seized perhaps by Finnish Jaegers fighting on the Eastern Front". A.R.G. Griffiths, "Finland, Norway and the Easter Rising," in Oliver MacDonagh, W.F. Mandle, and Pauric Travers, eds., *Irish Culture & Nationalism 1750–1950* (London, 1983), 149–60.
50 Finnish news stories and photographs were labelled either "SH" or "KC" (*Sensuurin Hyväksymä* or *Krigs Censuren*, in Finnish and Swedish respectively), to indicate approval by the wartime censor.
51 Ossi Päärnilä, "Irlannin Pääsiäiskapina Johtavissa Suomalaisissa Puoluelehdissä Kevällä 1916," Unpublished Pro-Seminar Material, University of Jyväskylä, 1974; Newby, *Éire na Rúise*, 91–105; Andrew G. Newby, "'Os Selve Alene': A Norwegian Account of the Easter Rising," *Studia Celtica Fennica* 13 (2016), 17–30.
52 *Helsingin Sanomat*, 27 April 1916; *Työmies*, 28 April 1916; *Hufvudstadsbladet*, 28 April 1916.
53 *Hufvudstadsbladet*, 27 April 1916. *Helsingin Sanomat*, 27 April 1916. *Aamulehti*, 27 April 1916; *Åbo Underrättelser*, 27 April 1916. *Aamulehti*, 28 April 1916.
54 *Hufvudstadsbladet*, 28 April 1916. *Novoye Vremya* was a pro-government newspaper.
55 *Hufvudstadsbladet*, 28 April 1916.
56 *Työmies*, 27 April 1916.
57 *Työmies*, 3 May 1916. See Paasivirta, *Finland and Europe*, 214.
58 *Työmies*, 4 May, 5 May 1916.
59 *Sosialisti*, 19 May 1916. The Swedish Socialist press presented a similar narrative: see Eskola, *Suomen Kysymys*, 150–51; *Social-Demokraten*, 5 June 1916.
60 He was recorded as a Russian national by the British at the time. "Antle Zecks Makapaltis, Finland" was listed in the *Sinn Féin Rebellion Handbook*. See Newby, *Éire na Rúise*, 77–79; The first published narrative account seems to have been "Inside the GPO: A Memoir by Two Participants," in *An t-Óglach*, 23 January 1926. Despite the public emergence of the story in Ireland in the 1960s, it was apparently President Tarja Halonen's speech in Dublin in 2007 that marked the first Finnish acknowledgment of their participant in the Rising. Newby, *Éire na Rúise*, 7.
61 Jimmy Wren, *The GPO Garrison, Easter Week 1916* (Dublin, 2015), 180.
62 Quoted in Kenneth J. Calder, *Britain and the Origins of the New Europe 1914–1918* (Cambridge, 1976), 233 [fn. 77].
63 Keith Jeffery, *1916: A Global History* (London, 2015), 103; Lyytinen, *Finland in British Politics*, 68–69.
64 *Helsingin Sanomat*, 31 May 1916.
65 *Hufvudstadsbladet*, 1 June 1916; *Oulun Sanomat*, 2 June 1916.

66 *Uusi Suometar*, 23 September 1916.
67 Pakaslahti, *Suomen Politiikkaa Maailmansodassa*, ii, 179.
68 Eskola, *Suomen Kysymys*, 150–51.
69 Ibid.
70 Jussi Jalonen, "From Volunteer Soldiers to Military Elites: Finnish Jägers and Polish Legionaries During and After World War I," *Zinātniskie Raksti* 93 (2014), 72.
71 John Foster Fraser, *Russia of To-day* (New York, 1916), 125.
72 Rosalind Travers Hyndman, "The Emancipation of Finland," *The New Europe* III.30 (10 May 1917), 105.
73 Hyndman, "The Emancipation of Finland," 106. For South Longford, see Marie Coleman, "Mobilisation: The South Longford By-election and Its Impact on Political Mobilisation," in Joost Augusteijn, ed., *The Irish Revolution, 1913–1923* (Basingstoke, 2002), 53–70.
74 Meinander, *History of Finland*, 121.
75 See for example, *Hansard*, HC Deb 20 February 1917 vol. 90, col. 1190 (Charles Trevelyan); *Hansard*, HC Deb 26 April 1917 vol. 92, col. 2707 (H. Dalziel); *Hansard*, HC Deb 10 April 1918 vol. 104, col. 1510 (John Dillon). F.P. Jones, *History of the Sinn Fein Movement and the Irish Rebellion of 1916* (New York, 1916), 50.
76 *Hansard*, HC Deb 2 April 1917 vol. 92, col. 885.
77 D. Fitzpatrick, "Militarism in Ireland, 1900–1922," in Tom Bartlett and Keith Jeffery, eds., *A Military History of Ireland* (Cambridge, 1996), 396–97; P. Karsten, "Irish Soldiers in the British Army 1792–1922: Suborned or Subordinate," *Journal of Social History*, xvii (1983), 47.
78 *Documents Relative to the Sinn Fein Movement* (London, 1921), 9.
79 Thomas St. John Gaffney, *Breaking the Silence: England, Ireland, Wilson and the War* (New York, 1931), 222, 239; *Dagens Press*, 16 February 1917; *Karjala*, 19 August 1917. Georges Chatterton-Hill was a Ceylon-born academic and journalist, who had allegedly never set foot on Irish soil. And yet, he was presented by Roger Casement to Count Georg von Wedel in 1915 as "a whole-hearted nationalist and most anxious to be of service in any way I desire". Quoted in R.R. Doerries, *Prelude to the Easter Rising: Sir Roger Casement in Imperial Germany* (London, 2000), 96.
80 In any event, Chatterton-Hill was well versed in the history and politics of Finland, having previously lived in Helsinki, working as an English teacher at the "Institute for Modern Languages" in 1907. Gaffney, *Breaking the Silence*, 195–96. Hannu Rautkallio, *Kaupantekoa Suomen itsenäisyydellä* (Helsinki, 1977), 104.
81 Newby, *Éire na Rúise*, 110.
82 "Germany and the Gulf of Finland," *Spectator*, 20 October 1917.
83 *Säkenia*, 1 October 1917.
84 Ibid.
85 Bill Kissane, "Victory in Defeat? National Identity after Civil War in Finland and Ireland", in J.A. Hall and S. Malešević, eds., *Nationalism and War* (Cambridge, 2013), 326.
86 *Kansan Lehti*, 3 November 1917.
87 Alan Titley, "Lá an Luain," *Irish Times*, 28 March 2016.
88 Michael Silvestri, *Ireland and India: Nationalism, Empire and Memory* (London, 2009), 211.
89 Lavery, *History of Finland*, 84–86. The Finns were glad to note that Ireland had apparently accepted Finnish independence after a "bloodless" revolution. *Wiipuri*, 16 January 1918.

90 Éamon De Valera, *Ireland's Case Against Conscription* (Dublin, 1918), 7.
91 Arthur Griffith, *The Resurrection of Hungary: A Parallel for Ireland*, 3rd ed. (Dublin, 1918), xii, 141, 163.
92 George Bernard Shaw, *John Bull's Other Island*, New ed. (London, 1918), 8.
93 Anders Ahlbäck, "Maculinities and The Ideal Warrior: Images of the Jäger Movement," in Tuomas Tepora and Aapo Roselius, eds., *The Finnish Civil War 1918: History, Memory, Legacy* (Leiden, 2014), 254.
94 Kissane, "Victory in Defeat," 322–23.
95 Newby, *Éire na Rúise*, 106–26.
96 Olof Enckell, *Jägarnas Historia* (Helsingfors, 1943), 9.

15 Early Risers and Late Sleepers

The Easter Rising and the Poznanian Uprising of 1918–1919 Compared

Róisín Healy

The oft-asserted notion of a historical parallel between Ireland and Poland in the long nineteenth century is especially plausible with respect to the years from 1914 to 1923.[1] In both places, the pressures exerted by World War I strengthened nationalist movements at the expense of the Great Powers, spurred anti-imperialist activity, and led eventually to the creation of independent states, the Irish Free State and the Second Polish Republic. In fact, the Easter Rising of 1916 had an echo in a lesser-known uprising which took place in the province of Poznania or Greater Poland [Wielkopolska], a province of the Polish-Lithuanian Commonwealth annexed by Prussia in 1793 and thus part of the German Empire since 1871. Lasting seven weeks, from late December 1918 to mid-February 1919, the Poznanian Uprising consisted of attacks on German military and administrative positions throughout the province perpetrated largely by Polish defectors from the German army. Their objective was to ensure that the whole province of Poznania, which consisted of 1.3 million Poles and 750,000 Germans, according to the 1910 census, and had been the centre of the medieval Polish Piast state, would be included in the borders of the new Polish state which were to be defined at the subsequent Paris Peace Conference.[2]

The roots of both the Irish and Poznanian uprisings were to be found in the mounting dissatisfaction with imperial rule, that is, with the British state and the German Empire respectively. Irish and Polish nationalists found their own political sovereignty, cultural traditions and economic interests compromised by the regimes that ruled them. Socialism played a secondary role to nationalism in both. While socialists figured prominently in the Easter Rising, in the form of the Irish Citizen Army, led by one of the signatories of the Proclamation of the Irish Republic, James Connolly, the goal of the majority of Easter rebels was the achievement of sovereignty rather than the immediate creation of a socialist order.[3] Despite the fact that the Poznanian Uprising took place at a time when many central and eastern Europeans had become Bolshevised as a result of terms in Soviet prisoner of war (POW) camps and frustration with the slow pace of economic reform, socialism had remarkably little influence over the Poznanian Uprising.[4] The Uprising occurred largely independently of the contemporaneous revolution among Germans in Poznania. Workers' and soldiers' councils were established in the province and Poles joined them, but without sharing the socialist sympathies of their German members.[5] If anything, opposition to socialism provided a spur in that the dominant political grouping in Poznania was the right-wing National Democrat Party or Endecja of Roman Dmowski and the rebels may have been seeking to pre-empt the spread of the Socialist Party of Józef Piłsudski into the province.[6]

The uprisings of 1916 and 1918–1919 were, moreover, both carefully planned by a coterie of committed revolutionaries and in that sense, were quite different from many other kinds of disturbances that were typical of World War I – food riots, street demonstrations, shirking on the front, desertions, surrenders, even mutinies – which were largely spontaneous and did not always signify treason or even disloyalty. The Russian Revolution offers a closer parallel in this respect. The Supreme Council of the secret military organisation, the Irish Republican Brotherhood (IRB), decided just after the outbreak of war that they would hold a rising as soon as possible and then in mid-January 1916 settled on Easter Sunday, in expectation that the British authorities would try to disband the Irish Volunteers, which had been formed in 1913 as a nationalist counterpart to a military organisation, the Ulster Volunteer Force formed in 1912 in order to oppose Home Rule for Ireland, and to disguise rebellion as a routine exercise.[7] For its part, the Poznanian Uprising was a concerted plan by the Polish Military Organisation of the Prussian Partition [Polska Organizacja Wojskowa], formed in February 1918, and the Endecja movement to wrest the province of Poznania from Germany in advance of the Paris Peace negotiations.[8] It was carefully designed to take advantage of the power vacuum that followed the collapse of the German war effort in the east and the official armistice in November.

Finally, despite the wartime context, these were largely domestic efforts to gain independence. The Proclamation of the Irish Republic referred to "gallant allies in Europe", but outside assistance proved minimal, consisting of arms, but no men, from Germany and bungled efforts to induce Irish POWs in German captivity to join an Irish brigade under the leadership of the former servant of the British Empire, Sir Roger Casement.[9] Similarly, the Germans' challengers in Poznania in 1918–1919 had to rely on their own strength. While Prime Minister Georges Clemenceau and Marshal Ferdinand Foch were keen to send the Polish army of France, led by Józef Haller, to Danzig (later Gdańsk) to help the Poles deprive the Germans of as much territory as possible, British Prime Minister Lloyd George vetoed the proposal at the Supreme Council of the Paris Peace Conference. Ostensibly concerned with the right of self-determination for the Germans in Poland, in reality Lloyd George feared that French influence in Poland might further weaken Germany and cause a future war.[10] France was thus obliged to leave the fighting to the Poles themselves, although it prevailed in its insistence that the Germans lay down weapons in February 1919.[11]

Notwithstanding these parallels, there is no evidence of direct transfer of military knowledge between Irish and Polish nationalists in this period. Some Irish people lived in Poland in the war years, but these were unlikely sources of revolutionary know-how – two Irish women, Annie Callanan and Mary Flanagan, were living in Russian-controlled Congress Poland, but they were working as governesses rather than conspirators, were evacuated to Russia proper after the German invasion of 1915 and returned to Ireland only in 1918.[12] Some Poles also reached Ireland during the War. Early in 1916, a Polish leader based in Chicago, Nicodemus Piotrowski, visited Dublin. His contacts appear to have been in the moderate rather than radical nationalist camp, the Irish Parliamentary Party, however.[13] Casimir Markievicz, the Polish husband of the Irish Citizen Army activist, Constance, had been living in Ireland for over a decade before the War and had done much to familiarise Irish people with the Polish revolutionary tradition, but he left to fight for Russia once the War broke out.[14] Moreover, there is little evidence of any effort on the part of the IRB to learn from the experience accumulated by the Poles in their various uprisings, in 1806, 1830–1831, 1846, 1848, 1863–1864 and 1905. While Irish military planners such as Ginger O'Connell examined several continental theatres, including Italy and Bulgaria, and James Connolly studied the revolutions of 1848 across the continent and of 1905 in the Russian Empire, Poland does not appear to have featured in their considerations.[15] Indeed the main model for the Rising's planners seems to have been an earlier Irish rising, that of Robert Emmet in Dublin in 1803.[16] Nor is there any evidence that Polish military strategists closely examined the course of the Easter Rising. As the inheritors of a strong revolutionary tradition and as World War I combatants, they had plenty of models closer to home to draw upon.

They also proved more successful than their counterparts in Ireland two years earlier. The reasons for the failure of the Easter Rising and the success of the Poznanian Uprising are fairly obvious – the Irish rebels had few arms to speak of because of the interception of the *Aud*, the ship bringing Casement and arms from Germany, while the Poles had their own weapons as soldiers in the German army and also managed to take many directly from the Germans, some of whom realised there was little point in fighting on. In April 1916, the Irish were facing a power that remained militarily strong, even if its defences in Ireland were temporarily weakened by the challenge of war. The Poles, by contrast, were facing in December 1918 a power that had been defeated after a draining four-year war, was in the midst of revolutionary upheaval, and had limited resources to defend its perimeter.[17]

The question of the timing is more complicated. If World War I provided the necessary context for both uprisings, the widespread nationalist resentment of Britain and Germany in evidence on the eve of the war should not be conflated with revolutionary fervour. The majority of Irish nationalists still supported Home Rule and Polish nationalists focused on cultural and economic issues rather than self-government. It should also be pointed out that, despite the oft-invoked motto "England's difficulty is Ireland's opportunity" and its German-Polish variant, war did not always lead to revolution. The Irish had, for instance, sat out the Crimean War and the Poles the Wars of German Unification. The discrepancy, however, between the considerable sacrifices demanded by the onset of total war in the form of extensive military service, food rationing and general deprivation, on the one hand, and the lack of meaningful political concessions to ethnic minorities, on the other, increased tensions throughout all belligerent states and made them particularly vulnerable to attack from disgruntled minorities. Both British and German governments worried about the loyalty of their minorities on the periphery, even those well behind the front, from the outset of the War. The British faced an uprising much earlier than the Germans, however. While the Irish proved "early risers", the Poles turned out to be "late sleepers". Polish anti-imperialists were very active politically during the war, but the Poznanian Poles waited until the last moment, just after the War and before the peace negotiations, to launch their uprising. This chapter attempts to explain why, against the shared background of World War I, Irish and Polish nationalists chose to revolt more than two years apart from one another.

In the case of Ireland, the Supreme Council of the IRB decided at the outbreak of hostilities to strike at some point during the War. Yet while this small group reserved the right to lead a rising, some of its members sought to wait until such a rising would enjoy at least some popular support.[18] This was not at all evident at the outbreak of war. Britain's Liberal government had passed the Third Home Rule Bill in 1914, over the objections of the House of Lords and the Unionist community, and promised to put it into operation once the War was over. Satisfied that nationalist demands had been met and anxious to realise Home Rule, the Irish Parliamentary Party leader, John Redmond, called on his supporters to go "wherever the firing line extends" in September 1914. As many as 200,000 Irishmen volunteered to fight in the British Army over the course of the war. While enthusiasm was greater within the Unionist community and the rate of recruitment in Ireland lagged behind that of Britain, nationalists dominated the ranks of Irish military recruits, and others worked to fulfil demands for increased production of food, clothes and munitions and to assist relief organisations.[19]

Conditions for an uprising were possibly more propitious in Prussian Poland than in Ireland in 1914. The War followed a decade of German-Polish conflict, sparked by the imposition of German-language religion lessons, a ban on the Polish language in public meetings, and attempts to expropriate Polish-owned estates. If ordinary Prussian Poles did not necessarily conclude that the only reasonable alternative was an independent Polish state, their leader, Dmowski, had certainly come to see Germans and Poles as being engaged in a zero-sum game.[20] Some Germans felt the same way. Just after the War broke out, rumours circulated within the German community in Posen, the capital of the province of Poznania, that an insurrection was imminent and that women were transporting ammunition in babies' prams.[21] While Polish deputies in the Reichstag voted for war credits in 1914 and conscripted Poles fought well, there was no public enthusiasm for the War among Prussian Poles.[22] The priests of Poznania distanced themselves from the hierarchy's loyalism and some were arrested for their hostility to the war effort.[23] The Poles were also slow to provide money towards the war effort. A collection for the German Red Cross elicited 17,000 marks from Poznania's Poles, compared with 900,000 from the province's Germans.[24] The Polish press selected official war reports that cast the German war effort in a poor light, prompting the local police chief in Posen to impose tougher censorship on Polish than German papers in his district in February 1915.[25]

Yet, while some Poznanian Poles were among those deserting and even defecting on the western front from late 1914 to mid-1915, those at home remained quiet.[26] This did not so much represent satisfaction with the regime – censors noted frequent expressions of support for the restoration of the Polish state in letters that they read – as the advantage of having options.[27] The Poznanian Poles were living in what Omer Bartov and Eric Weitz have called an "imperial shatterzone", at the juncture of several multinational empires.[28] While in many other respects and on many other occasions, this location exposed the Poles to enormous dangers and suffering, during World War I, it presented them with an opportunity to play the different powers off one another or at least an incentive to wait and see how the War progressed. As the Landrat or communal governor of Culm in neighbouring West Prussia suggested, Polish passivity in 1914 likely masked a process of political and military calculation – who would win the war and what they would give the Poles.[29] In this sense, the Poles did not have the luxury of principled anti-imperialism, but had the advantage of eager, if unreliable, collaborators in their efforts to topple at least some of the region's empires in order to achieve greater autonomy.

Throughout the War, it was difficult to calculate which side would triumph and Poles split over the most favourable ally, with Piłsudski opting for the Central Powers and Dmowski for the Entente.[30] Prussian Poles clearly favoured Dmowski and provided few volunteers for the Polish Legions that Piłsudski raised to fight alongside the Central Powers. The enthusiasm elicited by the Russians' offer of autonomy under Russian authority at the beginning of the war among Dmowski and his supporters in Poznania, however, waned in the wake of harsh Russification policies in occupied Galicia.[31] The Germans did little to endear themselves to the Poles either. They began the War with a massacre of Polish civilians in Kalisz, a town in Congress Poland which had once been part of Poznania, in August 1914. Once they took over Congress Poland, they offered substantial concessions to their new Polish subjects there, but only in exchange for heavy demands of them in terms of food, forced labour and military recruits.[32] By contrast, the Poznanian Poles experienced no improvement in their conditions, despite all their efforts on behalf of the Empire. The German administrators in Poznania continued to view the province as an integral part of the empire and insisted on the primacy of the German language there.[33] Food shortages and high inflation exacerbated the dissatisfaction of the Poles and hardened hostility to the Central Powers. Dmowski began a concerted campaign to win the support of the western Allies for the creation of a sovereign Polish state and his Endecja movement helped to form the Interparty Citizens' Committee [Międzypartyjny Komitet Obywatelski] to this end in Poznania in January 1916.[34]

A similar radicalisation was occurring in Ireland, but in a less favourable geopolitical context. Isolated on the western periphery of Europe, far removed from the theatre of war, there was little prospect of Ireland operating as a bargaining chip in the war. France, the traditional source of military assistance, was now allied with Britain and could not support Irish independence.[35] Germany was an unattractive alternative for most Irish nationalists, especially Catholics who disapproved of the attacks on their co-religionists in the Kulturkampf of earlier decades. A small group of advanced or revolutionary nationalists advocated an alliance with Germany from the turn of the century and claimed that Ireland would fare better, should Germany win a future war, implausibly citing the cases of Alsace-Lorraine and Prussian Poland as models of good government.[36] Moderate nationalists easily deflected such claims, however, and the actions of Germany during the War, especially its attacks on Catholic Belgium and the sinking of the *Lusitania* off the Irish coast, did nothing to improve its reputation in Ireland.[37] Indeed the liaison between the Irish Volunteers and the German government, Casement, gained few recruits from among Irish POWs in German camps in early 1916. The half-hearted assistance from Germany confirmed how little Ireland mattered in the War.[38]

Public support for a rebellion was also still doubtful in early 1916. In many ways, the War had been good for Ireland, boosting employment and agricultural prices without causing the kind of hunger that afflicted those closer to the action.[39] Yet the war was taking its toll, especially on families who had sent members to the front, and the delay in implementing Home Rule was beginning to irk the moderate nationalist majority and dampen military recruitment. Anxious to act on their long-standing plans and perhaps wary that the Irish Citizen Army might pre-empt them, the IRB planners decided in January 1916 to strike at the next provocation or expected provocation from the British side – they anticipated that the British would try to disband the Volunteers.[40] They settled on Easter so that they could disguise the mobilisation as a routine exercise of the Volunteers and thus confuse the authorities and buy time. Reactions to the Rising suggest that they had indeed jumped the gun. When news of the rebellion in Dublin filtered through to the front, Irish soldiers reacted with disgust. Some even burned an effigy of Casement in no-man's-land.[41] The population as a whole was also initially critical and recruitment even increased in the immediate aftermath of the Rising. Yet the British response to the rebellion – the execution of 15 leaders of the Rising in May, the imprisonment of thousands of others, and the trial and execution of Casement in August – played into the hands of the advanced nationalists, represented most effectively by the Sinn Féin Party, and encouraged the nationalist community as a whole to shift its sights from Home Rule to independence.[42]

These events were closely followed in Poland. Reports of "unrest" in Dublin circulated in *Kurjer Lwowski* and *Kurjer Warszawski* just two days after the outbreak of the Rising on 24 April. By 29 April, the latter had learned enough to describe the rebellion as "very serious and well planned".[43] The *Głos Narodu*, a conservative organ published in Cracow, carried a report on the Rising on 27 April and put another on its front page on 29 April. The *Gazeta Toruńska*, based in West Prussia, first mentioned it on 2 May, claiming that the fighting had broken out as a response to the threat of conscription, but had now ceased.[44] The *Kurier Poznański*, based in the city of Posen, published a short report of "rioting in Dublin" on the same day and a longer analysis that included an article by the Norwegian Celtologist, Carl Marstrander, who had lived in Dublin before the war. Marstrander attributed the Rising to the widespread dissatisfaction with Home Rule as a solution to the so-called Irish question.[45]

Like their Irish counterparts, Polish nationalists were also flexing their anti-imperial muscle at this time. On 3 May 1916, they organised a huge patriotic display, in which 300,000 people, including veterans of the January Uprising of 1863–1864, marched on the streets of Warsaw, the capital of the General-Government established by the German occupation authorities. The occasion, the 125th anniversary of the Constitution of 1791, came at what proved in hindsight the highpoint of German-Polish wartime co-operation as the Germans wooed the Poles in order to gain their support against the Russians and the Poles took maximum advantage to assert their claims to national self-determination.[46] While the anti-imperialism of the Poles took symbolic rather than violent form on 3 May, analyses of the Rising in the Polish press in the following days and weeks suggested the validity of the revolutionary option. An article on the front page of *Głos Narodu* on 4 May celebrated the Rising as a just response to foreign oppression. The author, Antoni Chołoniewski, a biographer of the leader of the 1794 uprising against Russia, Tadeusz Kościuszko, and himself a prominent patriot, acknowledged that Britain could easily overcome the rebels, but pointed out that harsh measures would make a poor impression on neutral powers and alienate the Irish community in the United States in particular. While the Rising's impact was as yet unclear, Chołoniewski concluded that Ireland had chosen the right time to recall its rights as a nation and insisted on Ireland's right to revolt.[47] Indeed a book he published in English in 1918, *The Spirit of Polish History,* suggested that it was the duty of Poles to support Irish anti-imperialism, in that he characterised Polish history as marked by a commitment to tolerance, democracy and a brotherhood of nations.[48] Another journalist, Dr Irena Pannenkowa, an assimilated Jew who had helped found the Polish National Revival Association [Związek Odrodzenia Narodu Polskiego] and whose husband served in the Polish Legions under Piłsudski, immediately claimed that the Rising held special significance for the Poles. She saw it as a warning to the Great Powers about the tenacity of national feeling and emphasised its importance in mobilising the Irish masses behind full independence.[49] She also justified the apparent recklessness of the rebels in taking on so great an enemy by reference to the Polish revolutionary tradition: "There is no one who better understands the Irish 'madness' than ourselves, the Poles. Weren't we equally, or even more, 'mad', and not only once but many a time?"[50] With her Polish surname, Constance Markievicz provided a convenient reminder of the Poles' revolutionary credentials and she was profiled in analyses of the Rising, such as in the *Kurjer Poznański* on 12 May.[51] The popular weekly *Świat* called her a "modern Irish amazon" and spoke of her husband as a "son of an oppressed nation fighting to the last breath for its national liberties".[52]

Polish anti-imperial forces were still optimistic enough about their bargaining power in May 1916, however, not to emulate the Easter Rising. Nonetheless, the Rising provided a vehicle to express their anxiety about the sincerity of the occupying authorities. An article in *Czas*, an influential conservative paper based in Cracow, depicted the British delay in implementing Home Rule in Ireland in terms that might have served as a warning to Poles about the self-serving and possibly hollow promises of the Central Powers to establish an autonomous Polish state. "It is very dangerous to feed the hope of regaining the rights once lost by the nation, so long and unjustly oppressed, and then postpone the promise, under unclear circumstances".[53]

The creation on 5 November 1916 by the Germans of the Kingdom of Poland, an autonomous state composed of the territory conquered from Russia, but not the provinces that had belonged to Prussia and Austria before the War, represented a major advance for the cause of Polish nationalism, but was received warily by the Poles. When it was announced in Warsaw, local leaders showed their disappointment about the exclusion of the historic Polish province, crying "Poznania lives!"[54] The Kingdom, which remained to be given a king and defined borders, was soon exposed as a German ruse to extract greater military resources from the region. Moreover, German concessions on the language question in the Kingdom did not extend into the Polish population to its west. Poznanian Poles had to witness Interior Minister Friedrich Wilhelm von Loebell pledge in the Reichstag that traditional *Polenpolitik* would prevail in Germany's original Polish provinces. The death of the patriotic novelist, Henryk Sienkiewicz, in Swiss exile on 15 November 1916 led to nationalist demonstrations that challenged the division of German Poland into its traditional Polish provinces and the new Kingdom of Poland with its capital at Warsaw. While demonstrations were officially tolerated only within the Kingdom, they spilled over into Prussia proper and the Prussian authorities there felt powerless to act against them.[55] In the summer of 1917, Piłsudski and the Polish Legions ended their cooperation with the Central Powers out of frustration with the lack of progress on meaningful autonomy in the Kingdom of Poland.[56] The patience of Prussian Poles was also wearing thin. Wojciech Korfanty, a National Democrat politician from Silesia, lambasted the government in the Prussian parliament in 1917 for the inadequacy of its concessions to the Poles.[57]

Yet the increasing support for Polish independence on the part of the Entente Powers suggested that Polish anti-imperialists might not need to resort to insurrection against the Central Powers in order to advance the cause of Polish independence. Prompted by the proclamation of the Kingdom of Poland by the Central Powers, in December 1916, Tsar Nicholas II promised a free and united Poland under Russian tutelage, should the Entente prevail in the War. Long sympathetic to the Polish national cause, Britain and France could now speak out publicly in favour of Polish independence without weakening the bonds of the Entente.[58] In this context and that of the February Revolution in Russia, Dmowski turned his attention to France, forming the Polish National Committee [Polski Komitet Narodowy] and a volunteer Polish army there in the summer of 1917. The defection of General Józef Haller from the Polish Legions of the Central Powers in July 1918 to this army, which became known as the Blue Army or Hallerczyki, boosted the Poles' credentials in the eyes of the Allies. The entry of the United States into the War in April 1917 suggested that the Allies might indeed prevail and emboldened the Poles in their demand for sovereignty. Polish optimism was evident in the numerous patriotic displays that marked the centenary of the death of Kościuszko that autumn.[59] Woodrow Wilson's inclusion of a Polish state with access to the sea in his Fourteen Points speech of January 1918 and its reiteration in the Versailles Declaration of 3 June 1918 gave further cause for hope. While the military strength of Germany in light of Russia's collapse following the revolutions of 1917 and the Treaty of Brest-Litovsk posed temporary, if serious, setbacks to Polish sovereignty, the defeat of Germany's subsequent Spring Offensive and the armistice of November 1918 were followed by the establishment of an independent Polish state, incorporating the Kingdom and Galicia.

While the Poles had refrained from insurrection during the War because of the greater advantage to be gained by cooperating with the empires, they recognised that, however great their support for the principle of Polish sovereignty, the Allies might not be so malleable on the question of the precise borders of the new state. Both the western and the eastern borders of the new state were disputed. While Dmowski favoured restoring the entire Polish-Lithuanian state, Piłsudski preferred a smaller Polish state at the head of a regional federation of national states.[60] They both agreed on the status of Poznania as an essential part of the new state. The problem was that Germans also regarded the province as an integral part of the German

Empire. The Poles of Poznania launched an uprising in order to ensure that the province become part of the new Polish state and thus pre-empt the negotiations at the postwar peace conference.[61] In this, they had the support of the local Polish population. There had been street demonstrations in favour of secession from Germany from 10 November with Poles hoisting red and white flags all over the city of Posen.[62] They also had the advantage of a weakened German army. They waited till it was clear that the German authorities would not send additional German troops to defend Poznania, but would rely on the German soldiers present there and the local militia [Grenzschutz].[63] The catalyst came with a rousing speech by pianist and associate of Dmowski, Ignacy Paderewski, in Poznan on 27 December 1918. The following day saw the opening of hostilities between Germans and Poles, which lasted into February 1919.[64]

As in the case of the Easter Rising, the Poznanian Uprising formed part of a longer military struggle to establish a sovereign state.[65] While the Rising helped to mobilise nationalist opinion behind a demand to move beyond Home Rule to independence, the new Irish state, which excluded the six counties of Northern Ireland, was established only after a guerrilla war against Britain from 1919 to 1921 and secured in a civil war from June 1922 to May 1923. In addition to the Poznanian Uprising, the Polish struggle included another three uprisings against German rule in Upper Silesia from August 1919 to July 1921 and four wars in the east, against Ukraine, Czechoslovakia, Lithuania, and the Soviet Union, between November 1918 and March 1921.

If the Easter rebels anticipated the popular tipping point in favour of a rising, one might say that the Poznanian Poles waited until well after popular support was assured. Yet public opinion turned out to be less important than a favourable international context in predicting the success of anti-imperialism. If, by 1918, Irish nationalist opinion had moved beyond Home Rule to some form of independence, it had to wait some years for the wider world to endorse this view. While Irish nationalists commented little on the Poznanian Uprising itself, they were envious of the privileged position of Poland at the Peace Conference and resentful of Wilson's refusal to offer similar public support for Irish independence.[66] From the start of the War, advanced nationalists had pointed to the hypocrisy of the British in criticising German and Austrian mistreatment of the Poles, while ignoring that of their ally, Russia, and failing in their support for self-determination at home. Yet while Irish nationalists had gained some support among radicals and liberals in the past for the notion that Britain oppressed the Irish just as much as others oppressed the Poles, this view was seen as disloyal during the War. In the long run, however, as Maurice Walsh has shown, the relaxation of censorship after the war and the scepticism engendered by wartime atrocity reporting allowed the international press to report in graphic detail the experience of the Irish during the War of Independence and effectively brought to Ireland the international sympathy that Poland already enjoyed.[67] The establishment of a Polish state was soon followed by an Irish state, which turned out to be far more secure than its counterpart in the shatterzone of east-central Europe.

Notes

1 For an analysis of Irish perceptions of this parallel, see Róisín Healy, *Poland in the Irish Nationalist Imagination, 1772–1922: Anti-Colonialism within Europe* (London, 2017).
2 On the course of the Poznanian Uprising see Zdzisław Grot and Antoni Czubiński, *Powstanie wielkopolskie 1918–1919* [Uprising in the Greater Poland Region] (Poznań, 2006) and for a recent discussion of its historical significance, see Janusz Karwat, ed., *Powstanie Wielkopolskie, 1918–1919: Wybrane aspekte z perspektywy 90 lat* [The Poznanian Uprising, 1918–1919: Particular Aspects 90 Years On] (Poznań, 2007). For more literature on the Uprising, see Andreas Lawaty and Wiesław Mincer, eds., *Deutsch-polnische Beziehungen in Geschichte und Gegenwart: Bibliographie, 1900–1998* (Darmstadt, 2000), 9550–709.
3 Ann Matthews, *The Irish Citizen Army* (Dublin, 2015). On Connolly, see Donal Nevin, *James Connolly* (Dublin, 2005).
4 See, for instance, Guido Hausmann, "The Ukrainian Moment," in Gearóid Barry, Enrico Dal Lago, and Róisín Healy, eds., *Small Nations and Colonial Peripheries in World War I* (Leiden, 2016).
5 Jens Boysen, "Simultaneity of the Un-simultaneous: German Social Revolution and Polish National Revolution in the Prussian East, 1918/19," in Klaus Weinhauer, Anthony McElligott, Kirsten Heinsohn, eds., *Germany 1916–23: A Revolution in Context* (Bielefeld, 2015), 242–46.
6 See strength of Endecja in 1919 elections, A.J. Groth, "Polish Elections, 1919–1928," *Slavic Review* 24 (1965), 653–65. On pre-empting the socialists, see Helmut Fechner, "Der Verlust von Westpreussen und Posen 1918/1920," in Helmut Fechner, ed., *Deutschland und Polen, 1772–1945* (1964), 94–115.
7 Charles Townshend, *Easter 1916: The Irish Rebellion* (London, 2006), 93.
8 Boysen, "Simultaneity," 240.
9 Christine Strotmann, "The Revolutionary Programme of the German Empire: The Case of Ireland," in Barry, Dal Lago, and Healy, eds., *Small Nations*, 19–36.
10 Piotr Wandycz, *France and her eastern allies, 1919–25: French-Czechoslovak-Polish Relations from the Paris Peace Conference to Locarno* (Minneapolis, MN, 1962), 30–39. On the importance of Poland to France, see Peter Jackson, *Beyond the Balance of Power: France and the Politics of National Security in the Era of the First World War* (Cambridge, 2013), 239–42.
11 Boysen, "Simultaneity," 241, 248.
12 "An Irish Girl from Russia," *Irish Independent*, 12 July 1918; "Thrilling Experience of an Irish Governess," *Freeman's Journal*, 13 July 1918; Mary C. Flanagan, "An Irish Girl in Russia, 1914–17," *The Irish Monthly* 49 (1921): 473–79.
13 *Irish Times*, 22 February 1915; *Freeman's Journal*, 17 April 1916. A Polish princess also came to raise funds in Ireland for the relief of Poles in 1915. See Healy, *Poland*, 237.
14 Patrick Quigley, *The Polish Irishman: The Life and Times of Count Casimir Markievicz* (Dublin, 2012), 51, and on his response to World War I, 156–57.
15 Townshend, *Easter 1916*, 97, 113.
16 Ibid., 48.

17 For a comparison of the two wartime armies, see Alexander Watson, *Enduring the Great War: Combat, Morale and Collapse in the German and British Armies, 1914–1918* (Cambridge, 2009).

18 Townshend, *Easter 1916*, 20.

19 On Irish responses to the war, see the classic local study by David Fitzpatrick, *Politics and Irish Life, 1913–1921: Provincial Experiences of War and Revolution* (Cork, 1998), 53–71, 90–97, and Catriona Pennell, *A Kingdom United: Popular Responses to the Outbreak of the First World War in Britain and Ireland* (Oxford, 2014), 163–97.

20 Boysen is sceptical about Poles' desire for independence on the eve of the War. See "Zivil-militärische Beziehungen in den preussischen Ostprovinzen Posen und Westpreußen während des Ersten Weltkriegs," in Alfred Eisfeld, Guido Hausmann, and Dieter Neutatz, eds., *Besetzt, interniert, deportiert: Der Erste Weltkrieg und die deutsche, jüdische, polnsiche und ukrainische Zivilbevölkerung im östlichen Europa* (Essen, 2013), 138.

21 Alexander Watson, *Ring of Steel: Germany and Austria-Hungary in World War I* (London: Basic Books), 76.

22 Jens Boysen, "Imperial Service, Alienation and an Unlikely National "Rebirth": The Poles in World War I," in Barry, Dal Lago, and Healy, eds., *Small Nations*, 171.

23 Landrat to Regierungspräsident, Neumark, 24 February 2016, and Report of Society for the Eastern Marches, Archiwum Państwowe w Gdańsku, Verhalten der Polen während des Krieges, 10/10230.

24 Piotr Wandycz, *Lands of Partitioned Poland* (Seattle, WA, 1984), 335.

25 Boysen, "Zivil-militärische Beziehungen," 137.

26 Boysen, "Imperial Service," 172. See also Mieczysław Wojciechowski, ed., *Spoleczeństwo polskie na ziemiach pod panstwiem pruskim w okresie I wojny światowej (1914–1918)* [*Polish Society in Prussian-Controlled Territory in World War I, 1914–1918*] (Toruń, 1996).

27 On attitudes to restoration before and during the War, see Boysen, "Zivil-militärische Beziehungen," 138, 145.

28 Omer Bartov and Eric Weitz, eds., *Shatterzone of Empires: Coexistence and Violence in the German, Habsburg, Russian and Ottoman Borderlands* (Bloomington, IN, 2013).

29 Oberpräsident to Regierungspräsident, 24 December 2014, Archiwum Państwowe w Gdańsku, Verhalten der Polen während des Krieges, 10/10230.

30 For a survey of Poland in World War I, see Piotr Szlanta, Poland, in: 1914–1918-online. International Encyclopedia of the First World War, ed. by Ute Daniel, Peter Gatrell, Oliver Janz, Heather Jones, Jennifer Keene, Alan Kramer, and Bill Nasson, issued by Freie Universität Berlin, Berlin 2014-10-08. doi:10.15463/ie1418.10255.

31 See Mark von Hagen, *War in a European Borderland: Occupations and Occupation Plans in Galicia and Ukraine, 1914–1918* (Seattle, 2007).

32 Jesse Kauffman, *Elusive Alliance: The German Occupation of Poland in World War I* (Cambridge, MA, 2015), 55–63. He stresses, however, that Prussian policies in World War I fell a long way short of the harsh German policies of World War II.

33 Boysen, "Zivil-militärische Beziehungen," 141–42.

34 Boysen, "Zivil-militärische Beziehungen," 147 and Tomasz Kamusella, *Silesian and Central European Nationalisms: The Emergence of National and Ethnic Groups in Prussian Silesia and Austrian Silesia, 1848–1918* (West Lafayette, IN, 2007), 248.

35 Jérome aan de Wiel, "Europe and the Irish Crisis, 1900–1917," in Gabriel Doherty and Dermot Keogh, eds., *1916: The Long Revolution* (Dublin, 2007), 30–44.

36 Joachim Fischer, *Das Deutschlandbild der Iren:Geschichte, Form, Funktion* (Heidelberg, 2000), 75–78.
37 Pennell, *A Kingdom United*, 171–72.
38 Séamus Ó Siocháin, *Roger Casement: Imperialist, Rebel, Revolutionary* (Dublin, 2008), 396–438 and Christine Strotmann, "The Revolutionary Program of the German Empire: The Case of Ireland," in Barry, Dal Lago, and Healy, eds., *Small Nations*, 19–36.
39 Niamh Puirséil, "Labour and the Great War," in John Horne, ed., *Our War: Ireland and the Great War* (Dublin, 2008), 181–94.
40 Townshend, *Easter 1916*, 113.
41 Ben Novick, *Conceiving Revolution: Irish Nationalist Propaganda during the First World War* (Dublin, 2001), 64.
42 Michael Laffan, *The Resurrection of Ireland: The Sinn Féin Party, 1916–1923* (Cambridge, 1999).
43 Adam Kucharski, "The 1916 Easter Rising: Irena Pannenkowa and the Polish Perspective," in Krzysztof Marchlewicz and Adam Kucharski, eds., *To the Cause of Its Freedom: Centenary of the 1916 Easter Rising* (Poznań, 2017), 130–31.
44 Mark Ó Fionnáin, "Éirí Amach na Cásca agus an Pholainn," in *Macallaí san Eoraip: Scéal éirí amach na Cásca i nuachtáin na hEorpa [Echoes in Europe: The Story of the Easter Rising in Europe's Newspapers]* (Dublin, 2016), 12.
45 "Rozruchy w Dublinie" and "Sinn Fein", *Kurier Poznański*, 2 May 1916. The same article by Marstrander appeared in the *Dziennik Poznański*, 2 May.
46 Kauffman, *Elusive Alliance*, 51–52.
47 Antoni Chołoniewski, *Tadeusz Kościuszko* (Lwów, 1902).
48 Heinrich A. Stammler, "Stanisław Przybyszewski and Antoni Chołoniewski: Two Interpreters of the Meaning of Polish History," *Jahrbücher für Geschichte Osteuropas* 20 (1972), 70–75.
49 Pannenkowa, *Irlandzkie Memento*, 38–39, cited in Kucharski, "Irena Pannenkowa," 135.
50 *Kurjer Lwowski*, 27 May–4 June 1916. The pamphlet was subsequently published by the newspaper. Irena Pannenkowa, *Irlandzkie Memento* (Lwów, 1916), 6, cited in Kucharski, "Irena Pannenkowa," 134.
51 Ó Fionnáin, "Éirí Amach,"14. See also *Kujrer Warszawski*, 14 May 1916.
52 Gerard Keown, "'Ireland of the East and Poland of the West': Reflections on the Intersections between Poland and Ireland," in Marchlewicz and Kucharski, *Polska i Irlandia*, 94. He does not provide the date of the publication.
53 *Czas*, 24 May, cited in Kucharski, "Irena Pannenkowa,"133. See also the characterisation of English government as adopting a "Two-Faced Policy," *Czas*, 28 April 1916.
54 William Mulligan, *The Great War for Peace* (New Haven, CT, 2014), 173.
55 Boysen, "Zivil-militärische Beziehungen," 147.
56 Arkadiusz Stempin, "Deutsche Besatzungsmacht und Zivilbevölkerung in Polen im Ersten Weltkrieg: Polen, Juden und Deutsche im Vergleich," in Eisfeld, Hausmann and Neutatz, eds., *Besetzt*, 159.
57 James Bjork, *Neither German nor Pole: National Indifference in a Central European Borderland* (Ann Arbor, MI, 2009), 191.
58 On French and British attitudes, see Jeffrey Mankoff "The Future of Poland, 1914–1917: France and Great Britain in the Triple Entente," *The International History Review* 30.4 (2008): 741–67.
59 Boysen, "Zivil-militärische Beziehungen," 147.
60 For a recent analysis of the attitude of the Polish Socialist Party to other ethnic groups in this period, see Paul Brykczyński, "Reconsidering Piłsudskiite nationalism," *Nationalities Papers* 42 (2014), 771–90.

61 The support of the Allies was not guaranteed. Britain and France had considered granting the province of Poznania to Russia in exchange for its continued support in the War in 1916, Mankoff, The Future of Poland, 763.

62 Fechner, "Der Verlust," 95.

63 Ibid., 100.

64 Dieter Vogt, *Der Großpolnische Aufstand* (Marburg, 1980), 43 ff.

65 For postwar comparisons, see T. K. Wilson, *Frontiers of Violence: Conflict and Identity in Ulster and Upper Silesia, 1918–1922* (Oxford, 2010); Julia Eichenberg, "The Dark Side of Independence: Paramilitary Violence in Ireland and Poland after the First World War," *Contemporary European History* 19:3 (2010), 231–48.

66 Healy, *Poland*, 250–51, 259–61.

67 Maurice Walsh, *Bitter Freedom: Ireland in a Revolutionary World* (London, 2015).

Index